The Macmillan Book of 366
BIBLE STORIES

Retold by
Roberto Brunelli

Illustrated by
Chris Rothero

Translation by
Colin Clark

Aladdin Books
Macmillan Publishing Company
New York

BIBLE STORY OF THE MONTH

God Creates the World and its Inhabitants

Along, long time ago, the sky, the earth, and all living things did not exist. There was nothing of what we now see all around us: there was only God, and it was he who created everything we see around us.

This is how it all happened. First, God said, "Let there be light!" And light began to shine. God saw that the light was good and decided to separate it from the darkness. He called the light "day" and he called the darkness "night." And it was morning and then evening: this was the first day.

Then God made the firmament over the waters, and it was like a great vault, transparent and clear. God called the firmament "sky." A morning passed and evening came, and this was the second day.

God then said, "Let the waters gather under the sky and let dry land appear:" And thus it was. God called the dry land "earth" and the waters he called "sea," and he saw that they were good. He spoke again, saying, "The earth shall produce buds, grasses, flowers, and trees that bear fruit, each according to its species!" And thus buds and shoots appeared from the earth, and grasses and flowers and fruit trees grew, each according to its species. And God saw that all of these things were good, and night came and that was the third day.

God said, "Let there be lights in the firmament of the sky, to distinguish day from night; they shall serve to indicate the passing of days, of seasons, and of years and they shall also illuminate the earth!" And thus it happened. God made two great lights. The larger was to illuminate the day, and the smaller was to brighten the night, and he then made many tiny lights. In this way God created the sun, the moon, and the stars, and he placed them in the firmament of the sky so that they might illuminate the earth, measure day and night, and separate the light from the darkness. God saw that all of this was good, and it was the end of the fourth day.

God said, "The waters of the sea shall be full of living things, and in the sky over the earth many kinds of birds shall fly." In this way God created all the creatures of the seas and oceans, from the enormous whale to the smallest fish, and also all the winged creatures, and set them to fly. At the end of the fifth day, God saw that this was good.

There were still no inhabitants of dry land and God said: "The earth shall be populated by living beings

of many different kinds: animals that are good to eat, wild beasts, reptiles, and every other species that moves on the land." This happened, and thus God created all the species of animals. And he saw that they were good.

At this point, God said: "I shall make man and he shall be different from all other creatures! I shall make him in my own image and likeness, and he shall reign over the fish of the sea, over the birds of the air, and over the animals on land!"

And so God created man in his own image and likeness, and he divided man into male and female and he blessed them, saying: "Give birth to other men and populate the earth; subject the earth to your will and rule over the fish of the sea and over the birds of the air, and over every other living thing that I have made!" And God continued: "I give you also all the plants that grow on the earth and all the fruit trees so that you may eat them. All green grass I give to the animals of the land and the birds of the air as food." And thus it was. When he had created man in his own image and given him the earth as his domain, God looked at everything he had made and he saw that it was good. Thus ended the sixth day.

The sky and the earth were thus finished and all their inhabitants completed. Therefore, on the seventh day God rested from his work, and he blessed the seventh day and made it holy. For this reason men do not work on the seventh day, which we call Sunday, but rest and worship God instead.

Oh Lord, Our God,
How great is thy name
In all the world:
Your magnificence
Crowns the heavens.
When I look at your sky,
The work of your hand,
The moon and the stars that you
   created,
I wonder why you remember
To take care of man.
And still you have made him
Little less than the angels.
And you have crowned him
With glory and with esteem.
You have given him power
Over the works of your hands,
And you have placed the world at
   his feet:
All the flocks and the herds,
All the beasts of the countryside,
The birds of the air
And the fish that swim in the seas.
Oh Lord, Our God,
How great is thy name
In all the world!

Genesis 1–2; Psalm 8

July

1 A Name for Every Animal

This is how the Lord God created man. He took dust into his hands from the earth and shaped it into the form of a man. Then God blew a breath of life into the nostrils of his creation and man became a living being.

God called him Adam.

Then the Lord created a magnificent garden in Eden, and it was full of beautiful trees which produced fruits that were good to eat. A great river watered the garden and then divided into four and flowed over the earth.

And there, in the Garden of Eden, God set down the man he had created, and nurtured and cared for him, for he wanted him to be happy.

God made all of the beasts of the earth and the birds of the air come before Adam, for he wished to see what name the man would give to them; whatever the man chose to call the living things was to be their name.

Thus Adam gave names to every animal of the earth and every bird of the air, and the name Adam gave to each has remained the same for all men since.

2 God Creates Woman

God had given the beautiful Garden of Eden to Adam. This, however, was not enough, for God wanted him to be happy.

Thus God said: "It is not right for man to be alone; I will make him a mate who will be like him." God made sleep fall on the man and then he removed one of his ribs and from it he shaped a woman.

God then led the woman to Adam, who greeted her with joy, saying: "This is flesh of my flesh and bone of my bones; she is just like me!" And he called her Eve.

3 The Serpent in the Garden

Adam and Eve were living happily in the Garden of Eden. Everything was beautiful to behold and they did not have to work, for the trees bore every type of fruit that was good to eat.

The Lord God had given everything to Adam and Eve, with one exception. He said: "You may eat the fruit of every tree in the garden except for one special tree in the middle. It is the tree of the knowledge of good and evil; and you must not eat of its fruits or you will die."

The most cunning of all the creatures that God had created was the serpent, and it did not like the man and the woman. Indeed, the serpent sought their downfall for, in reality, the serpent was the devil, the enemy of man.

One day, in the Garden of Eden, the serpent spoke to the woman saying: "Is it true that God has forbidden you to eat the fruit of the trees in the garden?"

"No," replied Eve. "We can eat every fruit except the fruit from the tree of knowledge. God told us not even to touch that fruit or we will die!"

"It is not true that you will die," lied the serpent. "On the contrary, God has forbidden you to eat from that tree because he knows that if you do then you will be like him and know good and evil."

Eve then looked at the fruit of the forbidden tree and found it desirable. She picked an apple from the tree and ate half, then gave the rest to Adam, and he too ate.

In that instant, their eyes opened, they realized they were both naked, and they covered themselves with fig leaves. Then Adam and Eve felt great shame and they understood the evil they had done. The Lord had given them everything and, in return, they had disobeyed him.

4 The Sin Is Discovered

Genesis 2–3

Adam and Eve, in the Garden of Eden, had disobeyed the Lord God by eating the fruit from the tree which he had forbidden to them.

A short time later they heard the Lord God walking in the garden and they hid themselves among the trees. The Lord called to the man: "Where are you?" and Adam replied: "I heard your footsteps and I hid myself in fear, for I am naked."

"Who told you that you are naked?" asked the Lord. "You have eaten the fruit which I commanded you not to eat!" And the man said:

"It was given to me by the woman whom you created and placed at my side."

"What have you done?" God asked Eve. "The serpent gave me the fruit," replied the woman. "It deceived me and I ate it."

And God then pronounced punishment. To the serpent he said: "You shall crawl on your stomach forever, as punishment for having done this." And to Adam and Eve the Lord God said: "You can no longer stay here in the garden; go forth and earn food to eat with the sweat of your brow." He then placed an angel with a flaming sword to guard the gates of Eden.

5 Cain and Abel

Genesis 4

Adam and Eve had two sons and they were called Cain and Abel. Cain was a farmer and Abel was a shepherd. One day the two brothers offered a sacrifice to God: Cain offered him the best fruits from his fields, and Abel his best lamb.

Abel made his offering with a sincere heart; this pleased the Lord. But Cain was angry and jealous of his brother, so his gift did not please the Lord. The Lord warned Cain, saying: "Why are you angry? Why do you glower? You must conquer your jealousy."

6 Cain Murders Abel

Genesis 4

Cain was jealous of his brother Abel because his gifts pleased the Lord, whereas those offered by Cain did not. His rage grew until one day he invited Abel into the fields and killed him there.

God, who saw everything, asked him: "Where is your brother?" and Cain, adding dishonesty to his crime, replied, "How should I know. Am I my brother's keeper that I should know where to find him?"

"The voice of your brother's blood cries out to me," said the Lord, "and for this reason you must flee from this place, and for the rest of your life you shall wander over the face of the earth."

Cain, then, was very much afraid that somebody would kill him because he was a fugitive. The Lord, however, did not desire anyone's death—even for sins as great as Cain's, so he marked Cain with a sign of warning so nobody would hurt him.

Thus Cain went away from the Lord and went to live in the land of Nod. After Cain had murdered Abel, God gave Adam and Eve another son and they called him Seth, and their descendants became ever more numerous on the earth.

7 Three Skillful Brothers

Genesis 4–5

In those days there lived three brothers named Jabal, Jubal and Tubalcain. They became famous because they taught the skills of their trades to those who followed. Jabal raised animals; Jubal played the lyre and the flute with great skill; and Tubalcain was a smith and a master of working iron and copper.

Early men behaved very badly, more like Cain than Abel. One of them, Lamech, father of the first three, was so evil and violent that he took revenge for every little wrong done to him.

8 Noah's Ark

Genesis 6–7

All the men living on the face of the earth were bad, for they did that which was evil in the eyes of the Lord. The only exceptions were the members of Noah's family.

God grew weary of so much evil and decided to rid the earth of all the wicked people. He therefore appeared to Noah and said to him: "I shall send a deluge, a great flood that will sweep away all life on the earth, except for the few whom I shall save." And he gave Noah this order: "You must build an ark, a great ship. It must have three levels, windows and a roof." And God told Noah exactly how long, how wide, and how high to build the ark.

Noah set to work with his three sons, Shem, Ham, and Japheth and his wife and the wives of his sons gathered food and clothing for their life in the ark.

Many laughed at Noah for trying to build a ship on dry land, a long way from the sea. But Noah paid no attention to them and went on with the work. When he had finished the building of the ark, Noah gathered together two animals of every species and made them enter the ark and then, finally, he and his family also went on board.

9 After The Flood

Genesis 8–9

A week passed and then it began to rain. As the Lord had foretold to Noah, it rained so much for forty days that a great flood came and covered everything—the houses, the trees, and then the mountains themselves. The ark floated, and when Noah looked out of the window he saw only the waters, but the people and the animals inside the ark remained safe, just as the Lord had promised.

At last the winds began to blow and the waters which had covered the earth began to ebb. The highest peaks began to appear above the water and the ark came to rest on Mount Ararat.

After forty days had passed Noah opened a window he had made in the ark and said: "I shall send out a dove to discover if there is dry land anywhere." But the dove, returned, having found nowhere to land.

Noah waited another seven days and then sent the dove out again. This time, too, it returned, but in its beak it carried a small olive branch, which was a sign that the waters had receded. Seven days later, Noah once again released the dove, and this time it did not return.

Four more weeks went by and then God said to Noah: "You, your wife, your sons and their wives, and all the animals of every species that you have with you must now leave the ark. All of you leave the ark, spread over the earth and multiply."

Obedient to the Lord, who had spared him and his family, Noah came out of the ark and he immediately built an altar to offer a sacrifice of gratitude to the Lord.

The Lord was pleased with Noah's sacrifice and he blessed him and his children and said to them: "Behold, life returns to the earth, and everything that is to be found on the earth, I now give to you and your children."

10 The Sign of the Rainbow

Genesis 8–9

When Noah, who had been saved from the flood with his family and the animals in the ark, set foot on the ground, he immediately gave thanks to the Lord, who had been so good to him. And the Lord then said to him: "From this day on, for as long as there is life on the earth, there will never be another flood like this one; there shall always be sowing and reaping, heat and cold, summer and winter. I make this pledge to you and your descendants, and to seal this promise, I place the rainbow in the sky."

11 The Tower of Babel

Genesis 11

After the days of the deluge, men had returned and multiplied on the earth and they were like a great family, with all of them speaking the same language. They lived on the plain of Shinar and thought themselves very important. "Let us build a great city," they said, "with a tower that is so high it will touch the sky. This will keep us united and well-remembered."

How proud they were of their idea! But they gave no thought to the Lord God and did not consider if their plan was in accordance with God's will. They believed that they had no need of God. For this reason, he intervened.

When the building work was already well advanced, the Lord changed the language of the people so that they could no longer understand each other and had to stop the work on the building of their great tower. Those who could understand each other came together and left the city to go and live in other countries, and thus spread all over the earth.

The city that they left behind, where every person spoke a different language, was named Babel, which means "confusion."

12 God Calls Abraham

Genesis 12

Abraham was born at Ur, an ancient city in Mesopotamia, the fertile land between two rivers. He moved to Haran, a city in the north, with his father and his family, where he earned his living as a shepherd and a breeder of livestock.

It was at Haran that an extraordinary thing happened to him: the Lord God spoke to Abraham. At that time men had forgotten God and they worshiped many different idols which they had invented and passed down from father to son. But Abraham recognized the voice of the one true God, the Lord, when he spoke to him.

The Lord appeared to Abraham and said: "You must leave here, leave your homeland and the house of your father, and go to the country I have chosen for you. From you and your descendants I shall make a great nation and I shall bless you. I will make your name great, and through you I shall give great gifts to mankind and all the earth."

Abraham trusted the Lord's word and, despite his great sadness at leaving Haran, he immediately set out for the south. He took with him his wife Sarah, his nephew Lot, his servants and his flocks.

13 Abraham's New Homeland

Genesis 12

Abraham followed God's instructions and arrived in the land of Canaan, later called Palestine.

Once there, he heard che voice of God again and it promised him: "This land I will give to your descendants." As a sign of his thanks and of his faith, Abraham at once built an altar to the Lord on that place.

He then began to travel around his new homeland. From Sichem, where the Lord had spoken to him, he moved to Bethel, where he built another altar, and then he went, eventually, to live in the south.

14 God Promises Descendants to Abraham

Genesis 14–17

Abraham owned a great number of beasts of the field and so, too, did his nephew Lot. Since the area they farmed was not large enough, they decided to split up. Lot took his flocks and his shepherds and went to live near Sodom, and Abraham remained in Canaan.

A short time later, during a war being fought by four kings against Sodom, Lot and his family and servants were taken prisoner and carried off. As soon as Abraham learned of this, he gathered his people together and set off in pursuit of the four kings. He caught up with them, fell on their camp by night, defeated them, and liberated Lot.

Upon his return Abraham met with Melchisedech, king of Salem and high priest of God, who gave him his blessing.

The Lord God had promised to give the land of Canaan to the descendants of Abraham. But Abraham and his wife Sarah were already old and they had no children. Where were these descendants? Abraham did not understand, but the Lord insisted, saying: "Look up at the sky and count the stars—there are not as many as shall be your descendants."

15 Three Strange Visitors

Genesis 17, 21

Abraham had set up his tents at the oaks of Mamre. One day, at the hour when the sun was at its height, he was sitting at the entrance to his tent when he raised his eyes and saw three men before him. At once he ordered that water be brought so that they might wash their feet, according to the custom of his people. He then went into his tent, told Sarah to prepare some cakes quickly, then ran to his herd and chose a tender young calf and had it cooked. When everything had been prepared, he invited his three mysterious guests to eat with him.

When the three men had finished their meal, they said: "We shall return in time and you and your wife, Sarah, will have had a son."

When Sarah, who was listening from inside the tent, heard these words, she gave a little laugh. For she believed that she had grown too old to bear a child. But the Lord—and the three strange visitors were sent by him—said to Abraham: "Why did Sarah laugh? Is there anything that is impossible for God?"

And, in fact, everything took place exactly as the Lord had foretold. Abraham and Sarah had a child and they gave him the name of Isaac.

16 Fire from the Sky Falls on Sodom

Genesis 18–19

The inhabitants of Sodom and its nearby cities behaved with great wickedness in the eyes of the Lord.

The Lord grew tired of such great evil and told Abraham that he intended to destroy the city of Sodom. Abraham, however, spoke to the Lord, saying: "Perhaps in Sodom there are fifty righteous men. You, Lord, would not want to slay the righteous with the wicked. This would not be just." The Lord replied: "If I find fifty just men in Sodom, then for their sakes I shall spare the whole city." But Abraham went on, saying: "Perhaps there will not be precisely fifty righteous men . . . perhaps there will only be forty." And, again, the Lord agreed.

"Lord, do not be angry with me," persisted Abraham, "but perhaps there will only be thirty . . . or twenty . . . or ten righteous men!" And at each of these figures the Lord promised to spare the city out of love for these few. But in Sodom there were not even ten just men and the Lord sent his angels to warn Lot to save himself and his family. And God then made fire and sulphur rain down from the sky over Sodom and the nearby cities, which were completely destroyed.

17 Abraham Is Put to the Test by God

Genesis 22

One day God said to Abraham: "You must offer me Isaac, your only son, in sacrifice." In those days it was not unusual for men to kill their own children in homage to their gods. Perhaps Abraham thought that the Lord was the same in this as all the other gods, but he was still very surprised, because God had promised that he would have many descendants and now required that Abraham sacrifice his only son. Abraham was very old and knew that he could not father any more children. How then did God intend to keep his promise?

Abraham did not understand, but he knew that he had to obey. One day he loaded his donkey with wood and set out with his son Isaac. When they reached Mount Moriah, Abraham loaded the wood onto Isaac's shoulders, and together they climbed the mountain. At the summit Abraham prepared an altar on which he laid first the wood and then his only son. Abraham took out his knife and was about to strike with it, when an angel of the Lord stopped his hand and said: "Do not kill the boy! Now God knows that you love him even above your only son."

18 A Bride for Isaac

Genesis 24

When Isaac came of an age to take a wife, his father, Abraham, called his most trusted servant and sent him to Haran to seek out a bride. Haran was the city from which Abraham himself had come.

The servant took ten camels and many precious things and set out. When he reached the city of Haran, he stopped outside the city walls, near the well where the women came to draw water in the evening, and he prayed to the Lord: "O Lord, I do not know how to find the maiden that you have chosen for Isaac. When I ask for some water let her be the one who not only gives me a drink, but also my camels."

A little later a beautiful girl approached with her water jar on her head. "Will you give me a drink?" asked the servant, and the maiden at once replied: "Of course, as much as you want; and your camels must be thirsty too."

The maiden's name was Rebecca and she was from the family of one of Abraham's relatives. When the servant explained to her father the reason for his journey, the girl was asked if she wished to become Isaac's bride. She consented and returned to Canaan.

19 The Veiled Bride

Genesis 24–25

The caravan had now arrived in the land of Canaan. The young Rebecca gazed at the land that was to become her home. Toward evening she saw a young man approaching the caravan. When she learned that it was Isaac, her husband-to-be, Rebecca dismounted from her camel and covered her face with a veil. Her husband, according to custom, should only see her face on their wedding day.

Isaac and Rebecca celebrated their wedding, and some years later they had twin sons, Esau and Jacob.

20 For a Mess of Pottage

Genesis 25

The Lord God had made a covenant with Abraham: Abraham had agreed to obey the Lord as the one true God, and in return the Lord had promised Abraham that he would give him the land of Canaan and that he would have descendants as numerous as the stars in the sky and the grains of sand by the sea. When Abraham died, this covenant held good for his son Isaac, and then for Isaac's firstborn son, Esau.

But Esau's twin brother, Jacob, wanted the rights for himself.

One day Esau came home tired and hungry from hunting and found that Jacob had cooked a mess of pottage. "Give me some to eat, for I am very hungry," demanded Esau. Jacob was ready with his reply: "In exchange you must hand over to me the rights of the firstborn." "I am dying of hunger, what use are the rights of the firstborn to me? You can have them," replied Esau. "You must swear it!" insisted Jacob.

Esau gave his solemn promise then ate. Thus, he showed how little he valued the covenant which God had made with his grandfather and it was only later that he realized how much he had lost with such a thoughtless action.

21 Jacob Deceives His Father

Genesis 27

Esau had thoughtlessly given up to his brother Jacob his rights as the firstborn. However, for this to have any real meaning it required the blessing of their father, Isaac. But everyone knew Isaac would never give this blessing to Jacob, because the firstborn son was Esau, whom he had always loved best anyway.

Rebecca, on the other hand, preferred Jacob to Esau, and she suggested a way for Jacob to find a way to obtain his father's blessing by trickery.

Isaac was now very old and his eyesight was failing. "He called Esau to him, and said, "I don't know when my death will be, but I know that I must offer my blessing to the firstborn. Therefore, take your bow and go out and hunt some deer for my meal, for you know that meat is the meal I enjoy most. When I have eaten the meal you have gotten for me, I will bless you before I die."

When Esau departed, Rebecca put into action her plan to have Isaac give his blessing to Jacob rather than Esau. She sent Jacob to fetch two kids from the herd of goats. When he brought them to her, she had them prepared for a meal for Isaac.

Next, she dressed Jacob in Esau's best clothing. Only, Jacob's arms were hairy, whereas Esau's were smooth. To make sure Isaac was fooled, Rebecca wrapped the smooth kidskins around Jacob's arms. Then Jacob carried in the meal to his father and asked for the blessing that rightfully belonged to his brother.

"Your voice sounds like Jacob's," said Isaac, "but the arms you hold out to me are definitely those of Esau." And so the deception worked. Isaac failed to recognize Jacob and he gave to him the blessing of the firstborn that was his favorite son Esau's by right.

22 Isaac Blesses His Son

Genesis 27

"Come and kiss me, my son," old Isaac said. Jacob obeyed. Isaac smelled the fragrance of Esau's clothes and gave him his blessing. With this, the covenant, made by the Lord with Abraham and then Isaac, now passed on to Jacob.

Isaac said: "Behold the fragrance of my son is like the smell that rises from a fertile field full of fruit, a field blessed by the Lord. The Lord will grant you dew from heaven and an abundance of the fruits of the earth. And all will respect you and bow down before you."

23 The Deceit Is Discovered

Genesis 27–28

With the help of his mother, Rebecca, Jacob had deceived his father. Pretending to be his brother Esau, Jacob had received Isaac's blessing, the right of the firstborn that also fulfilled the covenant made with the Lord God.

When Esau, who had been hunting, returned home with his catch, he prepared a meal and took it to old Isaac. The old man, who was by now almost blind, immediately asked him: "Who are you?" "I am your firstborn son," replied Esau. "Then who was here before you?"

Isaac went on, "And to whom have I already given my blessing?"

Thus, the deception was discovered. Esau was furious and vowed: "When our mother is dead, I will kill Jacob."

Rebecca became fearful at this threat and called Jacob to her, saying: "Go away from here until your brother has calmed down. Go to Haran for a while, to the house of my brother Laban. We will tell your father that you have gone to seek a bride at your relatives' home."

Old Isaac agreed that Jacob should do as he had done and should not take a bride from among the women of Canaan.

24 A Ladder from Earth to Heaven

Genesis 28

Jacob was in flight from his brother Esau, from whom he had deceitfully gained the rights of the firstborn, and so, also, inherited the promises that God had made to Abraham. Esau, naturally, was furious with Jacob. Who knows if even God had forgiven Jacob his deception?

One night on his journey, Jacob lay down on the ground to sleep with a stone for his pillow. After he fell asleep, he had a dream in which he saw a ladder that started from the earth and reached up to heaven. The angels of the Lord were going up and down the ladder. Then the Lord himself appeared before Jacob and said, "I am the Lord, God of Abraham and of Isaac. As I promised to them, so I do to you; you will have descendants as numerous as the stars and to them I will give the land on which you lie. I shall protect you wherever you go and I shall bring you back to this land."

Jacob, awed, awoke and said, "The Lord is present here and I did not know it! This is the house of God; this is the gateway to heaven." He then took the stone he had used as a pillow and blessed it and named the place Bethel, which means "House of God."

25 Jacob Is Also Tricked

Genesis 29

Laban, Jacob's uncle, had two daughters: Leah, the eldest, and Rachel. Jacob asked for Rachel as his wife; Laban agreed on the condition that Jacob work for him for seven years. But then Laban tricked Jacob into marrying Leah instead, saying, "It is our custom that the older daughter be married before the younger. If you want to marry Rachel, work seven years more."

At that time men often had more than one wife. And so Jacob worked another seven years to get Rachel because he loved her very much.

26 Peace between the Brothers

Genesis 32–33

Jacob remained with his uncle Laban for fourteen years, and during this time he worked for him and for himself as well, and he grew very rich. Then he decided to return to the land of Canaan, which God had promised to give to his descendants; so he gathered together his wives, his sons, and all his belongings, and he set off.

Along the way he grew afraid because of his brother Esau, whom he had tricked and whose revenge he feared. So he sent ahead to his brother a present of two hundred she-goats and twenty he-goats; two hundred sheep and twenty rams; thirty camels with their young; forty heifers and ten bulls; and twenty female and ten male donkeys.

The next day he saw Esau approaching him with four hundred men. Since he did not know if his brother was pleased with his gift, it was with great fear that he prostrated himself seven times on the ground before his brother to show the greatest respect. But Esau ran to meet him, hugged him and kissed him, and they were both moved to tears. And after the two brothers had spent some time together, they each went their separate ways.

27 Jacob Changes His Name

Genesis 32

A strange event once happened to Jacob. He was journeying with his family and his flocks, but at this moment he found himself alone on the banks of the River Jabbok. It was night when a man approached him and wrestled with him until daybreak. Then as the stranger prepared to leave, Jacob realized that perhaps this opponent was a messenger from God. So he said to him, "I will not allow you to go until you have blessed me." And the stranger blessed him, saying, "From this time on, your name will be Israel."

28 The Twelve Sons of Jacob

Genesis 35

While he was away from the land of Canaan, Jacob, who was also called Israel, became the father of many sons; he then had others when he returned to Canaan, the land that God had promised to his descendants.

These are the names of the twelve sons of Jacob-Israel: the firstborn Reuben, then Simeon, Levi, Judah, Issachar, Zebulun, Dan, Naphtali, Gad, Asher, Joseph and Benjamin. All together, with their wives and sons, they settled in Canaan as nomad shepherds.

29 Joseph the Dreamer

Genesis 37

Jacob loved Joseph more than all his other sons, because he was born during his old age of the wife Jacob cherished above all else, Rachel.

Then, Joseph was his youngest son, because at the time of these events Jacob's final son, Benjamin, was not yet born.

Jacob had given Joseph a coat with long sleeves which was a princely garment compared to the short coats of the Shepherds. When Joseph's brothers saw that Jacob favored Joseph so much they became jealous and no longer treated him kindly.

Once, when Joseph had grown to boyhood and had gone with his brothers to take the flocks to pasture, he had a dream and he told his brothers about it: "I dreamed that we were all working in the fields, tying bushels of corn, and while my bushel remained upright, I saw that your bushels bowed down, on all sides of mine."

The brothers understood what the dream meant and, in great anger, they replied: "Do you think that you will become more important than all of us, and that we will bow down before you?"

30 Joseph Dreams Again
Genesis 37

Joseph, who was seventeen years old at that time, had another dream, and on this occasion he spoke of it to his father and his brothers. "Listen," he said, "I dreamed that the sun, the moon, and eleven stars bowed down before me."

The meaning of this dream was also clear. This time it was his father who spoke up: "What sort of dream is this? Shall I and your mother and your brothers bow down before you? Do you, the youngest, believe that you will become more important than the rest of your family?"

31 Joseph is Sold by His Brothers
Genesis 37

One day, when Joseph was seventeen years old, his father sent him to see how his brothers were, for they were grazing their flocks a long way from home. The brothers did not love Joseph, for they knew that he was the one their father loved best and they were convinced that he considered himself more important.

Joseph walked a great distance and at last found his brothers with their flocks at Dothan. The brothers saw Joseph approaching from far off and they plotted among themselves. Here was the perfect opportunity to

be rid of him, and they decided to put him to death. "We will throw him in a well," they said, "and then we will tell our father that a wild beast has torn him apart."

But Reuben, the eldest brother, tried to save him. He said to the others, "He is our brother and we should not kill him. Let us throw him in a well, but not put him to death." Secretly Reuben intended to return later and save Joseph. So when Joseph reached them, his brothers stripped off his beautiful coat and threw him into an empty well. Then they saw a traders' caravan approaching and thought, "What do we gain by killing him? It

would be better to sell him to these merchants."

And that was what they did: Joseph was sold to the passing merchants as a slave for twenty pieces of silver. Then his brothers took his coat, killed a goat and having dipped the coat in the blood of the slaughtered animal, they took it to their father. "We found this," they told him. "Do you think it could be Joseph's coat?" Jacob took the coat in his hands and, recognizing it, began to weep in the belief that his youngest son had been torn to pieces by a wild animal. The merchant caravan was bound for Egypt and it carried Joseph there.

BIBLE STORY OF THE MONTH

Joseph in Egypt

Joseph, the young man who was sold into slavery by his brothers, was taken into Egypt and resold to Potiphar. Potiphar was an important man in Egypt; he was the chief of the pharoah's guards. He came to like Joseph because he could see that the young man was trustworthy and did his work well, and so he entrusted him with the running of the household.

Now that he was a slave in a foreign land, Joseph often thought of his own home and his father. But his situation became even worse when the wife of Potiphar turned against him, and before her husband she accused Joseph of behaving dishonestly. It was not true, but Potiphar believed his wife and had Joseph thrown into prison.

Some time later, both the chief cup bearer of the pharoah and his chief baker were thrown into prison with Joseph. One night each of his two companions had a dream, but they could not interpret its meaning. It was Joseph who explained it to them.

The chief cup bearer told him; "I dreamed of a vine with three shoots with bunches of grapes on them; I took the grapes, I squeezed the juice from them into a cup and gave it to the pharoah." Joseph explained: "The three shoots are three days; in

three days' time the pharoah will free you from prison and give you back your previous position. Then, I beg you to remember me: tell the pharoah that I am innocent."

Then the chief baker also recounted his dream: "I was carrying on my head three baskets of white bread and sweets for the pharoah, but then birds came and attacked the baskets and ate up their contents." Joseph said to him: "The three baskets are three days: in three days the pharoah will decide your fate, and he will have you executed." Everything happened exactly as Joseph had foretold. But the chief cup bearer forgot all about

Joseph and did nothing to have him freed from prison.

Two years passed, then one night the pharoah also had a dream. He dreamed that he was beside the Nile, the great river on which the very life of Egypt depended. Out of the river there came first seven fat cows, which began to graze; then out came seven lean cows, which promptly devoured the fat ones. Then he dreamed of seven big fat ears of wheat all growing on the same stalk; but afterward along came seven empty husks which swallowed up the full ears.

When he awoke the pharoah called upon all the wise men of his

kingdom, so that they might interpret his two dreams, but no one knew what they meant. Then the chief cup bearer remembered Joseph, and said to the pharoah, "In prison I met a young Hebrew who succeeded perfectly in interpreting one of my dreams."

The pharoah had Joseph brought before him. He told him of his dream, and Joseph said to him: "The two dreams have the same meaning: God is telling you what is going to happen. The land of Egypt will enjoy seven years of abundance, after which will follow seven years of famine. So take care to find someone able and intelligent, who will store up enough food during the first seven years, so that it can be distributed during the seven years of famine, when otherwise there will be nothing to eat."

The pharoah replied: "You have answered well, and God must be with you because he has revealed all these things to you. You are the right man. I hereby give you full powers, and all of Egypt will obey you; after me, you will be the most important man in the kingdom."

And so Joseph became the viceroy of Egypt; the pharoah gave him his ring, he dressed him in rich clothes, and around his neck he hung a golden chain of office.

During the seven years of plenty, Joseph amassed enormous quantities of grain and other supplies, so that when the seven years of famine arrived, no one in Egypt went hungry. In fact, people even came from countries all around to buy grain. Joseph's brothers also came, because the famine had struck the land of Canaan. They did not know what fate had befallen Joseph, and when he came before them, dressed as an Egyptian, they did not recognize him. Joseph, however, recognized them and, without giving himself away, he made inquiries about them and found out how his father was.

When they all came before him, Joseph was deeply moved and decided to make himself known to them. He said: "I am Joseph, your brother whom you sold into slavery. But do not be ashamed, because it was the Lord who brought me here before you, in order that our whole family might survive the famine."

The brothers then grew afraid that Joseph would now seek revenge. But he reassured them again, and said: "The famine will last another five years; therefore go and fetch my father, your wives, and your children, and bring them into Egypt: I will give you land where you can live in peace."

Genesis 39–45

August

1 The Hebrews Move to Egypt

Genesis 46

Joseph, the viceroy of Egypt, wanted all his family to be saved from the famine: For this they had to move from the land of Canaan, where they lived, to Egypt where Joseph, who was the favorite of the Pharoah, could guarantee them everything they needed to live on.

His father, Jacob, asked himself if it was good to leave the land of Canaan, the land that God had promised to him and his descendants.

He did not know what to do; but God came to his aid. In a dream, Jacob heard the Lord speak to him: "I am the Lord God, your father. Do not be afraid to go down into Egypt, because there I will make you a great people, and one day I will make your great people return to this land."

Then Jacob gathered all his sons, their wives, and their children, with their flocks and the other riches they had acquired in the land of Canaan, and they went down into Egypt. The number of the tribe of Hebrews who went down into Egypt was seventy in all.

And Jacob sent his son Judah on ahead to announce to Joseph the arrival of his whole family and their worldly possessions.

2 Jacob and the Pharaoh

Genesis 47

Seventy people, the entire family of Jacob, arrived in Egypt. Joseph, who had not seen his father for many years, had his chariot prepared and went out to meet them.

As soon as he saw Jacob he threw his arms around his neck and wept for a long time. Jacob was no less moved and he said: "Now I can even die, because I have seen that you are alive and well."

Joseph said: "Now I will go in person and announce to the pharoah the arrival of my father and my brothers with their wives and their children."

The pharaoh said to Joseph: "The land of Egypt is at your disposal. Have your father and brothers move into the richest part, into the fertile valley of Goshen."

Then the old man Jacob was brought into the pharoah's presence. "How old are you?" asked the king of Egypt. "One hundred and thirty," replied Jacob. "My years have been spent in wandering and hardships."

Jacob and his sons settled into the land of Goshen, in Egypt, where they continued to be shepherds and breeders of livestock. And Joseph took care of their every need.

3 The Lord Will Have You Return to Canaan

Genesis 48

One day Jacob-Israel sent for his son Joseph, viceroy of Egypt, and told him of a vision he had had many years before.

Israel said to Joseph: "When I was in the land of Canaan, the Lord appeared to me, blessed me, and made me a promise saying: 'You will have a large number of descendants, the sons of your sons will become a great people, and to that people I will give this land.'

"So remember, the Lord has promised you the land of Canaan and one day you will return there."

4 Jacob Foretells the Future of his Sons

Genesis 49

The old man Jacob, also called Israel, called all his sons to him one day and said: "Gather together, because I must tell you what will happen in future times."

One by one, his sons passed before him, and to each of them he foretold developments that would occur once they had all returned to the land that the Lord had promised them.

To Issachar, Jacob said: "You are as strong as a donkey, and you will be able to survive in spite of the domination of your enemies."

To Naphtali, he said: "You are as graceful as a doe, and you will also know how to use words gracefully."

To Benjamin, his last born, he said: "You will resemble the wolf which devours its prey."

To Zebulun, he said: "You will live by the sea in a place where the ships will shelter safely."

To Asher, he said: "You will live in a fertile region, rich in grain, with which you will bake bread fit for a king."

To Joseph, Jacob said: "You are like the sapling of a tree, growing up strong and green because its roots are near a spring of water. Almighty God will bless you."

5 Judah, the Young Lion

Genesis 49

Before he died, Jacob-Israel foretold his sons' futures.

He called together Simeon and Levi to tell them that they would be separated and dispersed, because they had been cruel.

But the most surprising predictions he made were to Reuben and Judah.

To Reuben, he said: "You are my oldest son, proud and strong, with blood that boils like water. But you will not be the most important among your brothers, because at one time you offended your father."

To Judah, Jacob said: "You will be the most important. You are like a young lion: you will overcome your enemies, and even your brothers will bow before you. You will be the ruler and the scepter will remain in your hands, until the one to whom it belongs will come, the one who all the peoples will obey."

After these predictions, people wondered who was this descendant of Judah, to whom the scepter of command belonged, who it was who would guide all the peoples. Only many centuries later was it realized that Jacob was speaking of the Messiah, the Lord Jesus, sent by God to save the whole world.

6 Ephraim and Manasseh

Genesis 48

After he had settled, with his whole family, in the land of Goshen, Jacob sent for his son Joseph, the viceroy of Egypt, to thank him again for the good that he had done.

As a sign of his gratitude, Jacob wished to adopt Joseph's two sons, Ephraim and Manasseh, who were still only boys. "They shall be sons of mine," Jacob said, "and their inheritance shall be equal to that of my other sons; the inheritance of the land that the Lord has promised to give to my descendants."

He then asked the two boys to approach him. Jacob embraced them, he kissed them, and he blessed them. In his blessing he placed his hands on their heads: crossing his arms he placed his right hand on the head of Ephraim who was the younger one, and his left hand, the less important one, on Manasseh, the firstborn son.

Joseph tried to correct his father, pointing out to him that he should change hands, so that the right hand was placed on the head of the older son. But Jacob refused. "Even though he is the younger son, Ephraim's descendants will be more numerous, prosperous, and powerful."

7 "Take Me away from Egypt"

Genesis 47–50

Jacob now knew that he had reached the end of his earthly life. He called Joseph to him and said: "When I am dead, take me away from Egypt to the land of Canaan and bury me in the tomb of my ancestors."

"I will do as you wish," replied Joseph. But Jacob wanted to be certain, so he added, "Swear it to me," and Joseph swore it.

The tomb of Jacob's ancestors was the cave of Machpelah, in the land of Canaan. It was a cavern that Abraham had bought as a burial place for his wife Sarah, and then Abraham himself had been buried there, as were Isaac and his wife Rebecca, and Jacob's first wife Leah.

When Jacob-Israel died, the whole of Egypt went into mourning because the father of their viceroy was dead. When some time had passed, Joseph asked the pharoah for permission to bury his father in the land of Canaan. With Joseph went his sons and his servants, his brothers with their families, the ministers and counselors of the pharoah, along with the war chariots and the cavalry. A mighty caravan accompanied the body of Jacob into Canaan, and then returned.

8 "Am I in the Place of God?"

Genesis 50

After Jacob was buried, his other sons became afraid of their brother Joseph. When they had sold Joseph into slavery he had suffered greatly. Afterward he had become an important man—no less than the viceroy of Egypt—but, the brothers thought, he certainly would not have forgotten the wrong they had done to him. The fact that he had refrained from punishing them, in fact had saved them from famine, they attributed to the respect Joseph had for their father. But now that Jacob was dead, the brothers thought that nothing was going to stop Joseph from taking revenge for the wrongs he had suffered.

So his brothers sent him a message saying: "Before he died, our father asked you to pardon us." Then they went and threw themselves at his feet, saying: "We are your slaves."

Joseph was deeply moved and said to them: "Do not be afraid. It is up to God to hand out rewards and punishments: am I in the place of God? Rather, the Lord our God has brought good out of bad, because he has used me to save your lives and make it possible for you to prosper!"

August

9 A Baby in the Bulrushes

Exodus 1–2

Many many years had passed since the Hebrews had come to Egypt. They had grown in number, they had become a great people, and had grown very strong in that land.

In fact, they became so powerful that the king of Egypt, the pharoah, began to grow worried: "These sons of Israel could take up arms and fight against us," he thought; "we have to stop them from growing any greater in numbers."

And to do this, he first made them into slaves, forcing them to work in the fields and build great cities. In his fear he then ordered that every male child born to a Hebrew family be put to death immediately by drowning it in the river Nile.

A short time after this cruel order was given, a male child was born to a Hebrew family, and its parents sought to save its life; so they kept it hidden for three months after its birth.

When they could no longer keep it hidden, the mother took a reed basket, and coated it with tar and pitch so that the water would not enter. Then she put the baby in the basket and placed it among the bulrushes on the riverbank.

10 Moses Is Rescued from the River

Exodus 1–2

A short time after his mother had placed the basket with little Moses in it in the water of the Nile, the pharoah's daughter came down to the river with her handmaidens to bathe. She saw the basket and sent one of her maids to get it. Inside she found the baby crying. "It is a child of the Hebrews," she realized, and she was filled with pity for the infant. The child's sister, who had been hiding, went up to her and said, "Do you want me to find a Hebrew nursemaid to look after the baby?"

The pharoah's daughter agreed and the young girl went away and brought back her mother, without revealing to anyone that she was the baby's mother. "Nurse this child for me," the princess said to her, "and I will pay you well."

And so the baby was raised safely by its own mother. When he was weaned, his mother brought him back to the princess, who adopted him as her own son and gave him the name Moses, a name which means "saved from the waters."

Moses remained at the pharoah's court, where he studied and became an important and respected man: in this way God prepared Moses for great tasks.

11 The Flight into the Desert

Exodus 2

The Hebrews lamented their condition as slaves in Egypt. Moses was in anguish to see his people so oppressed. One day he came across an Egyptian beating a Hebrew. Moses saw that there was no one else watching, and killed the Egyptian and hid his body.

The next day, he came across two Hebrews fighting among themselves, and when Moses tried to make them stop, one of them said to him: "You are not our judge. Perhaps you would like to kill me, just as you killed the Egyptian?"

Moses grew afraid because he thought: "Many people now know my secret!" In fact, the pharoah came to hear of it and tried to arrest Moses, so that he would be put to death. So Moses escaped from Egypt and fled into the desert.

After much wandering he came to a well, where he protected seven sisters, who had come there to water their flocks, from the bullying of the other shepherds. In gratitude, the sisters took him back to the camp of their father, Jethro, who welcomed Moses warmly, and gave him one of his daughters as a bride. So Moses remained with Jethro, and spent his days grazing his flocks.

12 A Fire That Does Not Burn

Exodus 3–4

Out in the desert Moses was grazing the flocks of Jethro, his father-in-law, when he witnessed a strange sight: a bush was burning, but although it burned the flames did not consume it. "I must go closer and look at this wonderful happening," cried Moses in amazement.

As he drew near the bush, he heard a voice coming out of the flames: "Moses, Moses." "Here I am," Moses replied. "Come no closer. Remove your sandals, because the place on which you are standing is holy ground."

So Moses did so, and the voice continued: "I am the Lord God. I have seen the misfortunes of my people in Egypt, and I have chosen you to free them. You will go to the pharoah and tell him to let my people go."

13 The Name of God

Exodus 3

"You command me to go to my people and tell them that you wish to free them from slavery," said Moses to the Lord, "but they will not believe me, and they will ask me who has sent me. What shall I say?"

The Lord answered him: "You will say this to the people of Israel: I have been sent by Jehovah, the God of your fathers, the God of Abraham, of Isaac, and of Jacob, to lead you out of Egypt, into the promised land."

The name Jehovah means "the true God, the only God."

14 Moses and the Pharaoh

Exodus 4–12

Moses set off toward Egypt, to carry out the difficult mission that God had entrusted to him. Along the way, he was met by his brother Aaron, and together they went to announce to the people of Israel that the Lord had taken pity on their tribulations, and had decided to lead his people back to the land of Canaan, the Promised Land, so rich and fertile that it was as if its rivers flowed with milk and honey.

But first Moses had to persuade the pharoah, who did not wish to let the Hebrews go because he used them as slaves to build his cities.

Through the mouth of Aaron, Moses warned the pharoah that many punishments would be sent by God to force him to free the people of Israel. These punishments, "the plagues of Egypt," soon came to pass. The waters of the River Nile were changed into blood, the land was invaded by frogs, by mosquitoes, then by flies. All the livestock died off, the Egyptians were stricken by ulcers, the fields were destroyed first by hailstones and then by locusts, and for three days there was only darkness.

As each plague arrived, the pharoah sent for Moses and promised him that he would let the people of Israel go free; but as soon as the plague was over, he changed his mind again. Then the Lord foretold the worst plague of all: the death of every firstborn child of the Egyptians, from the firstborn child of the pharoah, to that of the humblest servant.

And so it came about: on the ordained night all the firstborn of the Egyptians died, while the people of Israel were untouched.

Then the pharoah hastily called Moses before him and told him to leave at once, he and all his people, and to go out from the land of Egypt forever.

15 The Sign of Blood

Exodus 11–12

In order to free his people from slavery, the Lord had to bring about the death of all the firstborn of the Egyptians. So that the firstborn of the Hebrews might be saved, the Lord ordered his people to mark the doors of their houses with the blood of a lamb.

He then ordered that the lamb should be roasted on the fire and eaten quickly, along with bitter herbs, while the people were standing up, with sticks in their hands, all ready to leave as soon as the pharoah gave his permission.

This meal was called the Passover, and the Lord ordered that it be held every year from then on, in memory of the miracles he did for his people: to remind them of the *passing* of the Lord who, seeing the sign of the blood, spared the lives of his people.

The meal was also to be held in memory of the passing of the people of Israel from slavery in Egypt to freedom in the Promised Land.

And as soon as the Passover meal was consumed the people of God left Egypt forever and, with the help of God and under the guidance of Moses, set off toward their new homeland.

16 And the Sea Divided . . .

Exodus 14–15

The people of Israel were on their journey through the desert. After years of slavery in Egypt, Moses, sent by God, was at last leading them to the land that God himself had promised to the descendants of Abraham, Isaac, and Jacob.

The pharaoh had granted the Hebrews permission to leave, but he soon regretted it. He gathered his war chariots together and set off to bring them back. He caught up with them near the Red Sea.

Moses and his people were caught in a trap: the sea was in front and the pharaoh's army behind.

All seemed to be lost, until God intervened with one of the most incredible miracles: for a whole night a strong wind blew. It swept back the waves of the sea, and the waters divided, leaving a dry path across which the people of God could travel to the other shore, without even getting their feet wet.

The pharaoh's chariots raced to pursue them across the same pathway, but when they were out in the middle, the waters surged back into their proper place, and swept them away. The Hebrews were saved and together they all sang a hymn of praise to God.

17 Miracles in the Desert

Exodus 15–17

With his mighty hand, the Lord had freed his people from slavery in Egypt, allowing them to cross the sea without getting wet.

The Lord performed many other miracles for his people, as they journeyed across the desert toward the land he had promised them.

After three days of marching, the Hebrews reached the waters of Mara, hoping to be able to quench their thirst there, only to discover that the water was as salty as the sea. But, through Moses, the Lord made it drinkable again.

Later it seemed that they would die of hunger, and they protested bitterly to Moses. On the very next day, around their camp, they found a great flock of quails, so numerous that they could catch them with their hands. And on the ground was a sweet, white substance, good to eat and very nourishing. This was manna and from then on it was found wherever the chosen people of God wandered on their journey to the Promised Land.

At another time, God made water flow out of a rock for his people, and when they were attacked by the Amalekites, God granted Moses the victory he prayed for.

18 The Ten Commandments

Exodus 19–20

The people of Israel had long been journeying in the desert toward the Promised Land, when they put up their tents at the foot of a high mountain called Mount Sinai. There, God summoned Moses onto the mountain for forty days, and then gave to him two stone tablets on which were written the ten laws, the Ten Commandments.

The Lord said to Moses: "I will make a pact with all my people. If they observe these ten commandments, I will guide them to the promised land, and I will make them a prosperous and mighty people."

These are the ten laws:

1 You shall worship no other God
2 Do not take the name of the Lord thy God in vain
3 Remember to keep the Sabbath; the seventh day is holy to God
4 Respect thy father and thy mother, and you will live long
5 You shall not kill
6 You shall not commit adultery
7 You shall not steal
8 You shall not tell lies
9 You shall not covet anyone's wife or husband
10 You shall not covet anyone's possessions

19 The Golden Calf

Exodus 32–34

When Moses came down from the mountain, he found that the people had not waited for his return. They had done a great wrong, and had made a statue of God in the form of a golden calf. They were worshiping it, saying: "Here is our God who brought us out of Egypt."

Moses was outraged; in his anger he threw the two tablets of the laws onto the ground, and they broke into many pieces. Then he destroyed the golden calf and punished those who had made it, for it was forbidden to make images of him.

The next day Moses went back up the mountain and the first thing he did was to beg God to forgive the grave sin of his people. Out of his goodness, the Lord granted his pardon, and gave Moses another two tablets of the laws, as well as other instructions for the people.

After another forty days Moses went back to the camp. In the presence of all his people he spoke of the pact that the Lord had proposed, and he read out the laws that the people were to respect in exchange for God's mighty help. The people listened to him and promised that they and their descendants would be obedient.

20 Listen, Israel

Deuteronomy 6

In the desert Moses explained the laws of God to his people; and then he spoke these words.

"Listen, O Israel. The Lord is our God, there is only one Lord. You shall love the Lord your God with all your heart, with all your soul, and with all your strength. Let these laws that I give you today be fixed in your hearts; you shall teach them to your children, you shall speak of them when you are sitting in your home, when you walk on your way, when you lie down to sleep, and when you rise up in the morning."

21 The House of God

Exodus 35–40

The Ten Commandments that God gave to Moses on Mount Sinai were written on two stone tablets.

Moses commanded the people to make a magnificent chest to contain the tablets, out of acacia wood covered in gold. This chest holding the tablets was called the Ark of the Covenant. The Ark of the Covenant had a golden top surmounted by two cherubs: it represented the throne of God, who was invisible but present among his people.

In the desert there was no temple to which the people could go to worship the Lord, so Moses had a special tent constructed, to take down and put up at every resting place on their journey.

This special tent was made of the finest purple hemp, and divided into two rooms: one room contained the Ark, and the other, precious objects like the golden candelabrum with seven arms and a golden altar on which scented incense was burned.

Outside this tent on special occasions a sacrificial altar was set up, where Moses and the Hebrews offered burnt sacrifices of the best meat and the best crops.

22 A Land Flowing in Milk and Honey

Numbers 13

Before leading all the people into Canaan, Moses sent ahead a group of men to scout out the land. This group was made up of one man from each tribe, and with them was Moses' right arm, a man called Joshua.

After forty days they returned and reported to the people: "We have found a land so rich and fertile that it seemed to be flowing with milk and honey: look at some of its fruits," and with that they held up a bunch of grapes so large that it had to be carried on a pole by two men.

23 Forty Years in the Desert

Numbers 14

"The land of Canaan is very fertile," the scouts reported to the people, "as these wonderful fruits we have brought back will prove. But the land is inhabited by powerful nations who have built huge, fortified cities. Moreover, some of the people who inhabit the land are as big as giants."

When they heard these words many of the Israelites were afraid and said: "We will never conquer this land. It would be better for us to return to Egypt; otherwise we will die in the desert."

Moses and Joshua tried to calm the people by saying: "This is the land that the Lord has promised us. He is with us and without doubt he will give us the strength to conquer it." But the rebellious people did not want to listen and began complaining again.

Then, above the tent which held the Ark of the Covenant, the glory of God appeared to all the Israelites. And the Lord said: "You yourselves will not enter this land: I will give it to your children." And so it was that the people of Israel remained in the desert for forty years, before they were able to enter the Promised Land.

24 The Conquest of the Promised Land

Deuteronomy 34; Joshua 1

Moses, the beloved of God, who had spoken face to face with the Lord, was not permitted to lead the people of Israel in their conquest of the Promised Land. He was one hundred and twenty years old when the Lord, from the summit of Mount Nebo, allowed him to see the full extent of the Promised Land: from Dan to Jericho, from the river Jordan to the Mediterranean Sea.

Then Moses died and his place as leader of the people was taken by Joshua. The Lord said to Joshua: "Be strong and brave because you are to lead my people in the conquest of the land I promised them. If you obey all the laws I gave you through my servant Moses, then you need not fear, I shall be with you!"

Joshua commanded the armies of the people in many expeditions and victorious battles and conquered the land of Canaan. Then he divided the land into many parts, and he gave one to each of the tribes that made up the people of Israel.

However, he did not give any land to the tribe of Levi, because this tribe was to serve the Lord in the tent which was his dwelling place; it had no land because its only wealth was the Lord himself.

25 Rahab and the Spies

Joshua 2

To enter the Promised Land, the first city that Joshua had to conquer was Jericho, a mighty place with strong walls. To find out more about its fortifications, Joshua sent two men to spy inside the city.

The king of Jericho found out about this and ordered that the gates be closed and the spies, hunted down and captured. The two Israelites went into the house of a woman, Rahab, who hid them on her terrace. When the guards came to look for them, Rahab said: "They have already fled. Run and perhaps you can catch up with them!"

Then she returned to the terrace and said to the two Israelites; "I know that the Lord is with you, and you will certainly conquer this city. When you enter into it be kind to me and my family." The men reassured her: "When we enter the city, keep your family in the house with you; tie a red rope to your window, so that our warriors recognize your house and spare you."

Rahab's house overlooked the wall of the city, so the woman lowered the two Israelites out of the window with a rope, and they returned to their camp.

26 Over the Jordan

Joshua 3

Joshua struck camp on the other side of the Jordan, crossed over the river, and thus entered the Promised Land. The whole people moved, preceded by the Ark carried on the shoulders of the priests.

As soon as the priests' feet touched the water, the flow of the river was interrupted: the waters rose up, leaving a dry passage. Everyone was able to cross to the other side before the river began flowing again. This was another of the great miracles that God performed for his people.

27 The Walls of Jericho

Joshua 6

Joshua and his warriors were outside Jericho. Faced with the arrival of the Israelites, the city had closed the gates in its mighty walls. How were they to conquer it?

Once again the Lord intervened to help his people, who followed his instructions and succeeded in the conquest of the city. This is how it came about.

For six days, in complete silence, a procession wound its way around the walls: at the front were seven priests carrying trumpets, then came the Ark of the Covenant, then Joshua and the warriors.

On the seventh day, the people arose at dawn, and they walked around the city seven times: then the priests sounded their trumpets and all the warriors uttered a great shout. At this sound, without a hand being laid on them, the walls of Jericho collapsed, and the warriors swarmed in, overcame their enemies, and took the city.

The Israelites took no spoils of war from the city that the Lord had given over to them; the gold, silver, bronze, and iron that they found within were kept for the Lord and placed in the treasury of the house of the Lord.

28 The Day the Sun Stood Still

Joshua 10

The Israelites conquered the cities of the Promised Land one after another. So the inhabitants of Gibeon thought to themselves: "It would be better to seek peace with the people of Israel than fight them and suffer defeat the way the others have done." And they made an alliance with Joshua.

Five kings of nearby cities then decided to declare war on Gibeon; they gathered their armies and besieged the city. Its inhabitants sent messengers to Joshua to beg for his aid.

Joshua hurried to the place with his warriors, and did battle with the armies of the five kings. He attacked them by surprise, causing panic among their soldiers; but the night was beginning to fall and the battle had not yet been decided.

Then Joshua invoked the aid of the Lord, and said: "Sun, stop above Gibeon!" And to everyone's amazement, on that day the sun did not set until the people of Israel had won their victory. Never before had it happened, nor has it happened since, that the sun stood still in the sky. And Joshua became famous throughout the land, as a great war leader, and as a friend of the Lord.

29 Joshua Speaks in the Valley of Shechem

Joshua 24

When he had conquered the Promised Land and had divided it among the people of Israel, Joshua called representatives of all the tribes of Israel to Shechem. They came in great numbers, their elders, their leaders, their judges, their families, and Joshua spoke to them.

He reminded them of the history of their ancestors, of Abraham, Isaac, and Jacob. He reminded them of their slavery in Egypt and the great things God had done to liberate his people. He reminded them of the laws that God had handed down through Moses, the Ten Commandments, and of God's goodness in giving them the land they now inhabited.

Speaking in the name of the Lord, Joshua preached to them: "I have given you a land which you have not worked with your own hands; you live in cities which you did not build with the sweat of your own brow. You eat the fruit of vines and olives you did not plant."

"Now," Joshua went on, "you must decide if you wish to serve the Lord, or if you prefer the gods of the other races we have encountered. As for myself, and my family, we wish to serve the Lord."

30 The Israelites Choose the Lord

Joshua 24

Great was the crowd that had gathered in the valley of Shechem, and it was with close attention that they listened to the speech made by their leader, Joshua.

Joshua had invited the people of Israel to choose: either to serve the Lord forever, or to abandon him and worship the strange gods that they had found in the Land of Canaan.

The people of Israel answered Joshua with a great shout: "We will serve the Lord, our God, forever, and we will obey only his voice."

31 Deborah and the Iron Chariots

Judges 4–5

The people of Israel lived in peace in the Promised Land, but often they had to confront nations nearby who waged war against them. When this happened, the chiefs of Israel, who were called judges, would pray to the Lord for his help and call the warriors together to defend them from their enemies.

A woman named Deborah was a judge of Israel once, when the northern territory was attacked by the powerful army of Sisera. The men of Israel were all foot soldiers and feared they could do little against an enemy who possessed nine hundred iron chariots. Deborah, however, rallied the warriors and gave them hope, saying: "The Lord will give us victory, because he leads us into battle."

The enemy was crossing the plain in its iron chariots when it began to rain. So much rain fell that the plain was flooded and the chariots were bogged down and remained stuck in the mud. The enemy fled, pursued by the warriors of Israel, who had won a great victory.

After the battle, Deborah sang a hymn of praise and thanks to the Lord, who had fought for his people by sending the providential rain.

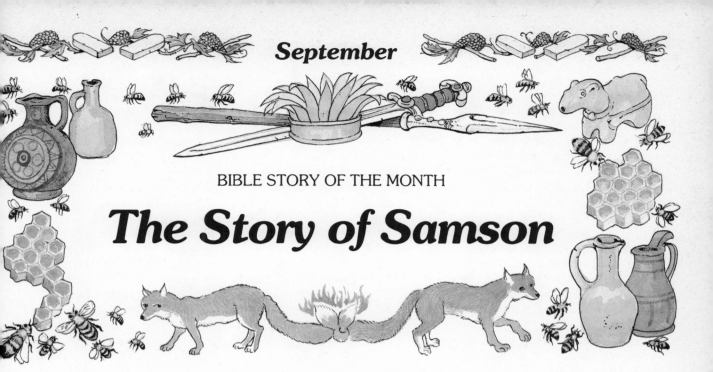

September

BIBLE STORY OF THE MONTH

The Story of Samson

Because the people of Israel had been oppressed for so long by their enemies, the Philistines, they raised up their voices in prayer to the Lord to ask him to come to their aid.

The Lord heard their prayers and from among the Israelites he set apart a child at the moment of his birth. His name was Samson and the sign that showed he was chosen by the Lord was that he was to allow his hair to grow and never cut it. In return, the Lord would give him extraordinary strength to fight the Philistines.

His strength was truly great: one day, when he was out in the countryside, Samson was attacked by a roaring lion. Although unarmed, he wrestled with the lion and killed it.

Some time after, he was passing by and decided to go and look at the remains of the lion. He discovered that a swarm of bees had made its home inside the carcass and had already begun to produce honey. There was so much that Samson was able to gather enough to satisfy his hunger.

It was the lion and the honey that inspired Samson to put a riddle to thirty young Philistines. He said to them: "If you can solve this riddle within seven days, I will give you thirty bed sheets and thirty changes of clothes."

The Philistines accepted the challenge and Samson put the riddle to them: "Out of the eater came forth meat, and out of the strong came forth sweetness."

The Philistines went to great lengths to solve the riddle, but they only succeeded by resorting to a trick at the end of the seventh day. Then they answered Samson: "What is sweeter than honey? What is stronger than a lion?"

Samson was obliged to give each of them a bed sheet and a change of clothes: these he obtained by killing thirty other Philistines, and in this way he began to fight his enemies.

On a later occasion, at the time of the corn harvest, Samson burned not only the Philistines' corn, but also their vines and their olives. The Philistines, in their fury, sent a great army against the people of Israel, who were filled with fear. So Samson said to the Israelites: "Do not be afraid. Bind me and hand me over to the Philistines, and then they will depart." The Israelites did as Samson commanded, but no sooner did he find himself alone among the Philistines, than he broke free from the bonds which restrained him and began to strike out at the enemy, killing a thousand of them.

On yet another occasion, Samson went into Gaza, a Philistine city. The enemy soldiers found out where he was staying and made plans to surprise him and kill him. But Samson

September

rose up at midnight and, since the gates of the city were barred, he used his mighty strength to lift up the great doors and the two posts, put them on his shoulders, and carry them off to the top of a hill nearby.

Since they could capture Samson in no other way, the Philistines decided to resort to trickery. It so happened that Samson was in love with a Philistine woman by the name of Delilah. She secretly made a bargain with the leaders of her people. Then she asked Samson again and again what the secret of his great strength was. He did not want to reveal this to her, but she insisted to such an extent that finally Samson explained: "My strength comes from

the Lord, my God; as proof of my love for him I have never cut my hair, and therein lies my strength."

Then, at night, while Samson slept, Delilah had his hair cut off and had him bound with strong ropes. When he awakened, Samson thought that he could break free but since his hair had been cut off, his strength had left him.

Then the Philistines led Samson away and they gouged out his eyes and chained him to the grindstone in the prison in Gaza.

Slowly, however, his hair began to grow again and his strength started to return. Some time later, on the day of a feast in honor of Dagon, their god, the Philistines

gathered in great numbers at their temple. There was great rejoicing among the Philistines that they no longer had to fear their great enemy, Samson. They decided to bring him out so that they might be amused by the spectacle of his defeat.

Samson was sent for and was brought from the prison to the temple, where a little boy led him by the hand because he was blind. Around the inside of the temple and on the roof were all the leaders of the Philistines and a huge crowd of about three thousand men and women. They laughed with delight at the man of whom they had been so afraid.

In his blindness, Samson asked the little boy who led him to guide him to the two pillars which supported the temple so that he could lean against them. He then prayed to the Lord: "Lord, remember me! I pray thee, only this once, to give me strength, O God!"

As soon as he had finished this prayer, he braced himself between the two pillars of the temple and began to push, crying out: "Let me die with the Philistines."

Then Samson pushed over the two pillars and the temple collapsed and fell upon all the people who were gathered there. In this way, Samson killed more enemies at his death than he had killed in his life.

Judges 13–16

September

1 The Lord Calls Gideon

Judges 6–7

For years the people of Israel had lived in fear of the Midianites, who stole or destroyed their crops and their livestock.

One day a messenger of the Lord appeared to Gideon and said to him: "The Lord is with you, mighty man of valor, and sends you to free his people from the Midianites."

"How do I know that it is the Lord who speaks? Show me a sign," Gideon asked the messenger. "Meanwhile, stay here while I go home to prepare food to offer you." Gideon went away and returned with bread and a pot of meat broth.

"Pour the broth over the bread," the mysterious visitor told him. Gideon obeyed, and then the messenger touched the meat and bread which were soaked in broth with the stick he held in his hand. At once they were consumed in flame and the visitor disappeared.

Then Gideon knew for certain that this mysterious visitor had been an angel of the Lord. The Lord himself then spoke directly to Gideon and commanded him to free his people from their enemies. Gideon now felt himself to be full of strength and when the Midianites returned, he gathered together a great army.

2 The Dew on the Fleece

Judges 6

Gideon wished to be certain that the Lord intended him to lead the army of Israel. So he prayed: "O Lord, tonight I shall lay a fleece of wool on the ground. If, tomorrow, I find dew only on the fleece, i will know that you will save Israel by my hand."

The next morning the fleece was soaked with dew while the ground around it was dry. "Help me to be certain, Lord," prayed Gideon, "and let it tomorrow be dry only on the fleece while the ground is bedewed." At dawn, he found the ground damp and the fleece dry.

3 The Victory over the Midianites

Judges 7

Gideon had gathered together his army to fight the Midianites and was camped at the well of Harod.

"The warriors who are with you are too numerous," the Lord said to Gideon. "They might think that the victory is a result of their own strength and not of my support. Therefore tell those who are afraid to leave and return home."

Gideon did this and twenty-two thousand men went home, leaving only ten thousand soldiers. "They are still too many," said the Lord. "Bring them to the well to slake their thirst. Keep with you those who drink by cupping their hands to their mouths and send home those who go on their knees to drink."

Gideon did as the Lord commanded and was then left with only three hundred men. "With these few men I will save the people of Israel and free them from the Midianites," the Lord assured Gideon.

When night was falling, Gideon divided his three hundred warriors into three companies and to each man he gave a trumpet and an empty pitcher containing a torch. He gave them precise orders and then, in the middle of the night, he led them to the enemy camp.

The three hundred silently positioned themselves around the camp where the Midianites were sleeping. Then, at a given signal, they smashed their pitchers and let their torches burn in the night, and they blew their trumpets and cried: "For the Lord and for Gideon!"

The Midianites awoke in surprise; when they saw the torches and heard the trumpets and the shouts, they were terrified. They too began to scream and fight among themselves confusedly, until they fled. Without using their arms and without even moving from their positions, the Israelites gained the victory, recognizing it as the work of God.

4 The Story of the Trees

Judges 9

The people of Shechem had chosen Abimelech, a cruel and ambitious man, as their leader. His brother, Jotham, warned the people, saying: "You have behaved as the trees did when they chose a king. They asked the olive to reign over them, but the olive replied: 'Should I stop producing oil, which is so useful to men, only to be king over you?'

"So the trees then asked the fig tree to come and be their king. But the fig replied: 'Should I forsake my sweetness and my lovely fruit only to reign over you?'

"The trees then asked the vine to be their sovereign. The vine, however, replied: 'Should I stop producing wine, which so cheers mankind, only to come and be your king?'

"Finally all the trees went and asked a mere bramble to be their king. The bramble accepted their offer at once, saying: 'I shall be your king, and if you are not good subjects I shall have you devoured by fire!' "

Jotham's parable turned out to be true. Abimelech showed himself to be wicked and inept, and some time later the people of Shechem had to rebel against him to free themselves from his dominion.

5 Ruth, the Faithful Daughter-in-Law

Ruth 1

In the days when the judges ruled the people of Israel, a great famine fell upon the land. For this reason, a certain man of Bethlehem went, with his family, to live in Moab.

His sons found wives among the women of Moab, but some time later they died and so did their father. Then the mother, whose name was Naomi, called her two daughters-in-law and said: "I can no longer look after you; therefore you should return to your families. I shall return to Bethlehem, my native city, to live among my own people."

One of the daughters-in-law returned to her own family, but the other did not wish to abandon her elderly mother-in-law and said to her: "Where you go, I will also go; and where you live, I too will live. Your people shall be my people and your God shall be my god. Only death shall separate me from you."

Naomi insisted, but when she saw her daughter-in-law was determined, they both gathered their belongings and left Moab for Bethlehem. The faithful daughter-in-law, willing to leave behind her own land and customs so as not to abandon her elderly mother-in-law, was called Ruth.

6 In the Fields of Boaz

Ruth 2–4

Everyone in the city of Bethlehem admired the young stranger, Ruth, who had risked so much and endured such hardship so as not to abandon her elderly mother-in-law.

Life was hard for the two women; they often had difficulties in finding enough food to eat. One day, at the time of the barley harvest, Ruth went out to gather grain and, without knowing it, she wandered into the fields of Boaz, who was a distant relative of Naomi's.

Ruth worked tirelessly for the whole day; Boaz noticed this, admired her, and wished to help her. He said to his men: 'Let some sheaves fall deliberately, so that the young woman may gather more."

On another occasion, Boaz made her a gift of six measures of barley and finally, moved by her unselfish manner to Naomi, he asked Ruth to marry him. Life was no longer hard for the two women, since Boaz was rich. But the marriage of Boaz and Ruth was also important for another reason: they had a son who was a great comfort to the aging Naomi and she gave him the name of Obed. He became the father of Jesse, who, in turn, was father to David.

7 A Child Is Offered to the Lord

1 Samuel 1–2

At that time a woman named Anna lived among the people of Israel and she was much loved by her husband. She, however, was very sad because the Lord had not granted her any children.

In those days, the Ark of the Covenant was kept at Shiloh and the priest Eli and his two sons served the Lord there in the sanctuary.

Many Israelites went there to pray, and one day, in tears, Anna offered up the following prayer and promise: "Lord," she said, "if you give me a son, I will consecrate him to you and he shall serve you all his life."

The Lord God heard Anna's prayer and she gave birth to a boy whom she called Samuel. She raised him with love and, years later when he was old enough to leave home, she took him to the sanctuary and entrusted him to the priest, Eli, to be trained in the service of the Lord.

Anna then offered up a sacrifice to the Lord, sang a hymn of praise, and returned home. Afterward the Lord rewarded Anna by blessing her with three more sons and two daughters.

8 God Speaks to Little Samuel

1 Samuel 2–3

Samuel lived in the sanctuary of the Lord, with the priest Eli and his two sons. These two sons behaved badly and carried out their work in a manner which offended the Lord.

Samuel was still a child when, one night, he heard a voice calling him: "Samuel! Samuel!" He thought it was the voice of Eli, sleeping nearby. Quickly, Samuel got up and ran to him. "Here I am," he said. But Eli replied: "I did not call you. Go back to sleep." A short time later, Samuel again heard his name called. He went back to Eli who again told him to go back to sleep.

When this occurred a third time Eli understood and said to the child: "If you hear your name being called again, you must say 'Speak, Lord, for your servant is listening.'"

Samuel went back to sleep, and when he heard his name being called a fourth time, he replied: "Speak, Lord, for your servant is listening." And it really was the Lord who had called him, for he gave Samuel a message: "I shall punish the sons of Eli for their wicked deeds," said the Lord, "for they have done evil in the eyes of the Lord and Eli has not restrained them. Tell Eli what I have said."

September

9 Samuel,
the Prophet of the Lord

1 Samuel 3–4

The priest Eli knew that the Lord had spoken to Samuel and he asked the boy what the Lord had said to him.

Samuel told him that the Lord was angry at the way in which the two sons of Eli behaved in his temple and had decided to punish them.

Not long afterward, the two wicked sons were both killed in battle and everyone then realized that the Lord had chosen Samuel as his chosen prophet, as a man to speak on his behalf.

10 The Ark in the Hands
of the Philistines

1 Samuel 5–6

It happened that the people of Israel were attacked by the army of the Philistines and the Lord allowed his chosen people to be defeated, for the Israelites had frequently ignored his will, and he wished to remind them to be faithful to him again.

When the Israelites realized that they were about to lose the battle, they sent for the Ark of the Covenant, which held the invisible presence of the Lord. They said: "If the Lord is among us, the victory will be ours."

But the Philistines were victorious instead, and they captured the Ark and carried it off to the temple of their god, Dagon.

The next morning the Philistines found that the statue of Dagon had fallen face down before the Ark of the Lord. They put it back in its place, but the following day they found that it had fallen down again and broken. Then strange diseases started to spread among the Philistines and they began to fear the Lord.

So they decided to return the Ark to the Israelites. They placed it on a new carriage, adding gifts of gold, and sent it back to the Lord's chosen people.

11 The Ark Returns
to the People of Israel

1 Samuel 6

The Philistines, who had taken possession of the Ark of the Lord, sent it back to the Israelites on a carriage drawn by two oxen, without a driver. Despite having no one to guide them, the oxen went straight to the land of the Israelites, straying neither to the left nor to the right.

It was the season of the grain harvest and the Israelites were at work in the fields. When they saw the Ark passing on the carriage they were filled with joy that the Lord, present in the Ark, was returning to be with his chosen people.

September

12 The Road to Salvation

1 Samuel 7

Once again, when the Philistines returned to threaten the Israelites, it was Samuel, the priest of the Lord, who showed his people the road to salvation. "Cast away all the false gods and turn your hearts completely to the Lord. If you serve only him, the Lord will deliver you from the Philistines."

The Israelites did as their wise priest had told them and succeeded in defeating the Philistines as well as their other enemies and recaptured the cities which had been taken from them.

13 The People Ask for a King

1 Samuel 9–10

One day the elders of the people of Israel came to Samuel with a request. "We," they said, "do not wish to be different from the other peoples. We, too, wish to have a king to keep us united, to give us just government, and to lead our armies into battle."

Samuel, however, replied: "We already have a king. The Lord God rules over us!" But they insisted and Samuel prayed to the Lord for guidance. "Listen to their request," the Lord told him. "Let a king reign over them. Appoint as king the man whom I shall choose for you, and I shall bless him."

Some time later it happened that a young man by the name of Saul was journeying from village to village in search of some of his father's donkeys which had been missing. Since he was passing close to the house of Samuel, he decided to go and ask the prophet whether or not he should continue to search for the donkeys.

Samuel saw that Saul was a tall and handsome young man. Samuel invited Saul to stay in his house for the night and the next day he was certain that he had found the man chosen to become king. Then Samuel took a jar of oil and poured it over Saul's head; in this way he blessed him and made clear what the Lord intended for him.

Samuel then said to Saul: "As for your donkeys, cease to trouble yourself, for they have already been found. Now you must go home; I will follow you and together we will offer up a sacrifice to the Lord. Then I will tell you what you must do."

On the road home Saul encountered a group of prophets with harps and flutes as Samuel had predicted. Then Saul knew that he really was chosen by the Lord and with the prophets he began to praise God.

14 Saul Is Proclaimed King

1 Samuel 10

Samuel had anointed Saul as king of Israel, but only in secret; now it was time to make the Lord's choice known to the people.

To do this, the prophet Samuel called the people together at Mizpeh. He made the men stand together according to their tribes, and then according to their families. Then he told the tribe of Benjamin to stand apart. From the tribe of Benjamin, Samuel then told the family of Matri to come forward. From this family Samuel chose a young man to stand forward and this was Saul.

They all looked for Saul and found him hiding among the baggage. He was brought before everyone and Samuel announced: "Here is the man whom the Lord has anointed." The whole assembly shouted: "Long live the king."

Sacrifices were offered to the Lord and a great feast was celebrated. Samuel then told the people what it meant to have a king and reminded them that all of them, both king and people, should seek above all else to do what was pleasing to the Lord. He then wrote all these things down in a book so that they should never be forgotten.

15 Saul Disobeys the Lord

1 Samuel 15

King Saul had decided to wage war on the Amalekites, so the prophet Samuel went to him and said: "The Lord will be with you and he will grant you victory, but all the spoils must be offered to the Lord. Neither you nor any other soldier must keep anything for yourself."

Saul went away to war and he defeated the Amalekites; but he disobeyed the Lord because he and his soldiers kept the best part of the spoils for themselves, instead of offering them to the Lord.

God then spoke to Samuel and said to him: "I regret having chosen Saul as king for he does not listen to my word."

Samuel went back to Saul and told him what the Lord had revealed to him. Saul then realized that he had acted against the will of God and asked for Samuel's forgiveness. "I cannot forgive you," replied the prophet, "for the Lord has rejected you and has already chosen another man to reign after you." He then turned to leave and Saul tried to detain him by grasping at his mantle, but it ripped. Samuel cried out: "Behold! In the same way the Lord will tear from you the kingdom which he gave you."

16 A Young Shepherd with a Kindly Face

1 Samuel 16

The Lord said to the prophet Samuel: "Go to Bethlehem to the house of Jesse. For it is from among his sons that I have chosen the king who will succeed Saul."

Samuel departed and when he arrived at the house of Jesse, he asked Jesse to let him see all of his sons. Jesse presented the eldest, Eliab, and Samuel wondered if he was perhaps the one that the Lord had chosen. But the Lord answered Samuel, saying: "Do not consider his stature, for I have refused him. Men look upon appearance, but I look upon the heart."

Jesse then presented his second, third, and fourth sons, and so on, until he had presented seven sons to Samuel. Samuel then asked him: "Are all your sons now here?" "There is still the youngest," replied Jesse. "Send for him now," said Samuel. The young shepherd was brought before them, and Samuel looked at him. He was golden-haired, with a beautiful face.

"It is he whom I have chosen," the Lord said, and so Samuel anointed him in front of his brothers. The young shepherd was called David and was to become the greatest king of Israel.

17 David at the Court of Saul

1 Samuel 16

King Saul knew that the Lord was not pleased with him, for he had disobeyed his command. Even the prophet Samuel no longer came to see him and no longer gave him advice. Saul was full of concern and from time to time he even had moments of madness.

His counselors advised him: "Find someone who plays the lyre well; when you feel agitated have him play and it will calm you." Saul accepted their advice and said: "Find me someone suitable."

"I know the right person," said one of the advisers. "He is David, the youngest son of Jesse. He has a handsome countenance, is strong and courageous, skilled in the use of arms, and wise in argument. What is more, he is an excellent player of the lyre."

David was sent for, and afterward he came often to the court of Saul, particularly when the king felt ill at ease. At these times, David would calm him by singing and playing his lyre.

Saul did not know that the young man had already been chosen by the Lord to become king of Israel after him, instead of Jonathan, his eldest son.

18 David Fights the Giant Goliath

1 Samuel 17

The Israelites were at war with the Philistines. The soldiers of Israel were terrified because every day a gigantic man strode out of the camp of the Philistines to challenge them. Each day, for forty days, the giant shouted: "Israelites: Send out one of your men to fight me. If he wins, the Philistines shall be your servants; if I win, then you become our slaves."

Then David came and said: "I will fight him!" He ran down quickly to the nearby stream, and picked up five stones and put them in his shepherd's bag. Then, with his sling, he moved toward the giant.

When Goliath saw this unarmed youth coming toward him, he began to laugh, but David said to him: "You come to me armed with your sword, your lance, and your club. I come to you in the name of the Lord, who will defeat you!"

When he was at the correct distance, David took a stone from his bag, fitted it into his sling, and threw it. He struck Goliath full in the forehead, and the giant fell to the ground unconscious. With a leap David, with Goliath's own sword, cut off the giant's head. At that, all the Philistines fled, pursued by the soldiers of Israel.

19 The Triumph of David

1 Samuel 18

With the help of the Lord, the young and unarmed David had defeated the giant Goliath, and had gained a great victory for the army of Israel, and put to flight the ranks of their enemies, the Philistines.

David returned home with King Saul from the field of battle and in all the villages and cities they passed through the women came out to praise them and sang and danced around them. As they danced for joy, they sang: "Saul has slain thousands of the enemy, but David has killed tens of thousands!"

20 Saul Tries to Kill David

1 Samuel 18–19

The people of Israel admired and loved David after he had killed the giant Goliath and put their enemies to flight. But King Saul became jealous of David and sought to kill him.

The king had promised the hand of his daughter in marriage to the man who overcame Goliath, but now he said: "I will give her to him, but first he must kill one hundred Philistines." Saul believed that if David had to fight one hundred enemies, then one of them would surely kill him!

But David, well within the allotted time, returned with proof of having killed not one hundred, but two hundred Philistines. And so David took as his bride Michal, the daughter of the king.

But Saul had not given up the idea of killing David. One day when Saul was at home and feeling ill at ease, David took up his lyre and began to play to calm the king. Suddenly Saul picked up his spear and threw it at David. If it had struck him, David would surely have been killed, but he avoided it and fled from the palace. Each time Saul made an attempt on David's life he was unsuccessful, for David was protected by the Lord.

21 Michal Helps David

1 Samuel 19

Michal, the daughter of King Saul, greatly loved her husband, David. When Saul tried to kill David with a blow from his lance, David escaped to his own home. Michal, however, warned David, saying: "I fear that my father will not change his mind; he will seek to kill you even here. You must flee tonight."

David listened to his wife's advice. She lowered him from a window and David ran off to hide in a nearby field. Then Michal made up David's bed as if he were still in it; she stuffed clothes under the blankets to look like his body.

Just as Michal had foreseen, men sent by Saul arrived the following morning to take David and kill him. Michal said to them: "Tell the king that David cannot come for he is sick," and she allowed them a glimpse of the bed, which seemed to be occupied.

"Bring him and his bed to me!" Saul ordered. Thus the trick was discovered and Saul was very angry with his daughter. He said to her: "Why did you deceive me and allow him to escape?"

And Michal, in ·her great love for David, lied: "He threatened to kill me if I did not help him to flee."

September

22 Jonathan, the Faithful Friend

1 Samuel 20

Jonathan, the son of King Saul, was a great friend to David and was very unhappy because his father wanted to put David to death.

David went in secret to Jonathan to ask him to find out what the king's intentions were. Jonathan promised he would try to tell him within three days. They agreed on a time and place to meet.

Saul said to Jonathan; "I know you are a friend to David! But if he lives you will not be king after me." Angrily, he added: "He must die!"

Jonathan tried to defend David and reminded his father that he had never done anything wrong; but Saul was unyielding. Then Jonathan took his bow and his arrows and, accompanied by a boy, he went out into the countryside.

At the place where he had agreed to meet David, Jonathan began to shoot arrows just as if he were practicing with his bow. Each time, the boy went to recover the arrows. At a certain moment, Jonathan shouted out to the boy: "Run! The arrow is farther away than that!"

This was the agreed signal. David, who was watching and listening from a hiding place, knew then what Saul's decision had been.

When Jonathan had sent the boy home with the arrows, David came out of hiding, walked up to Jonathan and embraced him. The two friends wept together. Then, when the moment of parting came, Jonathan said: "Now you must flee and hide; but do not be afraid, because the Lord is with you wherever you go. I beg you not to hate me for the wrong my father does you; be my friend always, as I have been and always will be a friend to you. Swear to me that, when you have defeated all your enemies, you will be kind to my children and their descendants." And David, moved by his friend, made a solemn promise.

23 The Sword of Goliath

1 Samuel 21

Under threat from King Saul, who wanted to put him to death, David fled. First, he went in secret to the sanctuary of the Lord, where he explained to the priest that he had to leave in haste, without arming himself. Immediately, the priest said to him: "We hold here the sword of Goliath. Use it if you wish."

David took the sword and went off to live in the desert. Many men gathered around him and together with them David fought against the enemies of his people.

24 David Flees from Saul

1 Samuel 23

David was living in the desert with his men. He did not declare war on King Saul, who planned to put him to death, but fought instead against the Philistines, the enemies of his people.

But Saul hated David so much that he wanted to kill him at any cost. One day some spies came to the king and informed him that David and his men were living in a certain part of the desert. Saul called up his army and set out.

He arrived near where David was and almost caught him in a trap. He would certainly have succeeded if David had not been under the Lord's protection, for the Lord had already chosen David to be the new king.

At one point during the pursuit the two armies were close enough to see each other. They had both entered a steep mountain gorge, and Saul and his men were on one side, David and his men on the other.

There would have been no escape for David if a messenger had not come unexpectedly to Saul to inform him that the Philistines had invaded the kingdom again, and the king had to hurry back to defend the land and his people.

25 Abigail, a Clever Woman

1 Samuel 25

David and his men were in the desert, preparing to fight the enemies of the people of Israel when David sent several of his young men to Nabal. Nabal was a very rich man whom David had helped. David sent a messenger to say to him: "Help me and my men, for it is difficult to find sustenance in the desert." But Nabal's reply was cold, for he did not want to give anything to David.

A servant spoke to Abigail, the wife of Nabal, and told her what had happened. She immediately realized the danger they were in: insulted by this reply, David and his men could easily take revenge on Nabal and his people. Without saying a word to her husband, Abigail hurriedly gathered two hundred loaves of bread, two bottles of wine, five cooked sheep, five measures of parched corn, a hundred clusters of raisins, and two hundred cakes of figs, and loaded it all onto the backs of donkeys. She sent servants to David with the laden donkeys, and she herself followed behind them.

When she came before David, she prostrated herself at his feet, saying: "Accept these gifts and forget the wickedness of my husband. The Lord will look on you favorably if you don't take revenge on him."

"Blessed be the Lord that has sent you to me," replied David, "for he has prevented me from taking vengeance with my own hands. You are a wise and clever woman."

Abigail returned home, where she found her husband feasting like a king. When she told him what had happened, he was so overcome with the thought of the risk that he had run that he became paralyzed with fear, and some days later he died.

When David learned that Nabal had died, he remembered how wise Abigail was and sent for her and married her himself.

26 David Spares the Life of Saul

1 Samuel 26

Saul, the king of Israel, was still determined to put David to death and prevent him from becoming king in his place. The king and his army were camped in the desert when David and one of his young men came down to their camp one night. They came to Saul's bedside and, everyone slept, so did not notice David. The man with David said: "Here is your chance to kill your enemy!"

"I will never do that," replied David, "even if Saul wishes my death, for he is the Lord's anointed!" Then he took the spear and the water jug which stood by the king's bedside and moved off. He climbed to the top of a nearby hill and shouted in a loud voice: "I am innocent. Why do you persecute me? I could have killed you and did not do so. If you do not believe me, send a man to fetch back your spear and your water jug."

Saul was overwhelmed by David's generosity and called: "I have sinned against you. Return and I will do you no further wrong." However, David did not trust him, and he replied: "Just as your life was sacred to me today, so is mine in the eyes of the Lord."

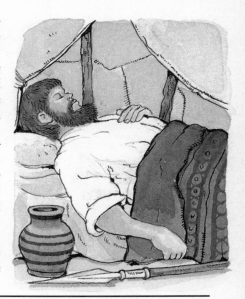

27 David Weeps for Saul and for Jonathan

1 Samuel 31; 2 Samuel 1

The king of Israel died on Mount Gilboa during a battle against his enemies, the Philistines. Many soldiers died with him, and among them was Jonathan, the son of the king and a great friend to David.

When David learned the news, he gave no thought to all the wrongs that Saul had done him. Instead he raised a cry of lament and said: "Neither dew nor rain shall fall again on Mount Gilboa, for heroes have perished there. Sons of Israel, weep for Saul! I am filled with anguish for you, Jonathan, my friend!"

28 David Becomes King

2 Samuel 2, 5, 8, 12

After the death of Saul and his son Jonathan, the people of the tribe of Judah, to which David belonged, came to him and proclaimed him their king.

David established himself in the city of Hebron, and there he reigned over the tribe of Judah for seven years. After seven years the men of the other tribes also recognized him as king and David reigned over all the people of Israel. He was thirty years old when he was made king and his rule lasted forty years.

During that time he fought many wars against his enemies. He subjugated many peoples and expanded the kingdom and amassed great wealth. He was a good king; he administered justice with wisdom; he praised the greatness of the Lord, composing beautiful prayers called psalms; and he ordered that the history of the people of Israel, the people whom the Lord had shaped, protected, and helped on so many occasions, be recorded in writing.

David had many wives, as was the custom then, and many children. Among these children was Solomon, the son of Bathsheba, and David promised Bathsheba that Solomon would be his successor.

29 The Conquest of Jerusalem

1 Chronicles 11

In the middle of the land of Israel there was a city inhabited by foreigners, the Jebusites. It was the city of Jerusalem, which stood on a hill and was surrounded by walls. It was a city that was impossible to conquer, and its inhabitants would say: "The blind and the lame would be enough to repel the attacks of our enemies."

David, who had become king over all the people of Israel, saw that Jerusalem was the ideal city for the capital of his kingdom. But how could he conquer it?

When he made a close study of how it was built, he noticed that the Jebusites had dug a deep well inside the city so that the water from the spring outside would reach the city. So David said to his men: "If there are any volunteers who will follow the spring up through the well, I will reward them greatly. Moreover, the first man to enter the city in this way will become a captain of my army."

A band of men went up through the well, entered the city, and took it by surprise. The first man among them was Joab, and David proclaimed him head of his army. In this way, Jerusalem became the capital of Israel.

30 The Ark Is Brought to Jerusalem

2 Samuel 6

The Ark of the Covenant, the golden chest which contained the tablets of the law given to the people of God through Moses, was the most precious to the people of Israel. On its lid stood God's two cherubim.

When David had conquered Jerusalem and made it the capital of Israel, he began to think about bringing the Ark of the Lord to the city, for until then it had remained in various places in the countryside.

The procession would have to be very solemn, thought David, to be worthy of the majesty of the Lord. For this reason he called all the people to celebrate at the Ark with music and songs, while he himself removed his royal garments and went dancing before it.

His wife Michal saw him from her window and when he came back into the palace she scorned him for having danced in front of everyone like a common man. David, however, said to her: "In this way, I chose to respect the Lord. And it was right, because he has been so good to me. I was a mere shepherd, a man of no importance, and he has made me the king of his chosen people!"

October

BIBLE STORY OF THE MONTH

Absalom, Son of David

King David was a good and just man, whose actions pleased the Lord; and even when David committed a sin, he asked the Lord's pardon immediately.

The same could not be said for his sons, who were often violent and selfish. Absalom was one of them: he was young, handsome, and brave, and many people thought well of him; but his heart was full of treachery. Absalom felt he had been offended by his brother Amnon. So, without showing his anger, he invited Amnon to a banquet and there he ordered his servants to kill him. Then he fled, to escape the wrath of David.

Absalom had a friend close to the king: Joab, the commander of the army. After three years, Joab found that the king had stopped mourning for his murdered son, Amnon, and he managed to obtain permission from David for Absalom to return to the land of Israel, as long as the king did not have to see him. Once he was back, Absalom tried so hard and insisted for so long, that in the end David agreed to pardon him and see him.

From that time, Absalom assumed an air of great richness and importance, and went with his men outside the gates of the city. When anyone came to the city to receive justice, Absalom said to him: "You are in the right, but no one will recognize your rights; no one will listen to you on behalf of the king. Oh, if only I could be named Judge of Israel: Then everyone who had suffered a wrong would receive justice."

Then Absalom would hold out his hand and hug and kiss the person, pretending to be very sorry for him. In this way young Absalom's popularity continued to increase throughout the land.

When the right moment arrived, Absalom went before David and said: "Let me go to Hebron, because I promised the Lord I would offer him sacrifices in that city." In reality his intentions were very different. Accompanied by some of the most important men in the kingdom, Absalom went to Hebron and sent out messengers to all the tribes, to announce that he was the new king.

When David was informed that Absalom had begun to plot against him, that he had proclaimed himself king and had a large following, David cried out: "Hurry, we must flee, otherwise none of us will escape the hand of Absalom."

Immediately, surrounded by his guards and his faithful friends, David set out from the palace, and a great number of the people of Jerusalem

went with him. He set off toward the desert, and in the valley of Cedron he stopped and waited for all of his followers to come to him. Then he saw that the priest Zadok was coming with the Levites, bearing the Ark of the Lord. David ordered him: "Return the Ark to the city! If the Lord is with me, he will allow me to return there and see it; if the Lord does not wish that I return, then his will be done."

Then David went off up the Mount of Olives. He went weeping, with his head covered and his feet bare, as signs of great suffering. Along the way a man insulted him. David's guards would have killed

this man, but David held them back saying: "My own son would take my life; what are the insults of this stranger compared to that? Leave him alone. Perhaps God will see the wrongs that I must suffer and repay me with a greater kindness."

Meanwhile Absalom had moved into Jerusalem and taken over the palace. His advisers then counseled him to chase after David, in order to kill him and all those who were with him. Absalom listened to them, called together his army, and set off after David.

David, too, was preparing for battle. He gathered all those who had remained faithful to him, organized

them into groups and, before all of them, he ordered the leaders to treat his young son Absalom with respect.

The battle took place in the forest of Ephraim, and David's soldiers overcame Absalom's. Absalom also fled, on a mule. All of a sudden the mule passed under the low branches of a great oak tree, and Absalom's head got wedged in the branches. The mule went on, leaving Absalom suspended in the branches. A man saw him and ran off to tell Joab, the army commander. "Why did you not kill him at once?" asked Joab, and the man answered: "With my own ears I heard the king's order that the life of his son be spared." But Joab killed Absalom himself.

David was sitting by the gates of the city, when a messenger arrived to announce the victory. "Is young Absalom well?" asked David. The man answered: "Would that all the king's enemies be as he!"

So David understood that his son was dead, and he began to shudder and weep. Through his tears, he cried: "Absalom, my son, if only I were dead instead of you, oh, my son Absalom."

And thus the victory was transformed into mourning; all the people were moved by the king's sorrow over his son, even though Absalom had betrayed him.

2 Samuel 13–19

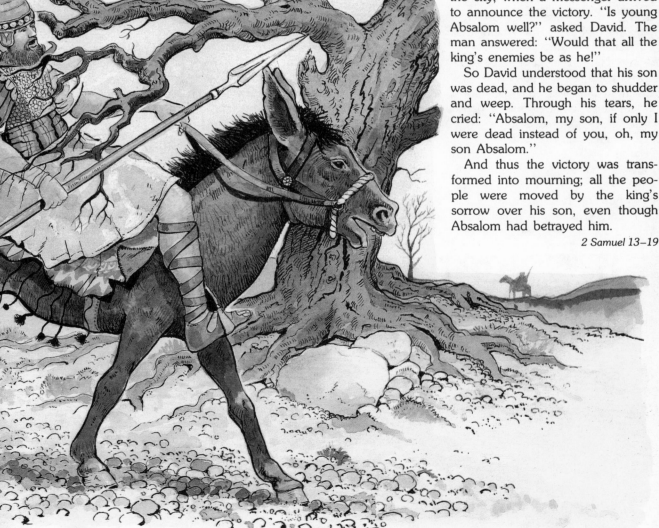

1 The Lord Is My Shepherd

Psalm 23

Throughout his whole life, King David continued to compose poems (or psalms), which he sang to the music he played on his lyre. There is one psalm that is full of joy for the protection that the Lord grants to those who trust in him: "The Lord is my shepherd, I shall not want. He makes me to lie down in green pastures; he leads me beside the still waters. He restores my soul; he leads me in the paths of righteousness for his name's sake. Though I walk in the dark valley, I fear no evil, for he is at my side."

2 A Prophecy for David

2 Samuel 7

David lived in peace in Jerusalem, where he had taken the Ark of the Covenant. One day he called the prophet Nathan to him and said: "Look. I live in a beautiful palace, while the Ark of the Lord is still in a humble tent. I want to build a great house, a temple suitable for the Lord, to enshrine the Ark."

Nathan, who, like all the other prophets, spoke in the name of God, said to him: "Do not worry about building a temple; the Lord has not asked you for it. The temple will be built by your son Solomon, who will be king after you; and after Solomon, Jerusalem will still be ruled by your descendants. Your throne will endure forever."

Then David went and stood before the Ark, in the presence of the Lord, and said: "Who am I, Lord, that you cover me with so many favors? And still you do not consider this enough: you now guarantee my descendants far into the future. You are truly great, O Lord, my God."

Nathan's prophecy came true with Jesus, the descendant of David and the Son of God: he is the King of the Universe, and his kingdom is without end; his throne will endure forever.

3 The Gratitude of David

Psalm 139

God knows the heart of man. David was aware of this, and so he sang his gratitude: "Lord you watch me and you know me, you know when I sit down and when I arise, when I walk along my path and when I rest. Where can I go to get away from you? If I go up into the sky, you are there, if I descend into the abyss, there you are. If I fly on the wings of the wind to go and live at the ends of the sea, it is your hand that guides me. For you the shadows are light and the night is clear as the day."

4 For Love of Jonathan

2 Samuel 4, 9

David ruled over Jerusalem, loved and respected by his subjects and feared by his enemies. He was very powerful, but he did not forget those who had helped him. In particular he did not forget Jonathan, the son of King Saul; nor did he forget his promise to Jonathan to treat his descendants with respect.

But were there any left? The king sent servants to find out, and they told him that only one of Saul's sons had survived. He was called Meribbaal, now a grown man, but he was crippled in both feet. He had been five years old when the news had arrived of the defeat of Saul and Jonathan; his nursemaid had picked him up to flee with him, but in her haste she had dropped him, leaving him crippled.

When David sent for Meribbaal he came, but full of fear, because he thought David wanted to take revenge on him for the wrongs he had suffered at the hands of Saul. But the king said to him: "Do not be afraid! I wish to be kind to you, out of love for Jonathan, your father. I will give you back all the fields taken away from you, and you will always feast at my table. For love of Jonathan."

5 Solomon Is Crowned King

1 Kings 1–2

King David had grown very old, and his eldest son, Adonijah, thought he would declare himself king. The most important men in the kingdom were on his side.

However, King David had decided a long time ago that on his death his place should be taken by another son, Solomon. So Nathan the prophet sent Solomon's mother to David, to remind him of his promise and tell David of Adonijah's intentions.

When he heard about Adonijah, David called the prophet Nathan and the priest Zadok to him, and said to them: "Take my guard at once, tell Solomon to go down to the well at Gihon: there you must consecrate Solomon as king; then sound the trumpets and shout: 'Long live King Solomon.'"

All this was done and Solomon became king of the people of Israel. When he felt that his time to die was near, David called Solomon to him and said: "Be strong and wise. Observe the laws of the Lord and you will succeed." Then the great King David died; Solomon took his place, and his kingdom grew prosperous and mighty, because the Lord was with him.

October

6 Solomon's Dream

1 Kings 3

King Solomon went to Gibeon to offer a great thanksgiving sacrifice to the Lord. And that night the Lord appeared to him in a dream and said to him: "Tell me what you desire from me."

Solomon replied: "O Lord. you have been so good to me to allow me to become king in the place of my father, David. But I am like a child, lacking in the experience to rule over your people properly. Help me to become wise."

The Lord was pleased by this request, and replied to Solomon:

"You did not ask me for a long life, nor riches, nor the defeat of your enemies, but you have asked me for the wisdom to rule over my people fittingly: so, I grant you a wise and intelligent heart, and I also grant you that which you did not ask for. Together with wisdom, I will grant you riches and glory and a long life for yourself."

Solomon awoke, returned to Jerusalem and went before the Ark of the Covenant, in the presence of the Lord. There he offered other sacrifices to the Lord, and the Lord kept his promises: Solomon ruled for forty years, and his rule was wise, rich, and glorious.

7 The Judgment of Solomon

1 Kings 3

Solomon was such a wise king that his judgments became famous all over the world.

On one occasion, two women came before him. The first one said: "We live in the same house and each of us had a child within a few days of each other. One night this woman's child died; and so she substituted it for mine: the child that she carries in her arms is mine!"

However, the second woman protested and said: "No, this child is mine. The one that died was yours!"

So Solomon had a sword brought and ordered his servants: "Cut the child in two and give half to each of these women!"

When she heard these words, the first woman said: "No, my lord, do not kill the child: I would rather have you give it to the woman who holds it in her arms than see it die!"

The second woman said: "Very well, let it be divided: so it be neither mine nor yours."

The wise King Solomon had given this order deliberately: he did not want to put the child to death, but he knew that the real mother would prefer to lose it rather than see it die. And he then gave the little baby to the real mother.

54

8 A House for the Lord

1 Kings 5–6

Solomon ruled in peace over the people of Israel, and he decided that the time had come to fulfill his father David's wish and build a permanent house for the Lord.

Until that time, the Ark of the Covenant, over which hung the invisible presence of God, had been housed in a tent which had been moved many times from the desert of Sinai until it reached Jerusalem. Now the Lord would have a permanent dwelling place among his people, a temple worthy of him.

For this reason, Solomon sent ambassadors to Hiram, the king of Tyre in Lebanon, and they spoke in the name of Solomon: "You know that my father, David, was not able to build a temple to the name of the Lord, because of the wars waged against him by all his enemies. Now that the Lord has granted me peace, I have decided to build a temple to his name. Order, therefore, that cedar trees of Lebanon be cut."

When Hiram heard these words, he sent a messenger back to Solomon saying: "I have received your message. I will do as you wish about the cedar and fir wood. My servants will take it down from Lebanon to the sea; I will have it loaded onto rafts and carried to the place you ask. Then I will have it unloaded and you can take it away."

After this agreement was reached, Solomon called upon thousands and thousands of workers from his people and sent them to dig out stone from the mountains and then he took skilled architects into his service. And in the fourth year of his reign, on the hill to the north of Jerusalem, Mount Zion, he began the construction. The building work lasted seven years, and the result was so magnificent, it became famous not only among the people of Israel but also in foreign lands.

9 The Temple on Mount Zion

1 Kings 6–7

The temple that Solomon raised to the Lord on Mount Zion was huge and magnificent.

An enormous terrace was raised high by thick walls on all its sides.

In the middle of the terrace was the sanctuary, made of nothing but marble embossed with gold, and of bronze, and precious wood like the cedar from Lebanon.

On the sides of the sanctuary there were wide courtyards, all covered in marble and surrounded by noble porticos on columns of pure marble.

10 The Sanctuary of the Temple

1 Kings 6

The main part of the great temple built by Solomon was the sanctuary. It rose up above the other buildings of the temple and it could be seen from afar in all its glory. It was made up of three rooms: the entrance, the sanctuary, and the Holy of Holies.

In the sanctuary there was a large elaborately carved seven-branched candelabrum and a table on which were laid twelve loaves, one for each of the twelve tribes of Israel. In the sanctuary there was also a small gold altar, the altar for holding incense.

11 The Holy of Holies

1 Kings 6

The third room in the sanctuary was the most sacred part of the whole temple; in fact it was the most sacred place in the whole world. This room was called the Holy of Holies, and contained the Ark of the Covenant, above which hovered the invisible presence of the Lord. The Ark of the Covenant was placed between two giant cherubs made of olive wood covered in gold. The two cherubs were taller than the height of two men, and their wings, which touched in the middle of the room, spread out over the Ark.

12 Offerings to the Lord

1 Kings 6

Outside the sanctuary of the temple of Jerusalem, in the open air, there was everything necessary to offer up to the Lord the sacrifices that the king and the people brought to the temple: animals without blemish or the choicest of the crops.

They were offered on the altar, a huge square piece of stone with a ramp on one side to allow access.

Not far from the altar there was a large washbasin of bronze, supported by twelve bronze oxen; it was full of water and was used for the purification of the priests.

13 Priests and People in the Temple

1 Kings 6–7

In the great temple of Jerusalem, built by Solomon, the main tasks were undertaken by the high priest and the other priests; the less important tasks were carried out by the Levites.

The priests wore special clothes while carrying out their tasks in the temple. Out of respect for the holy place, in the presence of the Lord, they went barefoot. They remembered that the Lord, when he spoke to Moses from the burning bush, out in the desert, commanded him to take off the sandals that he wore, because any place where the Lord is present is sacred.

Only the priests could enter into the sanctuary; only they could offer sacrifices. The people were not even allowed to approach the altar, but the men could watch the ceremonies from behind a screen. The women were only permitted as far as the courtyard before the one that admitted the men.

Foreigners, all those who did not belong to the people of Israel, could only enter the external courtyard of the temple, where notices in various languages warned them that, if they went beyond it, they risked certain death.

14 The Lord Enters into His Temple

1 Kings 8

The great temple built by Solomon on Mount Zion, in Jerusalem, was ready. It was a noble building, magnificent in its construction and furnishings. It was ready, but it lacked the essential element for which it had been built: the Ark of the Covenant, over which hovered the invisible presence of God. From the time of King David, the Ark of the Covenant had been in its tent in Jerusalem. When the temple was finished, King Solomon called together the elders, the princes, and the chiefs, and had them carry the Ark of the Covenant into the temple.

The priests and the Levites lifted it up, and amidst great exultation, the Ark was carried inside the temple, to the Holy of Holies. As soon as they left the temple, the glory of the Lord, in the form of a cloud, entered to fill up the temple: the Lord took possession of his house among men.

The king then went before the altar and, in front of all the people, he made a prayer to the Lord. He said: "Lord, listen to us when we come to this place to pray to you. You, from the sky, listen to our prayers and pardon our sins." Then Solomon offered a sacrifice to the Lord and blessed the people.

15 Pilgrims on the March

Psalm 84

Wherever Israelites lived, no matter how far away from Jerusalem, their greatest desire was to go to the holy city, to the temple of the Lord.

What could have been more important? That is why the Israelites composed this song:

How lovely is your house,
Lord, God of the universe!
My soul is sad because
it is far from your temple.
Even sparrows make their home
and swallows build their nests
there, near to your altar.
O Lord, my king and my God;
happy are those
who live in your house:
always singing your praise!
Happy are those who can make the
 holy journey.
Along the way their strength grows
until they come before you.
For me a day in your temple
is worth more than a thousand days
 elsewhere.

The journey that is spoken about in this song is the one that the Israelites made at Passover and on other major feast days, to Jerusalem, on the hill of Zion, where the temple of the Lord stood.

16 The Gratitude of the Pilgrims

Psalms 121, 130, 124.

The pilgrims who made their way to Jerusalem used to recite some psalms along the way:

"I raise up my eyes to the mountains: where will my help come from? My help comes from the Lord who made the sky and the earth."

The pilgrims prayed in this way, to ask for help with the dangers of the journey.

In order to go before the Lord they had to repent of their sins; and that is what the pilgrims did with this psalm:

From the depths I cry out to you Lord: Lord, listen to my voice.
If you look upon our sins,
then who could stand before you?
But we can find pardon in you!
I put my hope in the Lord;
my spirit awaits him
more than the watchmen await
the morning light.

After they had obtained his pardon, the pilgrims thanked the Lord with this psalm:

"If the Lord had not been with us, the waters would have swept us away, a torrent would have drowned us. We have been freed like a bird from the hunter's snare: the rope has been broken and we have flown away!"

17 The Pilgrims' Departure

Psalm 133; 134

The pilgrims journeyed in groups, and it was good for them to find themselves among other people with the same faith: good and sweet like the dew which comes down from mount Hermon.
Look, how good and right it is, that brothers should live together!
It is like the dew of Hermon which falls on the hills of Zion!

Hermon is the highest mountain in the land of Israel, and its snows were a symbol of coolness and delight for the inhabitants of that sun-parched land.

After the days spent near the temple, the pilgrims got ready to depart. First, however, they asked the priests, who had the good fortune to remain in the temple of Jerusalem, to continue to pray for them:
Bless the Lord,
All of you, servants of the Lord;
who pass your nights in
the house of the Lord.
Raise your hands up to the temple and bless the Lord.

In reply, the pilgrims received a last blessing from the priests: "The Lord who made the sky and the earth and all creatures great and small blesses you from atop Mount Zion."

18 The Feasts of Pentecost and the Day of Atonement

Leviticus 16, 23

Along with Passover, two major feasts were celebrated in the temple of Jerusalem.

Fifty days after Passover came the feast of Pentecost, when thanks were given to the Lord for the gifts of the earth, and the choicest of the crops were offered up in sacrifice.

And they also celebrated the Day of Atonement, when the Lord was asked to pardon the sins of the people. On that day, they would choose two goats. Through a random choice, one of them was put aside for the Lord; the other for the devil.

The high priest then performed a ceremony, during which he transferred all the sins of the people onto the second animal, which was then turned loose into the desert, to be consigned to the devil.

The other goat was offered up in sacrifice in the temple. Then the high priest took a little of its blood, and on this one day out of the whole year, he went into the Holy of Holies and poured it over the Ark of the Covenant.

This strange rite meant that the goat offered in sacrifice represented the people of Israel, and through this animal the whole population offered itself to the Lord.

19 The Feast of the Tabernacles

Leviticus 23

One of the main feasts celebrated by the chosen people of the Lord was the feast of the huts, or the tents, or the Tabernacles.

It was so called because on this day all the people left their houses to go and live in tents or temporary huts.

This was in memory of the forty years during which the people of Israel lived in the desert, after their flight from slavery in the land of Egypt.

During the eight days spent in the tents nobody worked; everyone meditated on the great miracles performed by the Lord for his people. He had kept his people fed and defended them from their enemies; he had made an alliance with them; he had given them his laws so that they would know how to behave in any circumstances in life; and last of all he had given them a fertile land in which to live.

Remembering how good the Lord had been also brought to mind all the other gifts that the Lord had given to his people, and they all praised him and thanked him, promising to repay him in the only way he desired: by loving him and observing his laws.

20 The Ships of Solomon

1 Kings 9–10

Solomon was a very wise and able king. His people were great traders and he levied a tax on all the merchant caravans which crossed his kingdom.

With the help of his friend Hiram, king of Tyre, Solomon also built a fleet of ships at Eloth, on the shores of the Red Sea.

Hiram sent his servants, sailors who knew the sea, onto the ships, and they went to the land of Ophir, along with Solomon's servants and sailors, to get gold and take it back to King Solomon.

21 The Greatness of Solomon

1 Kings 9–10

The greatness of Solomon spread over the whole kingdom of Israel. The fleet, loaded with gold from the city of Ophir, also brought back precious sandalwood with which pillars were made for the temple and the palace, as well as lyres and harps.

Kings from near and far paid homage to Solomon: visitors to his royal palace brought gifts of gold and silver, cloth, arms, rare perfumes, horses, and mules. It was said that during Solomon's reign silver was as plentiful as stone!

Solomon had gathered a great number of horses and chariots, which his merchants brought from the Hittite kings and from the kings of Aram. He owned one thousand, four hundred chariots and twelve thousand horses, which were distributed among Jerusalem and the other cities in the kingdom of Israel.

One day the Lord appeared to Solomon for the second time and said to him: "I have heard your prayer and your supplication and I have blessed this temple which you have built for me. If, however, you turn away from me to go and serve false gods, then I will destroy the temple which has been blessed in my name."

22 A Throne of Gold and Ivory

1 Kings 10

Solomon had also embellished the royal palace, which was built next to the temple of the Lord, and had enriched it with precious stones and golden ornaments.

Inside the palace Solomon had had his throne built: it was made of ivory and overlaid in pure gold; it had two armrests and beside these stood two lions.

The throne had six steps on which stood twelve more lions, six on each side. No other king on earth had a throne to equal the one King Solomon ruled from.

October

23 The Queen of Sheba's Caravan

1 Kings 10

King Solomon was richer and wiser than any king on earth. People from all over the world came to Solomon to listen to the wisdom with which God had filled his heart and which guided his decisions.

When the queen of Sheba, in Arabia, heard of the fame of Solomon she came to visit him in Jerusalem. She left her own country with a great caravan of camels loaded with gifts fit for a king: gold, precious stones, spices, and rare perfumes which she intended to give to Solomon.

24 Solomon and the Queen of Sheba

1 Kings 10

Having left her kingdom in Arabia, the queen of Sheba arrived in Jerusalem after a long journey. She presented herself to King Solomon and offered him the gifts she had brought. Then she wished to put his wisdom to the test: She put many difficult questions to him; when Solomon answered them all, she was filled with admiration. Solomon then showed the queen the temple of the Lord that he had built and the royal palace. He explained to her the laws of his kingdom and the work of his ministers.

The queen of Sheba was left breathless when she admired all of Solomon's wisdom and everything he had built. At last she said to Solomon: "Everything that I have heard in my own country, then, is true, concerning you and your wisdom! I would never have believed all that I heard unless I had come here and seen it with my own eyes. And still I have not even heard one half of the truth! Blessed are your ministers who benefit from your wisdom; blessed are the people that you govern, and blessed is your God who made you King!"

After this Solomon, too, gave many gifts to the queen.

25 The Kingdom Divided

1 Kings 11–12

Solomon reigned in wisdom and in glory for forty years—until in his later years his foreign wives attracted him to their gods and Solomon did evil in the eyes of the Lord.

For this reason the Lord said to Solomon: "You have not behaved as your father, David, did; you have not observed the covenant with me. Thus I shall now take away the kingdom which I have given you. But out of my love for your father, David, I shall leave one part of the kingdom for your descendants."

When Solomon died, his son Rehoboam became king in his place. He behaved in a foolish and evil way and a large number of the people rebelled against him. In this way, the kingdom was divided in two. The southern part remained under Rehoboam; it was called the kingdom of Judah and Jerusalem was its capital. The northern part became the kingdom of Israel, its capital Samaria and the first king was one of Solomon's ministers, Jeroboam.

Jeroboam did not wish his subjects to go to Jerusalem to pray in the temple of the Lord, so he built two other temples to the Lord in his own kingdom, one at Bethel and one at Dan.

26 The Prophets of the Lord

1 Kings 14–16; Amos 7; Jeremiah 1

The kingdom of Saul, of David, and of Solomon, had been divided into two. In Jerusalem, the descendants of David ruled one after the other. But they often behaved badly and had little faith in the Lord, and they often turned away from him to worship the false gods of other peoples.

The kings of Israel who reigned in Samaria behaved in exactly the same way. The people followed the bad example set by their kings and they too behaved wickedly.

The Lord saw how his people had betrayed him, but he never tired of inviting them to abandon their wicked ways and return to his love.

He did this in a number of different ways. For example, he permitted the enemies of his people to win in their wars, in order to make his people understand that they could only live in peace if they remained true to the Lord.

The Lord also sent special men to speak on his behalf: the prophets.

There were many prophets sent by the Lord, both in the kingdom of Judah and in the kingdom of Israel, but often neither the king nor the people listened to them; indeed they treated them badly, chased them off, or even killed them.

The Lord chose his prophets from among the people and it did not matter to which group they belonged. It was enough that they had a great love for the Lord in their hearts. Amos, for example, was a simple shepherd in the kingdom of Judah: the Lord sent him into the kingdom of Israel to warn the people of the grave punishments awaiting.

Jeremiah was a shy young man; when the Lord called to him, he replied: "Lord, I am not a good speaker, for I am young!" But the Lord said to him: "Do not say that you are young. You must only repeat that which I tell you to say."

27 The Lord Appears to the Prophet Isaiah

Isaiah 6

Isaiah was one of the great prophets of the kingdom of Judah. He discovered one day that he had been chosen by the Lord while he was in the temple in Jerusalem where he had a magnificent vision.

He saw the Lord on a high, raised throne and the hem of his gown reached down to the temple. All around him stood seraphim who proclaimed: "Holy, holy, holy is the Lord God of the universe; the heavens and the earth are full of his glory."

When he saw this vision Isaiah was filled with great fear and he said: "Woe is me! I am lost. For I am but a man and a sinner and yet my eyes have seen the Lord!"

At this, one of the seraphim flew toward him and seemed to touch his mouth with a glowing coal, saying: "Behold! Now your lips are pure and your sins are forgiven."

Isaiah understood at once what this gesture meant; the Lord had removed every obstacle and Isaiah could now speak in his name. Thus, when Isaiah heard the voice of the Lord asking: "Whom shall I send? Who will go and speak for us?", he replied at once: "Here I am, Lord. Send me!"

28 Amos the Prophet

Amos 5

There was once a prophet by the name of Amos. He was a shepherd in the kingdom of Judah, but God told him to go and speak in his name in the kingdom of Israel: Amos went, obedient to the command of the Lord.

One of the sins that Amos most condemned was the way in which the rich men in Israel treated their fellow men. Often the rich were very concerned about going to the temple and offering magnificent sacrifices while they behaved very badly with other people, cheating them and exploiting the poor.

All of this was very different from what the Lord had willed. He wanted them to help the poor and treat everybody with justice. Therefore, speaking through the mouth of his prophet Amos, the Lord said: "I detest your ceremonies, and your assemblies do not please me. You offer me animals in sacrifice, but I do not even pay them a glance. I would rather see your righteousness run like the water in a river. Do good, not evil, if you wish to live."

But the words Amos preached only annoyed them. "Go back to your own town," they said. "The words you say are of no interest."

29 Amos Speaks of Salvation

Amos 9

The prophet Amos warned the people of Israel that if they did not repent of their sins, then the Lord would punish them severely, and would go as far as to destroy the temple built by Solomon. But if they mended their ways, then God would love them once again.

Everyone had to learn to do the will of God. When that happened, Amos said, then the harvests would be rich and plentiful once again, wine would flow in streams from the hills, and the gardens would be rich in fruit.

30 The Trials of Jeremiah

Jeremiah 10

Jeremiah was a prophet born near Jerusalem. Speaking in the name of the Lord, he often chastised the Jewish people because, instead of worshiping the one and invisible Lord, they preferred the gods of other nations.

Jeremiah often said: "These false gods do not exist, even if they are represented in statues. They are only wood, cut in the forest and shaped by a carpenter. They are adorned with silver and gold but they cannot speak; and they must be carried everywhere. They are like scarecrows in a field of watermelons! You should not fear them for they can do you no harm. And it is useless to pray to them, for they can do no good either!"

Jeremiah also saw that the nearby nations were stronger than the Israelites and realized that God would make use of them to punish his chosen people. Jeremiah tried in every possible way to convince the people of Israel that if they continued to worship these false gods then they would be defeated by their enemies. Jeremiah repeated tirelessly: "God wishes you to return to him!" But the people of Israel did not listen to him.

31 Jeremiah Goes to the Potter

Jeremiah 18

The men of Israel made it clear that they did not believe the prophet Jeremiah, who feared that the Lord would punish all the Jews if they did not decide to worship the true God once again and renounce all the false gods.

One day, the Lord told Jeremiah to explain this to the people by way of a practical example. He said to Jeremiah: "Go down to the potter's workshop and there you will hear my words." Jeremiah obeyed: he went to the potter's workshop and found the potter making some clay vases on his wheel. Whenever he was not satisfied with the vase he would mix the clay all over again to shape a better vase.

"Behold!," the Lord spoke through the mouth of Jeremiah, "I could do with you, O people of Israel, just as the potter does with his vase. You are like clay in my hands; if you worship false gods you are like the badly-formed vase that must be reshaped."

These words of Jeremiah did not please the elders of the city and they complained to the king. But Jeremiah, like all the other prophets, continued to say what God ordered him to say.

November

BIBLE STORY OF THE MONTH

Jonah

At one time, the Lord chose as his prophet a man by the name of Jonah. "Get up," he told him, "and go to the great city of Nineveh and warn the inhabitants that they must cease their wicked deeds, for their evil has grown and is offensive to my eyes."

Nineveh was not a Jewish city, which showed that the Lord is God not only of his chosen people, but of all other people as well, and that he cares for everyone. Jonah, however, was afraid to go to this foreign city: what if the people should answer him with violence? Jonah, therefore, fled the Lord; he went down to Joppa and embarked on a ship going in the opposite direction from Nineveh.

During the voyage, however, while Jonah was fast asleep below deck, a great wind blew up and filled the sails and such a great storm began to rage that it endangered the ship. Each of the sailors cried out to his own god and they began to throw the cargo overboard so that the ship would be lighter and float better. When they found Jonah fast asleep, they asked him why he too was not praying to his god. Finally the sailors said to each other: "let us draw lots to see who has caused this disaster." So they drew lots and the lot fell to Jonah.

"Who are you?" they asked him. "Where are you from? Where are you going? With what evil are you tainted?"

"I am a Hebrew, and I fear the Lord, the God of heaven, who has made the sea and the dry land," replied Jonah. "Now, however, I am fleeing from his presence because I have disobeyed his command."

"What can we do to calm this storm?" the sailors asked him.

"Take me and throw me into the sea, and this great storm will subside, for I know that it is because of me that it rages," replied Jonah.

At first, the sailors did not want to do this, but when they saw the sea grow even more tempestuous they threw Jonah into the sea. The storm subsided at once!

The Lord then caused Jonah to be swallowed by a great fish and there, in the belly of the fish, Jonah prayed ardently to the Lord. He repented for not having followed the Lord's command and asked for his forgiveness.

After three days and three nights the Lord spoke to the fish, and the fish threw Jonah up alive and well, on the shore of his own land, from which he had departed.

Jonah had tried to avoid obeying the Lord's command, but in vain. He now made up his mind to do

what the Lord wanted and he went to the city of Nineveh to speak to the king and the inhabitants.

As he walked through the streets, Jonah cried out: "Forty more days and then Nineveh will be destroyed. If you do not change your ways, then you will not survive."

The people of Nineveh believed the words which God spoke through Jonah, and from the oldest to the youngest they dressed themselves in sackcloth as a sign of repentance and to show that they wished to change their evil ways.

Even the king of Nineveh dressed in sackcloth and said: "Who can tell if God might not have pity on us,

and put aside his anger at our behavior? This is our only hope of being allowed to continue to live!"

And, in fact, God saw the works of the king and the people of Nineveh; he saw that they had repented of their evil ways and he had pity on them and did not destroy the city.

Jonah should have rejoiced that the men of Nineveh had repented and so had been saved. Instead, he was angered by this because he thought that they would consider him a fool for having warned of a destruction which had not taken place. So Jonah complained to the Lord, saying: "I already knew that this would happen, from the first

moment that you ordered me to come to Nineveh. For this very reason I sought to flee to Tarshish. For you are a gracious and merciful God, and even when you threaten punishment you are always moved to pity afterward. Therefore take my life from me, for it is better for me to die than to live!"

"Do you think that it is right that you should be so angry?" the Lord asked him. Jonah, however, remained sullen and went out of the city and stopped a short distance away. He made himself a shelter from branches and sat down outside the walls to wait and see what would happen to Nineveh.

Then the Lord made a vine grow near Jonah so that he could take shelter in its shade, and Jonah was very grateful for this generosity. But the next day the Lord sent a worm to gnaw at the plant and it died. Jonah was left exposed to the sun and he said: "It is better for me to die than to live!"

"Do you think it is right for you to be so upset for a simple vine?" the Lord asked Jonah. And then he went on: "You feel pity for the vine which you did not plant and for which you had to do no work; should I not then feel pity for Nineveh, where one hundred and twenty thousand people live?"

Jona 1–4

1 King Ahab and the Prophet Elijah

1 Kings 16–17

Among all the kings of Israel, Ahab was the one who did most evil in the eyes of the Lord. As his wife, he took Jezebel, the daughter of the king of Zidon, a foreigner. Because of her, in the city of Samaria, a temple was built to Baal, a false god. Jezebel supported a great number of the prophets of Baal and was the enemy of all who remained true to the Lord.

In an attempt to change the hearts of the king and all those who had taken to worshiping Baal, the Lord sent the great prophet Elijah into the kingdom of Israel.

But Elijah's repeated calls went unheard, so, at the Lord's command, he presented himself to King Ahab and said to him: "I am the servant of the Lord. In his name I tell you that from this day forth neither dew nor rain shall fall on your kingdom, until I give the word."

And that is what happened. Without either dew or rain, the fields began to wither and gave no more fruit; the situation grew desperate and the king gave an order for Elijah to be found. However, with the help of the Lord, the prophet was able to remain in hiding.

2 Elijah Is Fed by the Ravens

1 Kings 17

Elijah, the prophet, was in danger. King Ahab and the wicked Queen Jezebel searched for him everywhere since he had announced the Lord's punishment to them: famine throughout the kingdom.

The Lord himself, however, hid his prophet and provided for him. First of all, he sent Elijah to hide near the brook Cherith, and said to him: "You shall drink the water from the stream and I will command the ravens to bring you food." And that is what happened. The ravens brought him nourishment in the morning and evening.

3 The Widow's Flour

1 Kings 17

The Lord was careful to keep his prophet Elijah hidden, because he was threatened by King Ahab. In order to keep him safe, the Lord sent him to another country. He said to Elijah: "Get up and go to Zarephath in Zidon: behold, I have commanded a widow of that town to feed you."

Elijah went to Zarephath. When he came to the gate of the town, he saw a widow: he recognized that she was a widow by the clothes she was wearing. The prophet called out to her: "Bring me a little water to drink, and also a bit of bread!" The woman replied: "All that I have left is a handful of flour and a little oil; I was gathering a few sticks so that I could cook the flour for myself and my son. We shall eat it and then we shall die, for nothing else remains to us!" But the prophet reassured her: "Do not be afraid. Use the oil and the flour to make me a cake and bring it to me; and then prepare something to eat for yourself and your son, because the Lord says that the jar of flour will not be empty, nor will the jar of oil run out." Thus, Elijah, the widow, and her son had food to eat, for the flour and oil lasted.

4 Elijah and the Widow's Son

1 Kings 17

Elijah was in hiding near Zidon, in the house of the widow who had taken him in and given him food.

After some time, the woman's son fell ill and the illness grew more and more serious, until the boy died. The poor widow began to weep and wail, suspecting in some way that the prophet was the cause of her son's death. In her great grief, the woman shouted at the prophet: "Did you come here to punish me by causing the death of my son?"

But the prophet lifted her son out of her arms and carried him to the loft where he slept and laid him on his own bed. Then Elijah called on the Lord, saying: "O Lord, my God, help this widow who keeps me in her house. I pray you to let the child's soul return to his body!"

The Lord heard Elijah's prayer; the boy's soul returned to his body and life returned. Elijah took the child in his arms again, carried him back downstairs and handed him over to his mother, saying: "Behold your son is alive!"

At this, the woman felt great joy and said to Elijah: "Now I am certain that you are a man of God; now I understand that when you speak, you speak in the name of the Lord."

5 The Faith of Obadiah

1 Kings 18

For three years now the famine had lasted in the entire kingdom of Israel, because, just as the prophet had warned King Ahab, neither rain nor dew had fallen on the land.

The time had come, however, to put an end to this punishment and the Lord said to Elijah: "Rise and go to Ahab, for I have decided to give rain to the earth."

Ahab had betrayed the Lord, but he had one minister, Obadiah, who had always been faithful to the Lord and had secretly helped all those who were opposed to the false for-eign gods. Obadiah was in the countryside when he met the prophet Elijah and recognized him as the man of God.

Elijah said to him: "Go and inform King Ahab that I have come to speak with him." Obadiah was surprised and replied: "The king has searched for you for a long time, in every corner of his kingdom. If I go and give him your message, and you disappear again before he comes here, then he will punish me by putting me to death!"

"Have faith: I shall not move from here," replied Elijah. Obadiah trusted him and went off, returning to Elijah with King Ahab.

6 Elijah Challenges the Priests of Baal

1 Kings 18

"You and your family are the ruin of Israel," the prophet Elijah told King Ahab, "because you have turned away from the Lord to worship the false god Baal. Now I will show you who is the true god. Call all the people to Mount Carmel, together with the prophets of Baal."

When all were gathered at Mount Carmel, Elijah spoke: "For how much longer will you limp on both feet? You must make up your minds: you cannot worship both the Lord and Baal. Behold: I am the only prophet of the Lord here, while the prophets of Baal, whom you see before you, number more than four hundred. And still, I challenge them: I shall offer a sacrifice to the Lord, and they will offer one to Baal. We shall not, however, light fires to burn them. The true God will send fire from heaven to burn the sacrifice offered to him. Let the followers of Baal begin, for there are many more of them."

The prophets of Baal built an altar, then they took a bull calf and placed it on top of the wood; then they began to call upon their god. They called on him for so long that Elijah began to laugh: "Call on him a bit louder: perhaps your god is asleep."

Midday came and went and nothing had happened. Then Elijah too built an altar, and he too placed a bull calf on top of the wood. Then, in a loud voice, he prayed with these words: "Lord, God of Abraham, of Isaac, and of Jacob, today everyone will see that you are the Lord God and your people will return to you." These words had hardly passed his lips before fire fell from heaven onto the altar Elijah had built and burned the sacrifice, the wood, and even the altar stones.

At this, everyone fell to the ground and proclaimed: "The Lord is our God! The Lord is God!"

7 The Return of the Rain

1 Kings 18

It had not rained for three years in the kingdom of Israel; but now this punishment would end because the king and the people recognized the Lord as the one, true God.

The prophet Elijah spoke to King Ahab: "Rise and go and eat and drink and be glad, for I hear the sound of torrential rain." Elijah then went to Mount Carmel, by the sea, where he sat down on the ground and began to pray.

He had taken with him a boy with very sharp sight and, after praying for a while, he called the boy and told him to look carefully out to sea.

"There is nothing there," the boy told him. "Go and look seven more times," the prophet ordered.

The boy obeyed, and after he had looked for the seventh time, he said: "There is a cloud as big as a man's hand rising from the sea." Elijah then said to him: "Run quickly to the king and tell him to fasten his horses to his chariot and hurry to the palace so that he will not be caught out in the rain."

And it happened that the sky darkened immediately with clouds, a strong wind blew up, and the rain began to pour down. The drought was over.

8 Elijah in Flight

1 Kings 19

Queen Jezebel worshiped the false god Baal, and because of that she persecuted Elijah.

In view of this danger, Elijah was forced to flee in order to save himself. From the kingdom of Israel he went down into the kingdom of Judah, crossing the desert. He walked next into the wilderness, and stopped and sat down under a juniper tree, to pray: "It is enough now, Lord; I am too tired. Take my life from me." Then he slept.

All at once an angel of the Lord touched him and said: "Get up and eat!" Elijah looked around and saw a cake baked on hot coals and a jug of water nearby. He ate and drank and then went back to sleep.

A short time later, the angel returned and invited Elijah to eat again, saying: "You have a long journey ahead of you!" Elijah got up and ate and drank. With the strength he got from this food, he walked for forty days and forty nights until he arrived at the mount of God in Sinai.

This was the same mountain on which Moses had met the Lord and where he had been given the tablet of the Ten Commandments.

9 Elijah Meets the Lord

1 Kings 19

Elijah arrived at the mountain of God, where Moses had already encountered the Lord. He had gone into a cave to spend the night, when he heard a voice that said to him: "Go outside and wait on the mountain, and the Lord will come." And the Lord did come.

A wind blew that was strong and fierce enough to break the rocks on the hills; but the Lord was not present in the wind. After the wind there was an earthquake, but the Lord was not in the earthquake. After the earthquake there was a fire, but the Lord was not present in the fire. After the fire, there was the whisper of a light breeze. As soon as he heard it, Elijah understood that the Lord was passing! He heard a voice which asked him: "What are you doing here, Elijah?" He replied: "The people of Israel have abandoned you, to follow false gods. I, alone, speak for you, Lord, and they seek to take my life!"

"I know those who have remained faithful to me," said the Lord. "Do not be afraid; retrace your steps and return to the land of Israel. There you will find Elisha, whom I have chosen as my prophet after you. Greet him."

10 The Vocation of Elisha

1 Kings 19

Elijah had been told to greet Elisha, who would become his successor. Elijah came across Elisha when he was working in his fields with a plow pulled by twelve pairs of oxen. Elijah went up to him and threw his cloak over him. This meant that he was passing onto Elisha his tasks and his responsibilities. Elisha stopped his oxen and ran after Elijah, who had already moved off, and said: "Allow me to go and kiss my mother and father good-bye, and I will follow you." Elisha then went with Elijah and became his disciple.

11 Naboth's Vineyard

1 Kings 21

A man by the name of Naboth owned a vineyard near the palace of Ahab, King of Israel. One day, Ahab said to Naboth: "Give your vineyard to me. It is close to my palace and I would like to make it my herb garden. In exchange, I will give you a better vineyard or, if you prefer, I will pay you in money."

Naboth, however, replied: "That vineyard has belonged to my family for many generations: the Lord forbids me to sell my inheritance."

King Ahab returned home, both sad and indignant at Naboth's reply.

He lay down on his bed and refused to eat. His wife, Jezebel, asked him: "Why are you angry? Why do you refuse to eat?"

Ahab told her what had happened: "I am angry because I said to Naboth, 'sell me your vineyard, or, if you choose, I will give you a better vineyard instead.' But his reply to me was: 'I will not give up the inheritance of my forefathers!'"

When she heard this, the wicked Queen Jezebel said,: "Are you or are you not the king of Israel? Do not despair! Get up, eat, and be merry! I shall find a way of obtaining Naboth's vineyard for you!" And Jezebel began to scheme.

12 The Prophet Elijah Confronts King Ahab

1 Kings 21

In order to possess Naboth's vineyard, the wicked Queen Jezebel wrote a letter in the name of King Ahab. She sealed it with the king's seal and sent it to the elders and chiefs of Naboth's city. The letter ordered that Naboth should be falsely accused, tried, and condemned to death.

And so it happened. After the unjust death of Naboth, Jezebel said to Ahab: "Behold! The vineyard that was Naboth's now belongs to you."

The Lord, however, spoke to the prophet Elijah and when Ahab went to visit his new vineyard the prophet was awaiting him. "The Lord knows that you killed Naboth to take possession of his vineyard!" the prophet told the king. "And since you have committed this great sin, a curse shall fall upon you, and Jezebel will die as Naboth has died!" At this, Ahab tore his clothes and began to fast and beg for forgiveness from the Lord for the sin he had committed. God spoke to Elijah and said to him: "Since Ahab has repented I shall forgive him." Jezebel, on the other hand, who had never repented, was later killed in a revolt and thus she suffered the Lord's punishment for her sin.

13 Into Heaven on a Chariot of Fire

2 Kings 2

Elijah was walking toward Jericho with his faithful disciple Elisha. That day Elisha knew that the Lord would take his master, the great prophet. When they arrived at the banks of the Jordan, Elijah took his cloak, rolled it up, and struck the water with it. The waters divided and the two prophets crossed the river without getting wet.

When they had reached the far bank, Elijah said to Elisha: "Ask me what you would like, before I am taken from you." "I wish that two thirds of your spirit would pass to me," replied Elisha, to show that he was ready to take the place of Elijah.

"God will grant this to you," said Elijah. And as they were speaking, a whirlwind came between them, and Elijah rose into heaven on the whirlwind as if borne on a flaming chariot pulled by horses of fire. When Elisha saw this, he cried: "My father, my father, the guide of the people of Israel."

Elisha then picked up the cloak of Elijah, which had fallen to the ground; with this he struck the waters of the river Jordan, which divided to let him pass. Thus, the spirit of Elijah lived on in Elisha; and with God's help he performed miracles.

14 The Spirit of Elijah Remains with Elisha

2 Kings 2

The prophet Elijah had been carried into heaven in a chariot of fire, while Elisha, his disciple, was watching.

When Elijah had disappeared from his sight, Elisha picked up the mantle that had fallen from Elijah's shoulders. Elisha said, "Where is the God Elijah served so faithfully?" He wanted a sign. Then, when he returned to the River Jordan, he used Elijah's mantle and smote the waters repeatedly until they parted before him, allowing him to cross, just as Elijah had done before him.

The prophets of Jericho witnessed this from a certain distance and they ran out to meet Elisha and bowed down before him. Then they urged Elisha to look for his former master, the prophet Elijah. They feared he had gotten lost in the mountains and some bad deed had befallen him.

The Prophets of Jericho offered to send fifty servants to look for Elijah, equipped with pack animals.

Elisha knew his master had gone to serve the Lord, but he could not stop the prophets from their search. At last they came back empty-handed, and avowed that Elijah's spirit had passed into Elisha.

15 The Healing of the Waters

2 Kings 2

The prophet Elisha was in Jericho when the people came to him and said: "Behold, this is a beautiful city, but the waters that feed it are polluted and make the land barren."

"Elisha then said to them: "Bring me some salt." They brought him the salt and he went to the source of the water. He poured the salt into the spring and pronounced these words: "The Lord says: 'I have healed these waters and from this day forth the water will be good to drink and will enrich the fields.'" And that came to pass.

16 The Widow's Oil

2 Kings 4

One day a woman came to the prophet Elisha and said to him: "My husband is dead. As you know, he always heard and obeyed the word of the Lord. Now, however, one of our creditors has come to take my two sons as slaves in repayment of our debt to him."

Elisha asked her: "What can I do for you? Tell me what you have in your house."

"The only thing I have at home is a pot of oil," replied the woman sadly.

"Go and ask to borrow pots from all your neighbors," the prophet told her, "and ask for a great many. Then go home and pour oil from your pot into all the other pots."

The woman did as she had been told; her sons held the pots while she filled them all with oil. And her pot only became empty when all the other pots were full. She then went back to the man of God and told him that her oil had multiplied.

"And now what shall I do?" the woman asked Elisha. The prophet replied; "Go and sell the oil in the pots and with the money you receive you will be able to pay off your debt. There will be enough left over to support you and your sons."

17 The Breath of Life

2 Kings 4

One day the prophet Elisha went to the home of a rich woman who always gave food to both him and his servants when they passed. Elisha knew that the woman had no children and very much wanted a child, so he said to her: "For all your kindness the Lord will grant you a son."

In due course, the woman had a son who grew up into a healthy boy. One day, however, when he was in the fields with his father, the boy suddenly felt a great pain in his head. He was taken home and there his mother held him on her knees

until midday, when the boy died.

The mother laid him on his bed; then, saddling her ass, she hurried off to find Elisha. When he found out what had happened, Elisha accompanied the woman home at once. When they arrived, he went by himself into the room where the child lay and closed the door.

First, Elisha prayed to the Lord; then he lay down on the boy and put his hands and his mouth on the child's mouth and breathed his breath into the child. The body of the boy grew warm again and then his eyes opened. Elisha called the mother in and said to her: "Behold, your son is well again."

18 Naaman's Leprosy

2 Kings 5

Naaman, the captain of the king of Syria's army, was a valiant man who had been greatly honored by the king. Unfortunately, he had the terrible disease known as leprosy.

One day the servant of the wife of Naaman, an Israeli girl, said to her mistress: "If Naaman goes to my country, there is a prophet there who can cure him of his leprosy."

Naaman, with the permission of his own king, presented himself to the prophet Elisha. When Naaman arrived at the house of Elisha and stopped before the door, Elisha sent word to Naaman that if he went and washed himself seven times in the River Jordan, he would then be cured of his disease.

When he heard this, Naaman was furious and left saying: "I thought that the prophet would come out to meet me, pray to his God, then touch me where I am diseased and my leprosy would disappear. Instead he sends me to wash in the Jordan! As if the rivers in my own country are not better than all the waters of Israel! For what reason have I come this far?"

His advisers, however, said to him: "If the prophet had commanded you to do something difficult, would you not have done it? All the more reason to do this simple thing that he has commanded you to do!"

Naaman heeded this advice and went down to the River Jordan. There he bathed seven times and, behold, his leprosy vanished! When he saw this, Naaman said: "Now I know that there is no other god than the Lord, God of Israel!" He went back to the prophet and offered him great gifts as thanks for his cure. Elisha refused them, saying that if Naaman was cured then it was not the work of the prophet but the will of God.

19 The Ax Head in the Water

2 Kings 6

One day Elisha and his followers decided to build a house where they could meet. They went to the banks of the River Jordan and set to work. While one of the men was chopping down a tree trunk, his ax head fell into the river. The man went to Elisha and explained what had happened and the prophet made him point out where the ax head had sunk. Elisha then threw a piece of wood into the river at the very same spot, and immediately the ax head floated to the surface to be picked up.

20 Joash, the Little King

2 Kings 11

Although the king and the people of Judah and Israel kept on doing great wrongs in the eyes of the Lord, he always kept his word. On one occasion, the king of Judah, Ahaziah, was killed in battle. His mother, Athaliah, ordered that all the princes be killed so that she could rule as queen. But when she died a man from outside the family would become king. And that would break the promise the Lord made to David that his descendants would always reign on the throne in Jerusalem. So the sister of king Ahaziah saved one of the king's young sons, Joash, and hid him.

For six years little Joash remained in hiding in the temple of the Lord, while Athaliah ruled the country. During the seventh year, the priest Jehoiada called the elders and the captains of the guard to the temple and showed them little Joash, who was then proclaimed king according to the will of the Lord.

When she heard the noise of the celebration, Athaliah went to the temple. There she found the little king surrounded by singers and trumpeters and rejoicing. In this way, Joash, the descendant of the house of David, became king.

21 The Lesson of the Arrows

2 Kings 13

When Elisha fell sick, King Joash went to visit him and said: "Oh my father, oh my father, the protector of Israel!"

Elisha said to him: "Pick up your bow and arrows." When Joash had done this, Elisha said: "Put your hand on the bow." When the king had done this, Elisha placed his hand on the king's hand and said: "Open the eastern window."

Once the window had been opened, Elisha said: "Shoot!," and Joash fired his arrow. Elisha said: "The arrow of victory for the Lord, the arrow of victory over the Syrians. You shall defeat the Syrians."

Elisha then told the king of Israel to pick up his arrows. When Joash had done this, Elisha said to him: "Beat the ground with your arrows." And Joash struck the ground three times, but then stopped.

Elisha was angry with Joash and said: "You should have struck the ground five or six times with your arrows! Then you would have defeated the Syrians forever! Now, instead, you shall defeat them only three times."

Having said this, Elisha, the man of God, foretold the end of the kingdom of Israel, then died.

22 Josiah and the Rediscovered Book

2 Kings 22–23

There was a king named Josiah who reigned for thirty-one years in Jerusalem. In contrast with many other kings, he always did what was good in the eyes of the Lord. In the eighteenth year of his reign, Josiah gave orders that the temple of the Lord should be repaired. During this work, the high priest Hilkiah found a long-forgotten book and he had it brought to the king.

The book contained, in full, the law of God and the sayings of Moses, together with the counsel he had given to the people. When the king heard the words that were written in the book, he tore his clothes to show his great pain, for he knew that the kings who had preceded him had failed to keep the law of God. Josiah then called the elders, the citizens, and all the priests and prophets, to the temple and had the book read aloud.

When the reading was finished, the king rose to his feet and renewed the covenant with the Lord, and in the name of the whole people he promised to keep the law of God. Then he ordered the destruction of all the statues and temples to false gods and celebrated a memorable Passover.

23 The Temple Is Destroyed

2 Kings 17—25

Despite the many proofs of God's goodness to them, the people of Israel continued to offend him and do evil. And so the Lord allowed a grave punishment to fall on them so that the people would then turn back to him.

Thus the two kingdoms, first one, then the other, were conquered by enemies. Everything happened just as the prophets had foretold. Nebuchadnezzar, the king of Babylon, came with an immense army and laid siege to Jerusalem. The city resisted for months until, finally, its inhabitants had nothing left to eat. Then, through a gap in the wall, the Babylonians entered the city. The king was captured and many were killed.

The temple, which had been built by Solomon, was destroyed. The soldiers of Nebuchadnezzar took all of its treasures, and all of the objects and ornaments in gold, silver, and bronze. A great number of Israelites were made slaves and sent to work in Babylon. There, in that foreign land, they suffered greatly. But, as God had planned, it was there that they came to understand the evil they had done and turned back to the ways of the Lord.

24 Four Boys at the Court of Babylon

Daniel 1

Nebuchadnezzar, king of Babylon, ordered the superintendent of his palace to choose several boys from among the Israelites sent to his kingdom. They had to be good-looking and intelligent and were to be instructed to perform certain tasks.

Among the boys chosen were Daniel, Hananiah, Mishael and Azariah. They, like the others who had been chosen, were given food from the king's own table. But good Israelites did not eat the food of foreigners, so Daniel asked the superintendent not to force them to eat the king's food. "But if the king sees that your faces are less healthy than those of the other boys," said the superintendent, "he will blame me and condemn me to death!" "Put us to the test for ten days," Daniel begged him. "Give us only water and vegetables. Then compare our faces with the other boys and make your decision."

The superintendent agreed and at the end of ten days the four boys appeared healthier and more handsome than the others. They also seemed wise and intelligent and so, when their instruction was finished, Daniel, Hananiah, Mishael, and Azariah served the king.

25 The Statue and the Little Stone

Daniel 2

One night, King Nebuchadnezzar had a dream. He saw an immense statue with a head of gold, the chest and arms of silver, the belly and the thighs of bronze, the legs of iron, and its feet partly made of iron and partly of clay. While Nebuchadnezzar was looking on, a stone flew from the mountain behind and struck the feet of the statue and broke the clay into pieces. When this happened, the entire statue crumbled, while the stone that had struck it grew and grew.

Since the wise men at the court of Nebuchadnezzar could not explain the dream to the king, a young Israelite named Daniel came forward. "My god has told me the meaning of your dream," said Daniel. "The golden head of the statue represents your glorious realm, O king. But after yours will follow other kingdoms, ever less glorious and strong, until God creates a kingdom which is greater than any other and it will grow until it covers the whole world and will endure forever."

The kingdom of which the prophet Daniel spoke was the one founded by Jesus, the Son of God and King of the Universe, when he came into the world.

26 Nebuchadnezzar and the Statue of Gold

Daniel 3

The king of Babylon, Nebuchadnezzar, had a statue of gold built, as high as a tower and very wide. He then called together all the important men in his kingdom, whereupon a herald announced: "At the sound of the musical instruments, you must all prostrate yourselves and pay homage to the golden statue. Whoever does not worship the statue will be thrown into a fiery furnace."

Hananiah, Mishael and Azariah, the three young Israelites at the Babylonian court, steadfastly refused to worship the statue. So the king had them arrested and asked them the reason for this refusal. "Only God is to be worshiped" replied the three young men. "You can have us thrown into the furnace, but if God wishes he will free us. And even if God does not save us, we will never act against his will."

Nebuchadnezzar was furious and ordered that the furnace be fired hotter than usual, and that the three youths be bound and thrown into it. To his amazement, he saw that they remained unharmed in the flames, praising God.

He had them brought out and saw that not a single hair on their heads had been singed by the fire.

November

27 The Fiery Furnace

Daniel 3

"Only God is to be worshiped" the three young Israelites, Hananiah, Mishael, and Azariah, had told King Nebuchadnezzar. For this the king had ordered them to be thrown into a fiery furnace. However, by the grace of God, they had been brought out again, unharmed.

The astonished king said: "These young men would not disobey their god, and he saved them. Therefore I now decree that no one in my kingdom speak against the god of these youths, since their god is so powerful."

28 The Writing on the Wall

Daniel 5

When Belshazzar became king of Babylon, he held a great banquet. A thousand nobles were invited and the king began to drink wine with them. The king ordered brought to him the precious cups and the vases of gold and silver which his father, Nebuchadnezzar, had brought from the temple of the Lord in Jerusalem. Belshazzar used them to drink to his false gods.

Suddenly, however, the fingers of a hand appeared and began to write on the wall of the banquet chamber. King Belshazzar was very afraid and

had his wise men brought to him but no one could make out what the writing meant, and the king and his counselors grew even more afraid. Then the queen spoke up and sent for an Israelite, who had been able to explain the dreams of the king. His name was Daniel and he was a prophet of the Lord.

Daniel said to King Belshazzar: "You have offended the Lord God, by using the cups and vases from his temple to glorify your false gods. These gods do not see, they do not hear, and they do not understand: they are nothing! But the Lord holds your life in his hands and you have

not worshiped him."

Daniel continued: "For this reason the Lord God has sent the hand to trace this writing on the wall. This is what is written: *Mene, Tekel, Peres.* And this is what these words mean: *Mene,* God has judged your kingdom and brought it to an end; *Tekel,* you have been weighed in the balances and you have been found wanting; *Peres,* your kingdom will be divided and will be given to the Medes and the Persians."

Just as Daniel had foretold, Belshazzar, king of Babylon, was killed that night. In his place, Darius the Mede became king.

29 Daniel Prays

Daniel 6

Daniel, the prophet of the Lord, was living in exile in Babylon, where he was the wisest and most intelligent of the king's counselors. The king had given him a position of high responsibility and placed him above all the other governors.

These governors, however, grew jealous of Daniel, and began to look for some fault in him so that he could be discredited in front of the king. In this way, they hoped he would be dismissed. Since they could find no fault in Daniel, they resorted to trickery. They went to the king and persuaded him to sign a law which said: "All the inhabitants of the kingdom must pray only to the king or else they shall be thrown into the lions' den."

Daniel realized that this law had been designed to trap him. In fact, he did not try to hide his faith: three times a day, every day, he opened the window in his room, turned toward Jerusalem, and got down on his knees to pray and praise God, who lived among men in Jerusalem.

Without paying any attention to the new law nor to the punishment for breaking it, Daniel continued to pray openly to the Lord.

30 Daniel in the Lions' Den

Daniel 6

Although the king had passed a new law forbidding the people to pray to anybody but himself, Daniel went on praying to the Lord, his God.

His enemies had been spying on him so that they could accuse him of this very practice. They went at once to the king and told him that Daniel was disobeying his orders. The king was very unhappy because he had great trust in Daniel. But the law had to be observed. Those who broke it were to be thrown into a den of lions.

The king spent the whole day trying to think of a way to save Daniel. But there was no escape. As Daniel was lowered into the lions' den, the king said to him: "Your God will save you."

The king spent the whole night unable to sleep for worry. At dawn, he went straight to the lions' den and called out: "Daniel, servant of the Lord, has your god, whom you love, been able to save you?"

Daniel replied: "My god sent an angel to close the jaws of the lions, and they have done me no harm."

The king was delighted that Daniel was safe. He was brought out of the lions' den and everyone could see that he was not scratched.

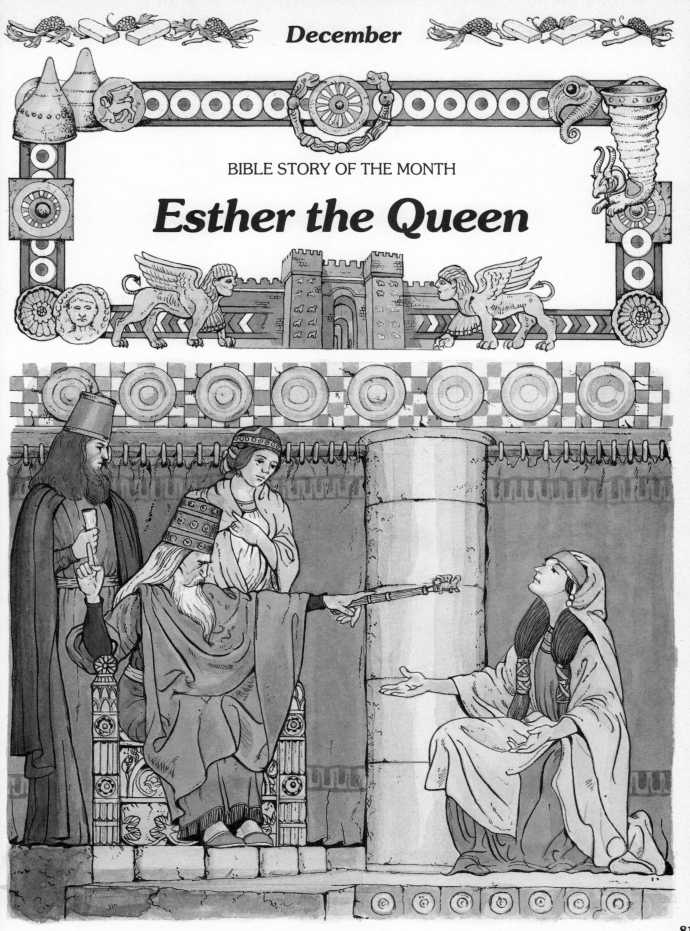

December

BIBLE STORY OF THE MONTH

Esther the Queen

In the palace of Ahasuerus, the king of Babylon, there lived an Israelite named Mordecai. He was part of the group of Israelites that had been taken from Jerusalem into exile in the east, and now he was working in the court of the king.

Mordecai had a young niece, called Esther. The daughter of his brother, she had been left without parents, so he raised her. It happened that Ahasuerus preferred Esther to all the other women of his kingdom: he married her and named her queen. One day, Mordecai overheard two ministers plotting to kill the king. Mordecai told Esther, who then went to tell the king. Investigations proved the two ministers guilty and they were put to death.

Some time later the king placed a man called Haman at the head of all the princes who governed the kingdom. Haman hated Mordecai and all the people of Israel, so one day he went before Ahasuerus and said: "There is a people spread over all the provinces of your kingdom. Its laws are different from those of the other peoples, and they do not observe the laws that you have made. If it pleases you, give orders that they be destroyed and their properties confiscated. I will put a part of what is taken into the treasury."

Ahasuerus took off the ring with the royal seal and gave it to Haman, to show him that he was granting him full power in this matter, and then said: "Keep the money for yourself; and do what you will with that people; they are yours."

Then Haman wrote to all princes in the kingdom that on a certain day in the month of Adar, all the Israelites were to be put to death and their goods confiscated.

When Mordecai came to hear of this decision, he tore up his clothes and dressed in sackcloth as a sign of great sorrow, and with his head covered in ashes he wandered the city, crying in pain and sorrow.

In this way he also meant to attract the attention of Esther. He could not go directly to her, because no one knew that Esther, the queen, was one of the people of Israel.

When Esther was told that her uncle was behaving in this strange way, giving signs of great sorrow, she called a trusted servant of the king and secretly sent him to Mordecai to find out what had happened.

Mordecai told the servant of Haman's plan and asked him to beg Esther to go to the king and protect her people. But this was very dangerous, as Esther knew well. If anyone—man or woman, stranger or

friend, even the ministers or the queen herself—went before the king without having been summoned, he would be put to death; unless the king pointed his scepter at the person, sparing his life and giving him permission to speak.

But Mordecai persisted in begging Esther to intervene, to try and save her people, even at the risk of losing her own life. The queen sent him this reply: "Go and gather all the Israelites who live in this city. Tell them to fast for me for three days; I and my handmaidens will also fast to ask for God's help. Then I will go before the king, and if I must die, I will die."

On the third day, after a long prayer to the Lord, Esther put on her royal gown and thus dressed, she went before the king.

The king was pleased by her and he pointed his scepter at her, saying: "What do you desire, Queen Esther? Anything you ask of me I will grant you, even if it be half of my kingdom."

"I ask that you come to the banquet today that I have prepared for you and for Haman," the queen replied.

So the king and Haman came to the banquet and Ahasuerus again asked: "What is it you desire, Queen Esther? Any request you

make will be granted."

Then Esther said: "If I have found favor in your eyes, oh king, my first wish is that you grant me my life, and my second is that you spare my people. Because I and my people have been condemned to be put to death, and all our belongings confiscated."

"Who is it and where is the person who would dare to plan such an act?" asked the king in surprise and fury.

"The enemy, our oppressor, is none other than that wicked man Haman!" Esther said bravely, pointing her finger at the king's minister.

Haman was gripped with fear; he tried to beg forgiveness for what he had done, but Ahasuerus would not listen and condemned him to death. Then he sent an order throughout his kingdom that the lives of all those belonging to the people of Israel be spared.

Later on Mordecai came before the king, because Esther had told Ahausuerus that Mordecai was really her uncle. And Ahasuerus took the ring with the royal seal, which he had taken from Haman, and gave it to Mordecai, ordering that his new minister be granted royal honors. On that day all the Israelites were filled with joy and thanksgiving because of Esther, the queen who had saved her people.

Esther 1–8

December

1 By the Waters of Babylon

Psalm 137; Ezekiel 11

Led away into a foreign land, the king and the inhabitants of the land of Israel suffered greatly.

Later on, they remembered that time with this song:
By the waters of Babylon,
we sat down and we wept
at the memory of Jerusalem.
There they asked us to sing,
those who had taken us away:
to sing songs of joy,
for them, our oppressors.
"Sing the songs of Zion for us,"
   they said.

But how could we sing the songs of the Lord
in a foreign land?
On the willows of that land
we hung up our lyres.

There in that foreign land, they realized that it was a bad thing to be far from the Lord. The Israelites understood that they had done wrong by abandoning the Lord, and so, just as the Lord desired, they turned back to him. They asked him to pardon the sins they had committed, and they begged him to give them back his love. And the Lord, who is good and pardons willingly, sent the prophets to them, to show them that he had not forgotten them.

2 The Visions of the Prophet Ezekiel

Ezekiel 11, 37

The Lord sent his prophets to give heart to his people who were suffering in exile and had repented of their sins. One of the prophets, Ezekiel, spent almost all of his life with the exiles. He remembered clearly the temple in Jerusalem and assured the Lord's chosen people that God would allow those who remained faithful to him to worship in the temple again. Ezekiel told them the Lord would change their very hearts, and instead of harboring evil, they would love the Lord.

Ezekiel explained to the people the visions which God sent him. One of these visions concerned the reuniting of the people of Israel. The prophet told them that God had led him into a valley full of dry bones and said to him: "Ezekiel, speak to these bones: Tell them that I will bring them back to life and all will know that I am the Lord!"

Hardly had he said this than he heard a great noise, and saw the bones coming together again. Ezekiel looked on astonished as the dead rose to their feet and life came back into them and they were as numerous as a great army.

God explained this vision to the prophet: "These bones are all the children of Israel. At the moment they are like the dead, like dry bones. In the exile in which they find themselves, they think there is no hope for them. But go now and tell them that I, the Lord God, will bring them back to life and take them to their homeland, the land that I have promised to Abraham and his descendants.

"My spirit will enter into them, and they will live again," the Lord continued to Ezekiel, "and they will know that I am the Lord. Thus I have spoken and thus I will do!"

3 The Return from Exile

Ezra 1–6

The people of Israel had had to pass many years in exile. But for the tribe of Judah this exile ended when Cyrus became king in the east.

In the first years of his reign, King Cyrus made the following proclamation: "The Lord, God of heaven, has told me to build a temple to him in Jerusalem. All of the people of the Lord in my kingdom are now free to return to Jerusalem to build the temple. Furthermore, I command that the people of God be given gold and silver, goods and livestock, over and above offerings for the temple to be built in Jerusalem."

Thus the Jews returned to Jerusalem and rebuilt the temple: in this way the promises that the Lord had made to his people through the prophets were fulfilled.

The rebuilding of the temple took a long time and there were many difficulties; in the end, however, it was completed and the occasion was commemorated with great joy by all of God's people. Everyone celebrated the Passover and sacrifices were again offered to the Lord in the temple. Hymns of praise were sung to God who had brought his people out of exile.

4 The Joy of the Returning Exiles

Psalm 126

The people who returned home from exile in Babylon commemorated the event with this song:
When the Lord led the prisoners
    home to Jerusalem, it
seemed like a dream to us!
Our mouths opened with laughter,
    and our tongues sang songs of joy.
Even foreigners said God has done
    great things for them!
Indeed the Lord has done great
    things for us; he has filled us full
of joy, like those who go out to sow
    and return home carrying
    sheaves!

5 Nehemiah and King Cyrus

Nehemiah 1–2

The Jews of the tribe of Judah rebuilt the temple as soon as they returned from exile. But the city of Jerusalem, which had been destroyed by their enemies a long time before, was still in a terrible state.

Nehemiah, who was one of the Jews who had remained in Persia, learned of the condition in which the city had been found. Saddened by this information, he went to the king. "Why are you so unhappy?" the king asked him, and Nehemiah replied: "Because Jerusalem, the city of my fathers, is ruined. Permit me, O king, to go and repair it!"

The king gave his consent and Nehemiah departed. When he reached Jerusalem, he rested for three days. Then, by night, he got up and went with a few men to inspect the walls. He saw that at many points there were open breaches and that the gates had been destroyed by fire.

Having seen this, Nehemiah went to the chiefs of the people and said: "You see clearly the situation we are in: Jerusalem is destroyed and the walls are useless. We must take heart and set to work!" And everyone replied: "We shall set to work at once. Jerusalem will be rebuilt!"

6 Nehemiah Rebuilds the Walls

Nehemiah 2-7

Under the direction of Nehemiah, the Jews had decided to rebuild the walls of Jerusalem. Some people laughed at them, but Nehemiah said: "Let us set to work and the Lord will see that we finish it!"

The work was begun. But enemies of the Jews in the surrounding region did not wish the Jews to become a powerful people again. These enemies united, planning to attack the city, stopping the rebuilding, and enslaving the Jews.

When Nehemiah learned of their plan, he divided his men into two groups. One half worked on the rebuilding of the walls, while the other half remained fully armed on guard. Those who were working also were ready to fight if necessary.

The work proceeded rapidly from dawn to dusk each day, and after fifty days it was finished. When it was done, Nehemiah declared: "The city gates shall be opened when the sun is already high in the sky, and they shall be closed while the inhabitants are still on their feet. Choose sentinels and guards from among you and make sure they are always at their posts."

The Lord had given great wisdom to his servant Nehemiah.

7 The Renewal of the Covenant

Nehemiah 7-13

The Jews lived in safety in the city of Jerusalem, now that the walls had been rebuilt and were well guarded.

Everyone thought that it was now time to give thanks to the Lord. All the men and women gathered together and told Ezra to bring out the book of the law of Moses, which the Lord had given to his chosen people. Ezra was a scribe and an expert in the explanation of the law.

Therefore Ezra brought the book out before the assembled people and stood up on a wooden pulpit which had been built for the occasion. He blessed the Lord and the people replied, "Amen." Then they listened to Ezra as he read and explained the law of God to them.

They all realized that they had often broken this law and said, "You, Lord, have not dealt with us as our sins deserve, but have showered us with blessings! We now promise to keep every commandment of your law."

Then, full of joy, and singing hymns and songs of praise, they made two great processions around the walls and came together in the temple. There, they offered sacrifices to the Lord and held a great feast in his honor.

December

8 Job Is Put to the Test

Job 1–42

By now, everyone clearly understood that if he was not faithful to the Lord, he would encounter great problems. But is this the only reason that we should be faithful? Should we avoid doing evil only to avoid God's punishment? Or should we always do good, no matter what happens? The story of Job gives us the answer to this question. . . .

In the land of Uz lived Job, who feared God and did no evil. He had three daughters and seven sons, and many herds of livestock. He was the most important of all the men of the east.

One day the Lord said to Satan: "Have you seen my servant Job? There is no man on earth as upright as he." But Satan replied, "Try taking some of his possessions from him, and he will curse you!" The Lord then said to Satan: "All that Job owns is in your power, but do no harm to his body."

And thus, one day soon afterward, a messenger came to Job and announced: "Marauders have attacked and carried off your oxen and your asses, killing your servants who were guarding them!"

He was still speaking when a second messenger arrived and said: "A fire has destroyed the sheep and the shepherds who were watching over them!" These words were barely out of his mouth when a third messenger arrived to say: "Robbers have killed your servants and stolen all your camels!"

Finally, yet another messenger arrived with the news: "Your sons and daughters were eating together when the house collapsed on them and killed them all!"

At this, Job threw himself to the ground and said: "All that I had was given to me by the Lord. Now the Lord has taken it away. Let his will be done."

9 Job Is Struck Again

Job 2–42

Through the will of the Lord, Job had suffered severe blows to his fortune and his family: his sons and his daughters were dead and he had also lost all of his possessions. And still Job accepted this as the will of the Lord: but he had never turned against God.

Satan, however, still was not satisfied: he wanted Job to turn away from God. Therefore Satan said to God: "I know why Job continues to praise your name: he is still alive and in good health. Strike him on his body and he will curse you!"

And the Lord replied to Satan: "Let Job be in your power, but his life must be spared. In this way we shall see if he truly does love me!"

Thus, Satan struck Job with boils all over his body. At this point, his wife said to him: "Do you still insist on accepting the will of God? After everything that has happened, you should curse his name!"

"You are speaking foolishly," replied Job. "If we accept the good things that God gives us, should we not also accept the bad things?"

Nevertheless, as Job endured his suffering he complained, "Perish the day that I was born! I have no peace, no comfort and no rest."

10 Job and His Three Friends

Job 1–42

Job had suffered every misfortune imaginable: his sons and daughters and all his wealth gone, and his body was covered with boils. Yet he remained faithful to the Lord.

One day, three of his friends came to visit him. They showed great sympathy for Job's pain, but they argued that if Job was suffering so much, then he must also have committed some great sin.

Poor Job replied that this was not true in his case. He had committed no great sin, and he suffered without knowing the reason why.

11 Job Questions God

Job 1–42

Tried by so much suffering, Job at last raised his voice up to God, to ask him the reason for his great misfortunes. But the Lord replied that men could not understand everything. Only God knew the reason for many things.

Moreover, the Lord said: "Who is this man that would try to teach me? Where were you when I laid in place the foundations of the earth? Tell me this, you who claim to understand so much! Who decided the dimensions of the world? Who made it strong? Have you ever ordered the morning to come or told the sun where to rise? Have you ever been to the source of the sea, or walked in the depths of the abyss? Which way do you go to arrive at the source of all light? Have you ever reached the place where the snow comes from or seen the home of the hail? Can you raise your voice to the clouds and order the rain to fall?"

When he heard this, Job replied to the Lord, saying: "I have spoken of things which are too great for me. Therefore, Lord, I ask pardon for having dared to request an explanation. I will ask no more and will not repeat my error. Instead, I will repent in dust and ashes!"

12 Job Is Rewarded

Job 42

Although he had been struck by many misfortunes, Job did not rebel against the Lord, and the Lord recognized and appreciated the patience and humility of Job, and gave back to him both his health and his wealth. All his friends came to congratulate him and to show their sympathy for his misfortunes.

In this way, the Lord blessed Job in later life even more than he had blessed him in his youth. He lived to see his children and his grandchildren as far as the fourth generation of his descendants.

December

13 Waiting for the Messiah

Daniel 7

Finally, at the time decided by God, there came the Messiah, whose arrival had been foretold for so long by the prophets and so long awaited by the people of Israel. Thus came true the prophecy made by Daniel, the last and greatest of the prophets who foretold the Messiah.

This prophecy, known as "the vision of the Son of man," is a vision of the Ancient of days, who is surrounded by angels. The Son of man comes before him and on him is bestowed eternal power and a kingdom with no end.

14 The Vision of the Son of Man

Daniel 7

These were the words of Daniel: "I saw thrones cast down, and the Ancient of days was seated. His garment was as white as snow, and the hair on his head was as pure as wool. His throne was like a flame.

"And in the night I saw visions more. I saw one, like the Son of man, appear on the clouds of the sky. He came before the Ancient and was given the kingdom, the power, and the glory. All nations shall serve the Son of man. His power is everlasting and his kingdom can never be destroyed."

15 The Long-Awaited One Is Here

Daniel 7

When the prophet Daniel wrote of the vision that he had of the Ancient of days and the Son of man it was as if he were putting forward a riddle: What could it mean?

All was made clear later when Jesus talked of his life on earth and his mission and on several occasions referred to himself as the Son of man. Jesus is God because he came down from heaven. He is man and, in fact, appears as a son of man. God the Father, the Ancient in Daniel's vision, has made him king of the universe for all eternity.

16 Zacharias and Elisabeth

Luke 1

At the time when Herod reigned in Palestine, there was a man named Zacharias among the priests who served in the temple. Both he and his wife, Elisabeth, were elderly.

Zacharias and Elisabeth were good people who were careful to obey the Lord's commandments in everything that they did. Only one thing made them sad: the Lord had not granted them any children, although they had both prayed a great deal for a child. Now that they were old, they had given up hope for such a blessing. When Zacharias

was working in the temple, it was his duty to go into the sanctuary, the chamber which only the priests could enter, to offer incense to the Lord, while the people outside waited and prayed.

Zacharias was busy putting the incense on the brazier that stood on the altar, when the angel of the Lord appeared to him, standing to the right of the altar. Zacharias was filled with fear at this apparition, but the angel said to him: "Do not be afraid, Zacharias. The Lord has heard your prayer and will grant a son to you and your wife, Elisabeth, and you will call him John, which means 'God is favorable.'"

17 Zacharias and the Angel

Luke 1

The angel had spoken to Zacharias in the sanctuary of the temple and had told him that he and his wife, Elisabeth, although they were very old, would have a son. Zacharias could not believe this news, but the angel said to him: "You will feel great joy at his birth, and many will rejoice. For your son will prepare the people for the Lord who is coming. I am Gabriel and God has sent me to speak to you. Since you do not believe my words, behold, you shall be dumb until what I have foretold has been fulfilled."

18 Zacharias Returns Home

Luke 1

As the angel Gabriel had said, when Zacharias came out of the temple he could no longer speak and had to try to explain himself with gestures. When the people outside the sanctuary saw Zacharias gesturing, and moving his mouth in speechlessness, they understood that he had had a vision in the sanctuary. Quietly, Zacharias went among them, his head filled with the promise the angel Gabriel had brought that he would be father to a child that would grow to help to be a savior to all the world.

As soon as he had finished his priestly duties, Zacharias returned home. Some time later, his wife, Elisabeth, realized that the Lord's will was going to be fulfilled: she was going to give birth to a child. She knew that this was a great gift from God, and she thanked with all her heart the Lord who had answered her prayer.

That child, to whom the angel Gabriel himself had given a name, was John, and was later known as John the Baptist. To him the Lord had given the great task of preparing the people of Israel to accept Jesus, the Messiah whom the prophets had foretold.

December

19 A Young Woman Named Mary

Luke 1

The angel Gabriel was sent by God to a village called Nazareth in Palestine. A young woman named Mary lived there, and God knew that her heart was filled with faith and love for him.

For this reason, the Lord had already done an extraordinary thing for Mary: he had filled her with his grace and she had, therefore, always been full of his love.

God had done this because he had decided that Mary was the worthiest of all women to become the mother of his son.

20 Mary, the Mother of God

Luke 1

The angel Gabriel had been sent by God to the village of Nazareth. He entered Mary's house and said to her: "Hail Mary, full of grace, the Lord is with you."

This was an unusual greeting and Mary wondered what these words could mean. The angel went on speaking: "Do not be afraid, Mary: you have found favor with God. Because of this you will be the mother of a child and you will call him Jesus. He shall be great! He shall be called the son of the highest and God will give him the throne of David, his forefather. His kingdom will have no end."

Mary then asked: "How can I have a child if I am not married?"

"The Holy Ghost will descend upon you," explained the angel Gabriel, "and the power of almighty God shall overshadow you like a cloud. The child that is born to you will be holy, the Son of God. Know that your cousin Elisabeth is also expecting a child, despite her great age, because it is God's will."

At this, Mary said: "Behold, I am the handmaiden of the Lord; I wish to do his will: let it happen as you have said!"

December

21 Mary Goes to See Elisabeth

Luke 1

Mary had been told by the angel Gabriel that her elderly cousin Elisabeth was expecting the child she had wanted for so long. She knew that this child was a sign that God had listened to the prayers of Elisabeth and her husband, Zacharias.

Mary, therefore, decided to go and visit Elisabeth and tell her the wonderful news that she too would have a child, and that he would be the Son of God. Elisabeth, however, did not have to be told, for, when Mary arrived at her house and began to greet her, Elisabeth felt inspired by God and said: "Blessed are you among women and blessed is the fruit of your womb! What honor and what joy, that the mother of my Lord should visit me!"

Elisabeth then told Mary how her husband Zacharias had doubted the words of the angel who had told him that God would grant them a son, and how on account of this doubt he had been struck dumb. Mary, on the other hand, had never doubted, and so Elisabeth added: "Blessed are you Mary, because you believed that the Lord would fulfill all he has said to you." And Mary replied with a hymn of praise to God.

22 His Name Is John

Luke 1

Mary, who was to become the mother of Jesus, stayed with her cousin until Elisabeth gave birth to a baby boy—the same baby boy that the angel Gabriel had spoken of to the incredulous father Zacharias, who had been struck dumb.

Eight days after the birth of the child, according to custom, it was time to give the boy a name. Since the father could not speak, his relatives decided the child should be called Zacharias, but Elisabeth cried: "No! He will be called John!"

"John?" asked the puzzled friends and relatives. "Why? You have no relatives of that name." Then they made a sign to the boy's father, asking him how he wanted to name the child. Zacharias made signs requesting a tablet to write on and wrote: "His name is John." Hardly had he written the name of the child than his voice came back and he could speak again, just as the angel Gabriel had foretold. At once, Zacharias sang a hymn of praise to the Lord. The relatives and friends who were present were filled with wonder at these incredible events and asked: "What kind of child will this be?"

23 Joseph the Carpenter

Matthew 1

Mary was about to become the mother of the Son of God. She was engaged to be married to Joseph, a humble carpenter from Nazareth, a descendant of King David.

When Joseph found out that Mary, his bride-to-be, was going to be the mother of a child, he decided to free her from her promise to marry him. But an angel appeared to him and explained to him: "Joseph, do not hesitate to take Mary as your wife, for her child is the Son of God!"

The angel also told him the name of the child: Jesus, which means "God is the Savior," and the angel added: "This name is fitting, because this child, the Son of God, will save his people from their sins."

When he heard this, Joseph remembered many things which the prophets had said and written in the sacred books which were read every Sabbath day in the synagogue. In particular, he remembered that the prophet Isaiah had spoken of an unmarried woman who would bear a child called Emmanuel, a name which means "God with us."

Mary's child, then, was to be this Emmanuel, Joseph realized. God made man like us, to be with us!

Joseph felt his heart fill with the love of God. He realized what an important task God was entrusting to him: to be the guardian and protector of the Son of God on earth.

When he understood all these things, Joseph did not break off his engagement with Mary. He took her as his wife and he watched over her with great care. When the child was born, everyone thought it was Joseph's son. As far as the law was concerned, he was the son of Joseph and since Joseph was a descendant of the house of David, Jesus too was a descendant of the great king. This, too, was as the prophets had foretold.

24 The Journey from Nazareth to Bethlehem

Luke 2

At that time, the Roman emperor was Caesar Augustus and he also ruled over Palestine. Augustus wished to know how many people lived in his empire and he therefore ordered a census to be taken.

For the census, each person had to register in the place from which his family came. Since Joseph was a descendant of David of Bethlehem, Joseph had to travel from Nazareth to Bethlehem. And so he helped his pregnant wife, Mary, onto a donkey and they set off.

25 Jesus Is Born

Luke 2

Joseph and his wife, Mary, were traveling from Nazareth to Bethlehem. This was a long and difficult journey, especially because it was nearly time for Mary to give birth to her child. However, they had no choice, because the Roman emperor, who ruled in Palestine, had ordered everyone to return to his place of birth for the census.

In those days, when people had to make a journey, they would walk during the day and they would stop and spend the night in an inn along the way. To make the journey less tiring for Mary, Joseph made her travel on the back of a donkey.

After many days on the road, Joseph and Mary arrived in Bethlehem, the city of David, which was crowded with strangers who had also come for the census.

Joseph went to seek lodgings at the inn, but found that it was completely full. Mary was about to give birth, and shelter had to be found for her. At last Joseph found a cave which shepherds and farmers used as a stable. And it was there, in that cave, that Mary gave birth to Jesus, the Son of God. With great care, she wrapped him in swaddling clothes and laid him in a manger.

26 The Song of the Angels

Luke 2

In the fields around Bethlehem there were some shepherds who spent their nights out in the open, watching over their flocks.

One night, an extraordinary thing happened to them: all of a sudden they were surrounded by a great light and in the light they saw an angel of the Lord. The shepherds were filled with fear, but the angel said to them: "Do not be afraid: I bring you good news, news that will bring great joy to you and all men. Today, in Bethlehem, the city of David, is born the Savior, the Messiah foretold by the prophets, the Lord! Go and see him; he is wrapped in swaddling clothes and lying in a manger." And, suddenly, other angels joined with the one who had spoken and they began to sing in praise of God: "Glory to God on the highest and peace on earth and good will to men."

When they had finished their song of praise, the angels left the shepherds and disappeared back into heaven. The shepherds, who were still amazed by what they had seen and heard, said to each other: "Let us go at once to Bethlehem to see this thing which has happened and which God has made known to us."

December

27 The Good News Given to the Shepherds

Luke 2

The angel of the Lord had brought joyous news to the shepherds who were watching their flocks in the fields around Bethlehem. A child had been born in Bethlehem who was Christ the Lord, the Messiah of whom the prophets had spoken so often. And they now had the chance to see him. They, who were so poor and looked down on by everyone, had the honor of being the first to see him.

Truly, all men are equal in the eyes of God, and perhaps he even prefers the poor and humble.

28 Mary Praise the Lord

Luke 1

Mary, who was called by God to be the mother of his son, Jesus, praised the Lord with a great hymn that even today many people repeat as a prayer. This is the hymn that Mary sang to the shepherds and all who gathered:

My soul does magnify the Lord and
  my spirit rejoices in God my
Savior, who has looked on me, his
  humble handmaiden.
Henceforth all men to come shall
  call me blessed.
Almighty God has done great things
in me.
Holy is his name; he will be merciful
  to those that love him
  from generation to generation.
He has shown his great strength: he
  has caused the plans of
  the proud to fail
  and has brought to ruin
  the powerful;
And he has exalted the humble and
  filled the hungry with good things;
While he has sent the rich away
  empty-handed.
He has remembered to be merciful
  and has sent help to his people of
  Israel, according to the promise
  he made to Abraham and his
  descendants forever.

29 The Homage of the Shepherds

Luke 2

The shepherds had been told by the angel the news that the baby Jesus had been born in Bethlehem. They then hurried to Bethlehem and found the baby wrapped in swaddling clothes and lying in a manger in the stable where Joseph and Mary had found shelter. The shepherds immediately gave thanks to God, because the baby Jesus was the proof of the great love that God had for all mankind. Afterward, the shepherds did not keep their joy to themselves, but spoke to everyone they met of the miraculous events that had taken place.

30 Zacharias Gives Thanks to the Lord

Luke 1

When his son John was born, Zacharias sang a hymn of praise to the Lord.

Blessed is the Lord God of Israel; for he has visited and
redeemed his people.

Among the descendants of David he
has caused a savior to
be born, as he had promised
through the words of his holy
prophets.

He has been merciful. Now we can
serve him without fear;
faithful to him all our days.

And you, my son, will be the prophet of Almighty God: you will
walk before the Lord himself and
prepare the way for him.

You will announce to his people
that God
will save them and forgive all their sins.

The Lord will shine for us, like the
sun among the shadows,
and he will guide our steps onto
the path of peace.

And so it happened; the child who was born to him, and who was named John, grew in body and in spirit and prepared himself for the mission that awaited him. He was to be the last of the prophets, who was to proclaim that Jesus, the long awaited Messiah, had arrived.

31 Unto Us a Child Is Born

Isaiah 9,11,35,62

The child born in Bethlehem was the Messiah, the Savior so long expected by the prophets and the people of Israel. This is the way the prophet Isaiah foretold his coming: The people who walk in darkness have seen a great light. Unto us a child is born! On his shoulders he wears the emblems of a king. Great will be his dominion and there will be everlasting peace in the kingdom which he establishes. In his kingdom all men will do what is good and right before God.

He, a descendant of David, will have the spirit of God in him. He will not judge according to appearances, but with justice, and he will have no respect for the powerful or the wicked.

In the kingdom he establishes, the wolf shall lie down with the lamb, the leopard with the kid; the calf and the lion shall go to pasture together and a small child will be able to watch over them. The cow and the bear will feed together, with their young. The lion will dine on straw and kill no more, and the child will play in safety with snakes.

In the whole Kingdom of God, no one will ever do evil again: everyone will live in peace and harmony.

Behold, the Savior is coming!

January

BIBLE STORY OF THE MONTH

Baby Jesus in the Temple

The angel of the Lord had said to Mary: "When your child, the Son of God on high, comes to be born, you will name him Jesus."

The baby was born in the stable in Bethlehem, and according to the Hebrew custom he was given his name eight days later. Naturally it was the name that the angel had indicated, Jesus, which means "God is the Savior." In fact, through this child, God intervened to save his people.

The prophets had foretold this centuries beforehand: one day God would send a Savior, and they had named him the Messiah, "the consecrated of the Lord." The name Christ means the same as Messiah: that is why Jesus was also later called Christ.

Jesus was Mary's first son, and Hebrew law stated that the firstborn son belonged to the Lord. So in a certain sense the child had to be bought back from the Lord, by an offer to exchange two doves or two wild pigeons.

For this reason, forty days after her son's birth, Mary and her husband Joseph took Jesus to the temple of the Lord in Jerusalem, and they also took two turtle doves to offer up to the Lord.

Inside the temple they met a man who was called Simeon. He was a good man, and all his life he had tried to please the Lord. Simeon remembered the words of the prophets, and he anxiously awaited the day when the Lord would send the Messiah.

And the Lord had promised him that before he died he would know the joy of setting his eyes on the long awaited Messiah.

The day that Mary and Joseph took Jesus to the temple, Simeon also felt inspired to go to the house of the Lord, and when he saw the child, God led him to understand that this was the Messiah.

So he picked the infant up, and thanking the Lord with all his heart, he said: "Now Lord, you can let me, your servant, go in peace, as you have promised, because my eyes have seen the Savior that you have sent.

You have placed him before all the peoples of the earth, like a light which illuminates all nations and all races of men and gives glory to your people, Israel."

Mary and Joseph were amazed to hear these words. Simeon blessed them and then turned to the mother of the child, Mary, saying: "This child will be the cause of the ruin or the salvation of many men from the people of Israel. He will be a sign from God, to reveal the intentions of

many people, those intentions which are kept hidden in their hearts. And for you Mary,' a sword will pierce your soul."

With these mysterious words, Simeon meant that in the future, Jesus was to be accepted by a part of the Jewish people, while the other part of his people would reject him.

Those who would accept him, believe in him, and love him, would be saved and go to heaven, while those who refused him would be ruined. As for Mary, she was to suffer upon seeing her son refused: She was to suffer as if she had been pierced by a sword.

That same day, in the temple, Mary and Joseph met a woman named Anna. She was very old, eighty-four, and since being widowed she had dedicated herself to God; she lived in the temple, and day and night she showed her most devout love for him with prayers and sacrifices.

When she saw the child, Anna, too, understood who he was; and so, like Simeon, she gave praise to God, and spoke of the child to all those who awaited the coming of the Messiah.

This was not the only time that Jesus' parents took him to the temple in Jerusalem.

Every year Joseph, with his wife, Mary, went to Jerusalem for the feast of the Passover, and they took Jesus with them.

When he was twelve years old it happened that, when the feast was over and Joseph and Mary were returning home, Jesus remained in Jerusalem.

Joseph and Mary were traveling with a large number of other pilgrims, the men divided from the women, as was the custom. During the first day of their journey, they did not realize that Jesus was missing: Joseph thought he was with Mary and the other children, and Mary thought he was with the group of men.

It wasn't till evening that they realized Jesus was missing, so they immediately left the others and returned to Jerusalem.

After searching for three days they found him in the temple, busy talking with the elders and teachers, who were amazed at his intelligence and the things that he knew.

Then his mother said: "You have made us very worried!" But Jesus answered: "Why are you looking for me? Didn't you know that I have to look after the affairs of my father?"

The child Jesus knew that his father was not Joseph, as everyone believed, but God himself.

Luke 2

1 The Wise Men from the East

Matthew 2

On the night Jesus was born, not only did the Lord send an angel to the shepherds, he also sent a message to three Magi (wise men) who lived in the east. This message was in the form of a bright star which suddenly began to shine in the sky.

When the Magi saw the star they knew, from all their studies, what it signified, and they said: "This star announces the birth of a very important person, the birth of a king, the king of the Jews. We must follow the star and find this child who is born, and worship him!"

2 They Will Bring Gold and Incense

Genesis 49; 2 Samuel 7; Isaiah 60

The birth of Jesus was, at first, an event of which very few people were aware. Later, when the people of Israel knew of him, many realized that in him the words of the prophets were fulfilled.

Through the words of the prophet Nathan, the Lord had promised to David of the tribe of Judah that one of his descendants would be king forever.

All of this was fulfilled in Jesus: He was a man born in the tribe of Judah, and a descendant of David. And he was God, a king who reigns forever, because he never dies!

There was, therefore, reason for rejoicing, as the prophet Isaiah had foretold: "Arise Jerusalem, bathed in light, for the glory of the Lord shines on you and illuminates you!

"Behold, shadows cover the earth, but the Lord shines on you and his glory covers you!

"The peoples of the world will move toward your light. Their kings will be drawn to you, led by he who illuminates you.

"Foreigners will bring you their treasure; a host of camels will be brought to your land; they will bring gold and incense and will come to praise the Lord."

3 The Journey of the Magi

Matthew 2

Large and bright, a new star had suddenly appeared in the sky to show that a new king of the Jews had been born, and the Magi of the east had decided to follow it. At once they prepared a great caravan of camels and chose the proper gifts for the newborn king.

After following the star for a long way, the Magi arrived in Jerusalem.

"Where is the king of the Jews who has been born?" the Magi asked. "We have seen his star rise, and we have come to pay homage to him!"

4 Herod, King of the Jews

Matthew 2

At the time when Jesus was born in Bethlehem, a cruel and bloody king called Herod ruled over the Jews.

He had come to the throne with the help of the Romans, who had conquered the whole land of Palestine and given him this kingdom so that they could keep better control over the country. Herod ruled over Palestine until a few years after the birth of Jesus. Out of spite, he had had many members of his own family put to death. His jealousy and suspicion caused him to persecute the infant Jesus.

5 King Herod and the Magi

Matthew 2

It was a common belief among the people of the east that a new star in the sky meant the birth of a great person. Thus, when King Herod learned that the Magi had arrived in Jerusalem following the star and seeking the new king of the Jews, he was filled with suspicion that this new king of the Jews would lay claim to his throne. What was he to do?

Herod called the high priests to him and asked them where this Messiah, of whom the prophets had spoken for centuries, should have been born. "In Bethlehem," he was told, "for the prophet Micah explained this clearly when he said these words 'And you Bethlehem, are certainly not the least of the cities of Judea, for in you will be born the ruler to lead my people, Israel!'"

Herod then secretly called the Magi to him and made them tell him precisely when the star had first appeared in the sky. He advised them to go at once to Bethlehem, with these false words: "Go to Bethlehem and carefully seek out the child. And when you have found him, come back and tell me so that I too can go and pay homage and worship him!"

6 The Adoration of the Magi

Matthew 2

King Herod wanted the Magi from the east to help him discover where to find the child whom they said would become king of the Jews. In reality, Herod had absolutely no intention of going to pay homage to a rival; he wished to know where to find Jesus in order to kill him!

The Magi departed from Jerusalem again and the star they had seen in the east shone over their heads and guided them. When they looked at it, they were filled with a great joy. The star finally stopped over the spot where Jesus lay with his mother, Mary. At once they went down on their knees and worshiped Jesus; then they offered their gifts to him. Opening a casket, one of them offered him gold, truly a gift fit for a king. Another brought from his casket incense, which would spread its sweet perfume when it was burned on the fire, and this also was a gift fit for a king. The third of the Magi opened his casket and brought out myrrh, a perfumed resin which was also precious for its medicinal properties; this too was a rare gift, and fitting. Thus, it was not only the humble shepherds who came to pay homage to Jesus, but also the illustrious wise men.

7 King Herod and the Children of Bethlehem

Matthew 2

The Magi, led by the star, had arrived at the cave in Bethlehem and worshiped the baby Jesus. It was now time for them to begin their journey back to their own country. The Lord, however, warned the Magi in a dream to say nothing to Herod of what they had seen and not to go back to him in Jerusalem. Thus the Magi did not return to Jerusalem, but went back home by another route. When Herod realized that the Magi had deceived him and had departed without telling him where the child was, he flew into a rage and sought another way to kill the infant whom he feared.

Thus, Herod sent his soldiers to Bethlehem and the surrounding countryside with orders to kill all male children under two years of age. This was the amount of time that had passed since, as the Magi had revealed to him, the star had first appeared in the sky.

Unfortunately, this cruel order was obeyed and the result was a massacre. All the male children in Bethlehem and the surrounding countryside who were under two years of age were put to death. However, even this cruel measure proved futile against Jesus.

January

8 The Flight into Egypt

Matthew 2

The cruel massacre of the children of Bethlehem, ordered by Herod, did not succeed in killing the baby Jesus. In fact, an angel of the Lord had appeared to Joseph in a dream and given him these commands: "Arise! Take the child and his mother with you and flee into Egypt, for Herod is seeking to kill the child. You must all stay in Egypt until I tell you to return!"

Joseph awoke at once and immediately did what the angel had ordered him to do; he took the child and his mother Mary and fled by night into Egypt, where he remained until the death of Herod. In this way the baby Jesus was saved and what the Lord had foretold through the prophet Hosea came true: "I have called my son from Egypt!"

When Herod died, Joseph was still in Egypt and an angel of the Lord appeared to him a second time and said: "Arise! Take the child and his mother with you and return to the land of Israel. For those who threatened the child are dead!"

Once more, Joseph did exactly as the angel had ordered him to do; he got up, took the baby Jesus and Mary with him, and set out from Egypt to the land of Israel.

9 Jesus in Nazareth

Matthew 2; Luke 2

From Egypt, where he had fled to save the life of the baby Jesus, Joseph returned to the land of Israel and, more exactly, to his home village of Nazareth.

There, Jesus grew up and became strong; he was filled with wisdom, and the grace of God was upon him. He lived in Nazareth, ever obedient to Mary, his mother, and to Joseph until he was about thirty years old. For this reason, although Jesus was born in Bethlehem, he was called the Nazarene. No one yet realized that he was the Son of God.

10 John Preaches Repentance

Luke 3

John, the baby born to Zacharias and Elisabeth a few months before the birth of Jesus, grew in body and in spirit. When he became a man, the Word of God came to him.

John would stand on the banks of the river Jordan and say: "The Messiah foretold by the prophets is soon to come among us! You must ask God's forgiveness for your sins and change your way of life."

Everyone held John in great respect, for he was the first to put into practice what he told others to do. He had spent many years in the desert, eating locusts and wild honey, and he dressed very poorly.

The people who were prepared to change their way of life came to him in the waters of the Jordan, and he poured water on their heads and thus baptized them. For this reason John was called the Baptist, which means "One who baptizes."

Some of the people asked him: "What must we do to become better people?," and John replied: "Whoever has two coats should give one to someone who has none. And whoever has more than enough to eat should do the same!"

Several tax collectors also came to be baptized and they, too, asked him: "Master, what must we do?" To them John replied: "Do not take a penny more than is due in taxes." Even the soldiers asked him the same question: "What should we do?" And John said to them: "Do not exploit your strength or take advantage of the weapons you carry. And do not maltreat anyone."

Everyone had so much admiration for John that they wondered if, perhaps, he himself was not the Messiah. But he explained to them: "No! The Messiah is much greater than I! I am not even fit to tie his sandals! I baptize you with water. But he, along with the water of baptism, will give you the Holy Spirit!"

11 John and Jesus: "Behold the Lamb of God"

John 1

Thus, John the Baptist stayed on the banks of the Jordan. He invited the wicked to change their way of life and to prepare themselves for the Messiah who was soon to come among them. Those willing to change were baptized by John.

His behavior was surprising and everyone wanted to know more about him. For this reason they asked him: "Are you, yourself, perhaps the Christ, the Messiah foretold by the prophets?" "No I am not the Messiah," replied John. "Then you must be Moses or the prophet Elijah, returned to this world?" "No," replied John.

"Well then, who are you?" To this question John replied: "As the prophet Isaiah foretold a long time ago, I am a voice that cries in the wilderness: prepare ye the way of the Lord who is coming among us!"

One day the Lord, Jesus, really did arrive. He had left Nazareth and come to the banks of the Jordan where John was baptizing people. When John saw who was coming toward him, he said to the crowd that surrounded him: "Behold the Lamb of God, behold he who will take away the sin of the world. He is the Son of God!"

12 The Baptism of Jesus

Matthew 3

Jesus had come to John, who was baptizing the Jews on the banks of the river Jordan. Like all the others, Jesus also went into the water as a sign that he wished baptism.

John, however, had not expected this at all: he baptized sinners, while Jesus was without sin. Moreover, he was the Son of God who had come into the world especially to take away the sins of mankind.

John, therefore, said to Jesus: "It is not you who should be baptized by me. It is I who should be baptized by you." But Jesus replied, saying: "Do as I ask, for there is a reason."

John understood the reason shortly afterward. Hardly had he baptized Jesus than he saw the spirit of God descend upon him like a dove and he heard a voice say: "This is my beloved son, in whom I am well pleased."

The voice of God the Father, while God the Son was before him, hardly out of the water, and God the Holy Spirit had come down upon him! The three persons of the Holy Trinity all present together! This was a solemn moment: Jesus was beginning the work for which he had come into the world.

13 Jesus Defeats the Devil

Matthew 4

Jesus' great task lay before him. To prepare himself well, he retired for forty days into the desert and did not eat in order to pray to his father in heaven and be ready for what he had to do. At the end of the forty days, he was very hungry. So Satan sought to tempt Jesus. He said to Jesus: "If you are truly the Son of God, then make these stones into bread." Jesus, however, replied: "Man does not live by bread alone, but also by every word that comes from God."

The devil then carried him to Jerusalem, to the highest pinnacle of the temple, and said to him: "If you are the Son of God, then throw yourself down. God will send his angels to protect you and prevent you from hurting yourself." But Jesus did not fall into the trap; he replied: "It is wrong to put yourself in danger and expect God to save you with a miracle."

The devil did not give up. He took Jesus to a very high mountain and showed him the whole world and all its wealth. "All that you see, I will give to you if you bow down before me and worship me." But Jesus replied: "Be gone Satan! Only God is to be worshiped."

14 Jesus Announces the Good News
Matthew 4

Jesus was about thirty years old when he began the task he had come into the world to accomplish. He had gone to be baptized by John, and his Father and the Holy Spirit had been present. He had meditated for forty days in the desert and had then defeated the devil who had come to tempt him into sin.

By now everything was ready and Jesus began to go around the cities and the villages of Palestine and to repeat to everyone he met: "Repent, for the Kingdom of Heaven is at hand!" He told the people to change their way of life and truly love God, and he would open the gates to his kingdom where happiness is eternal.

The words of Jesus constituted a happy announcement for the people of Palestine. This was the gospel, the "good news" that they had long awaited.

Hadn't the prophets spoken of this? Hadn't even John repeated it to those who came to him for baptism? The Christ, the Messiah had come to make true friendship possible between mankind and God. And the Messiah, the Christ, the Lord Jesus, had arrived!

15 The First Disciples
Luke 5

One day, Jesus was talking to the crowd by the lake of Gennesaret. Among the crowd there was a fisherman by the name of Simon, and Jesus said to him: "Launch out into the deep and let down your nets to fish." Simon replied: "Master, we have toiled and fished all night, and caught nothing. Nevertheless, if you say so, I will go out again."

And, together with his brother Andrew, that is what Simon did. When they pulled in their nets, they held such an enormous quantity of fish that the nets almost broke. They had to ask for help from their partners, the brothers James and John, who were on a nearby boat. They had caught so many fish that they filled both boats to overflowing.

Simon and the others were astonished, but Jesus said to Simon: "From this day, you shall be a fisher of men!" By this Jesus meant that Simon would bring men to accept the good news. In this way, Simon, Andrew, James, and John left their work in order to follow Jesus. They were his first disciples.

Simon, who lived in Capernaum, accepted Jesus into his house. Jesus changed the name of his disciple and called him Peter.

16 Jesus Calls Philip and Nathanael
John 1

One day, Jesus met a man called Philip and asked him to become one of his disciples. Philip consented and when, in his turn, he met his friend Nathanael, he said to him with great happiness: "We have found the Messiah, prophets foretold! He is Jesus of Nazareth."

Nathanael, however, was not impressed, and replied: "From Nazareth? Can anything good come from that tiny village?" But Philip insisted, saying, "At least come and see for yourself!" When Jesus saw Nathanael approaching, he said: "Behold a true Israelite, with no falsity."

Nathanael was surprised and said: "You know me? How is that?" Jesus replied: "Before Philip called you, I saw you beneath the fig tree."

It was true that, before his meeting with Philip, Nathanael had been in the shade under a fig tree. Thus, Nathanael realized, this was not a man like other men. He understood and exclaimed: "Master, you are the Son of God, you are the king!"

Jesus replied to him: "You believe only because I told you that I had seen you in the shade of the fig tree? You shall see much greater things than these!"

17 The First Miracle at Cana

John 2

A marriage was being celebrated in the village of Cana in Galilee. Jesus had been invited with Mary, his mother, and his disciples.

During the wedding feast the wine ran out and there was a risk that the celebration would be ruined. Mary realized this and said to Jesus: "They have no more wine." Jesus replied to her: "The hour has not yet come for me to perform miracles." Mary, however, said to the servants: "Do as he tells you."

In the house there were six large stone waterpots which could each hold two or three barrels. Jesus said to the servants: "Fill the jars with water." When the servants had done as Jesus asked, he said: "Now take a little of the contents to the head of the table."

The water had become wine, and the wine was excellent! When the head of the table had tasted it, he said to the bridegroom: "Normally, at a celebration, everyone gives the guests their best wine first. Then, when the guests have all had some to drink, they give them their poorer wine. You, on the other hand, have saved the best wine till last!"

In this way, in Cana in Galilee, Jesus began to perform his miracles.

18 Jesus Drives the Merchants from the Temple

John 2

The feast of the Passover was approaching and Jesus went to celebrate the holy day in Jerusalem. When Jesus entered the temple, in the courtyard he found a great number of merchants, dealing in foreign currencies or selling oxen, sheep, or doves to people who then offered them in sacrifice.

The temple, the Passover, and the sacrifices offered to the Lord all meant nothing to the merchants. They were only concerned with making as much money as possible. Jesus grew angry. He took small cords and made a scourge to topple the tables and drive out the merchants. "Take these things away," Jesus said. "You have transformed the house of my father, the temple, into a market!"

"Who are you to do these things?" they asked him. "Who has given you the authority?" Jesus replied: "Destroy this temple and in three days I will raise it up again."

At that time they did not understand, but his disciples were later to understand. Jesus was referring to the temple of his body. With these words he spoke of his own death and resurrection, his return to life after three days.

19 A Nocturnal Visit

John 3

A man named Nicodemus, one of the rulers of the Jews, felt a great desire to speak with Jesus. However, he did not want anyone to see him because he did not want to be considered a disciple of the person that the other rulers viewed with suspicion and distrust.

Therefore, Nicodemus decided to visit Jesus at night, and said to him: "Master, we know that you have come from God, because no one else can do what you do!" And in reply Jesus explained: "I tell you in truth, that if a man is not born again, then he cannot enter into the Kingdom of God."

"How can a man be born again when he is already old?" asked an amazed Nicodemus. And Jesus explained to him: "A man must be born of water and in spirit to enter the Kingdom of God."

With these words Jesus spoke of baptism. Whoever receives the holy water receives the life of God himself; the Lord adopts him as his son and opens the doors to his house to him.

"God loves the world so much," Jesus concluded, "as to send his only son, so that whoever believes in him shall have eternal life."

20 The Parable of the Sower

Matthew 13

"The sower went out to sow. And while he sowed, some of the seeds fell by the wayside and the birds came and ate them. Other seeds fell among stones, where there was very little earth; they grew up at once, but with shallow roots and, as soon as the sun came out, they withered away. And some of the seeds fell among thorn bushes which grew up and suffocated them. But other seeds fell upon good ground and gave fruit, some a hundredfold, some sixtyfold and some thirtyfold."

Jesus recounted this parable to his listeners one day. Parables are almost like riddles and those who listened to Jesus tried to understand them. Who is the sower? What are the seeds he is sowing? And the ground?

Sometimes, Jesus himself gave them the explanation. On other occasions his listeners understood the meaning by themselves. Jesus explained the parable of the sower in this way: "The seed is the Word of God; the different types of ground are the hearts of men.

When a man hears the Word of God and does not understand it, he is like the arid ground by the wayside; the seed does not take root, and the devil comes and takes it.

The word that falls on stony ground is like a man who hears it with joy, but he is inconstant and easily refuses the word of God which has no deep roots in his heart. The ground covered in thorn bushes is like the person attached to money and things of this world: these prevent the Word of God from bearing fruit.

The good ground, on the other hand, is like the heart of the person who listens seriously to the Word of God and accepts it gladly, so that he can put down healthy roots and produce the abundant fruits of good works."

21 The Kingdom of God and the Grain of Mustard Seed

Mark 4

To what can we compare the Kingdom of God? With what words can we describe it? This is what Jesus said about it:

"The Kingdom of God is like a grain of mustard seed. When it is sown it is the smallest of all seeds, so small that it is almost invisible. But, once it has been sown, the mustard seed grows and grows until it becomes the greatest of all the herbs. And the branches shoot out so large and strong that the birds of the air find shade beneath them and build their nests among them."

22 The Son of the Nobleman

John 4

Jesus was in Cana, in Galilee, the town where he had changed the water into wine, when he was approached in great haste by a nobleman who lived in Capernaum. The nobleman was very worried and distressed, and said to Jesus: "Master, my son is so ill that he is on the point of death. I beg you to come with me to Capernaum, to come and heal my son!"

"Go, your son is well again," Jesus said to him, without moving, to show to all those present that he could even perform miracles at a distance. The nobleman believed the words of Jesus and set off home. Before he even got there, his servants ran out to meet him and said: "Your son is well again!"

The nobleman wanted to know at what time his son had started to feel better again. The servants answered: "It was yesterday afternoon, about one o'clock, that the fever left him. And the nobleman realized that this was precisely the time at which Jesus had said to him: "Go, your son is well again!"

Jesus performed many miracles. He could do this because, although he was a man, he was also God and God has the power to do all things.

23 The Yeast and the Treasure

Matthew 13

In order to be sure that everyone understood him, Jesus explained himself with stories and comparisons. In this way, talking about the Kingdom of God, Jesus said: "The Kingdom of God is like a little yeast that a woman mixes with a large quantity of flour, until the whole mixture is leavened!

"The Kingdom of God is also similar to a treasure hidden in a field. A man finds it and hides it again. Then, filled with joy, he goes and sells everything he owns and buys the field!"

24 Jesus Heals a Leper

Mark 1

At the time of Jesus there were many lepers in Palestine. They suffered from a horrible disease of the skin and were forced to live far off. One day a leper approached Jesus and said to him: "If you want to, you can heal me!" Jesus was moved with compassion for him and stretched out his hand to touch him, saying: "Be healed!"

The disease left the man at once: He was healed! The man was so happy about this that he told everyone. And the fame of Jesus spread throughout the land.

25 Jesus Calls Levi Matthew to Him

Mark 2

In Palestine at the time of Jesus there was one group of people that everybody hated and tried their best to avoid. These were the tax collectors who were considered traitors and sinners by the people.

One day at Capernaum, Jesus passed near the stall where people went to pay their taxes. He saw among the tax collectors a man named Levi and he said to him: "Come with me." At this the man got up and followed Jesus.

Levi, the tax collector, is the disciple also known by the name of Matthew, and he is the same man who also wrote one of the Gospels.

Happy and moved that Jesus had actually chosen him, a man despised by everyone, Levi Matthew invited Jesus to dinner at his own house with his friends, the other tax collectors. Jesus accepted, and this caused several masters of the law to marvel. They asked some of the disciples of Jesus: "Why does your master eat with all those sinners?" But Jesus overheard these words and he himself replied: "Healthy people do not need the doctor. Those who are sick, on the other hand, do need him. I did not come to call the righteous, but to call sinners to me!"

26 The Fishing Net

Matthew 13

To what can we compare the Kingdom of God? On one occasion Jesus said: "The Kingdom of God is like a net that is thrown into the sea and catches fish of every kind.

"When it is full, the fishermen draw the net to the shore and put the fish that are good to eat into baskets; the poor fish are thrown away.

"This is what will happen at the end of the world: The angels will separate the good men from the bad. The good will be carried into the Kingdom of Heaven, but the bad will be cast away."

27 The Man Lowered from the Roof

Mark 2

Jesus was in a house in Capernaum and the crowd had thronged to the door to listen to him speak.

Four men arrived carrying a paralyzed friend on a stretcher. They wanted to present him to Jesus and ask Jesus to cure him, but they could not get near the door of the house because of the crowd. Thus, they climbed onto the roof of the house and removed the straw covering over Jesus and then lowered the paralyzed man through the opening. When Jesus saw the great faith of these men, he said to the paralytic: "My son, your sins are forgiven."

When they heard these words, some of the learned scribes who were present thought, "What is he saying? Only God can forgive sins! This man is blaspheming!"

Jesus, however, knew what they were thinking and said: "Why do you think this? I will prove to you that I have the power to forgive sins. At this, Jesus turned to the paralyzed man and said: "Arise, take up thy bed, and walk!"

While everybody looked on, the paralyzed man stood up, lifted his bed, and walked off. Everyone was amazed and said: "We have never seen anything like this!"

28 The Man with the Withered Hand

Mark 3

For the Jews, the Sabbath was a holiday, because they obeyed the commandment of the Lord which told them not to work on that day. For this reason, they did nothing on the Sabbath, not even good works.

One day Jesus taught them, with an example and a miracle, that the Lord had meant something else when he had given them this commandment. One Sabbath Jesus went into the synagogue at Capernaum and saw a man with a withered hand. The enemies of Jesus constantly spied on him, hoping to accuse him of disobeying the law of God, and now, too, they watched carefully to see what he would do.

Jesus was well aware that they were watching him and he said to the man with the withered hand: "Come here, to us." Then he turned to the onlookers and said: "Is it permitted to do a good work on the Sabbath? For example, is it permissible to save a life?"

They said nothing: these men would not even save the life of a man in danger on the Sabbath. Jesus was saddened by the hardness of their hearts. To the man, he said: "Hold out your hand!" The man stretched it out and Jesus cured it.

29 Jesus Chooses the Twelve Apostles

Mark 3; Matthew 5

One day Jesus chose twelve men from among all his disciples. They are the twelve apostles, which means "Those who are sent," and he gave them a very special task.

These were their names: The first was Simon, to whom Jesus gave the name of Peter. After him, Jesus chose his brother Andrew. Then came the two brothers James and John, whom Jesus called "the Sons of thunder." And then Jesus chose Philip, and Nathanael who is also known as Bartholomew, and Levi who is called Matthew. Then he chose Thomas and James the son of Alphaeus, Thaddaeus, Simon the Canaanite, and Judas Iscariot who was later to betray Jesus.

Jesus said to his disciples one day: "You are the salt of the earth. Be careful not to lose your flavor, for salt without flavor is good for nothing and has to be thrown away. You are the light of the world. A city built on a mountain cannot be hidden. Men do not light a lamp to put it under a bucket, but rather to put it up high so that it can give light to everyone. The light of your good works must shine in this way so that all can see the good that you do and give thanks."

30 A Group of Women Help Jesus

Luke 8; Mark 15

Jesus moved through the cities and villages to tell everyone the good news about the Kingdom of God. He was accompanied by the twelve apostles and there were also several women who helped him. Jesus had cured these women from various illnesses and they, out of gratitude, gave their goods and belongings to him. Among these women were Mary Magdalene, and Joanna, the wife of Herod's steward; Mary, the mother of the apostle James Alphaeus; and Salome, the mother of the apostles James and John.

31 The Parable of the Weeds

Matthew 13

One day Jesus recounted the following parable to his disciples: "The Kingdom of Heaven is like the man who sowed good seed in his field. But at night, while everyone was sleeping, his enemy came along and sowed weeds among the wheat, and then stole away. Thus, when the wheat began to spring up, the weeds also grew. The field workers then said to their master: "Do you want us to go and pull out the weeds?" But their master replied: "No, because you might root out the good wheat along with the weeds. Let them both grow together until harvest. Then we will gather the weeds and burn them and we will gather the wheat and store it."

After he had told this parable to the crowd, Jesus went into the house and his disciples asked him: "Explain the parable of the weeds in the field to us." And so Jesus said: "I am the man who sows good seed. The field is the world. The enemy is the devil. The harvest is the end of the world, when wicked and evil men, who are like the weeds, will be sent to the devil, while the men who have produced good fruits in their life will be gathered into the Kingdom of God."

BIBLE STORY OF THE MONTH

Jesus and his Disciples

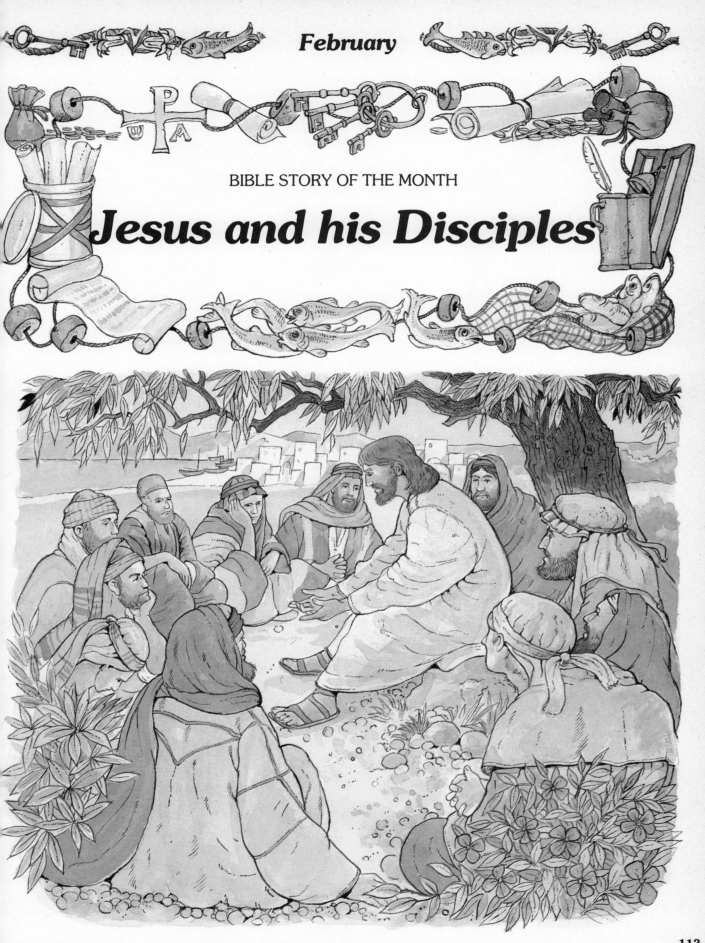

When it was time for Jesus to begin the work he had come down to earth to do, he left his native village of Nazareth and moved to Capernaum.

In Nazareth he had lived a quiet life, and no one knew that he was the Son of God; only his mother, Mary, was aware of it. So he went to live in Capernaum, an important city on the left shore of the Sea of Galilee. Here Jesus chose his first disciples from among the fishermen: one of them, Simon, whom Jesus later called Peter, welcomed him into his own home.

From Capernaum Jesus took to wandering through the villages of Galilee on foot, announcing the Gospel of the Kingdom of Heaven. In fact the word Gospel means "Good News." Jesus brought the good news that God the Father loves all men very much, and wants them to be happy with him.

One day Jesus went out from Capernaum and headed toward a nearby mountain. His disciples followed him. When he got to the top, he sat down with his disciples around him, and taught them the "Beatitudes," telling of those who will be blessed in the Kingdom of Heaven.

Jesus said: Blessed are those who are poor in the eyes of God, be-cause God will offer them the King-dom of Heaven.

Blessed are those who mourn, because God will comfort them.

Blessed are the meek, because God shall reward them with paradise.

Blessed are those who want to do God's will with all their hearts, because God will fulfill their wish.

Blessed are those who show mercy to others, because God will show mercy to them.

Blessed are the pure in heart, because they shall see God.

Blessed are those who spread the word of peace, because God will welcome them like children.

Blessed are those who are persecuted when trying to do the will of God: God will give them his kingdom. Rejoice if you are persecuted because you are my disciples: God has prepared a great reward for you!"

Sometimes Jesus would take a boat with his disciples to cross to the other side of the sea. On one occasion, being tired after a hard day, Jesus lay down in the bottom of the boat and fell asleep with his head resting on a cushion. It was evening, and the weather was calm. But all of a sudden, as happens on the Sea of Galilee, a great storm arose. The water became agitated. The waves

rose up higher than the boat, and the disciples began to feel frightened. When the water began to pour into the boat, they feared they were going to sink. So they went to Jesus, who was still sleeping, and they woke him, saying: "Lord, save us or we will all drown!"

So Jesus arose, and said to the wind: "Be silent!" and to the water he said: "Be calm!"

Suddenly the storm ceased, and Jesus said to the apostles: "Why are you so afraid? Do you have no faith in me?"

The disciples looked at each other with expressions of wonder and amazement, and they said: "Who, then, is this man, this teacher of ours, whom even the winds and waters obey?"

The disciples began to understand. God created the winds and the water and everything that exists, and he has power over everything. If Jesus was able to command the forces of nature, then it meant that he had the same power and the same authority as God.

This experience, which had so frightened the apostles, helped them to get to know their master better, and to have more faith in him.

On another occasion, the disciples were out in their boat without Jesus when the wind picked up, making the surface of the sea rough. The boat began to rock about in a dangerous manner.

Meanwhile, evening had fallen. The disciples rowed very hard in an attempt to get back to land as quickly as possible, but the shore was still a long way off.

Jesus, who was waiting for them on the shore, saw that his disciples were in danger and wished to help them. So he started off toward them, walking on the water.

When they saw a figure approaching them, walking on the water, the disciples grew fearful.

"Take courage, it's I, do not be afraid!" Jesus said.

"Lord, if it is truly you, command me to come to you by walking on the water!" Peter said to him.

"Come here!" Jesus ordered him.

Peter went out of the boat and began walking on the water. But he soon became afraid and began to sink. Then he begged Jesus to help him and he shouted: "Lord, save me!" So Jesus went to him, he took him by the hand and raised him up saying: "Why did you not have faith in me?" Then he climbed into the boat with Peter.

On seeing this, the other disciples went down on their knees before Jesus and exclaimed: "You are truly the Son of God!"

Mark 1; Matthew 5; Matthew 8; Mark 4; Matthew 14

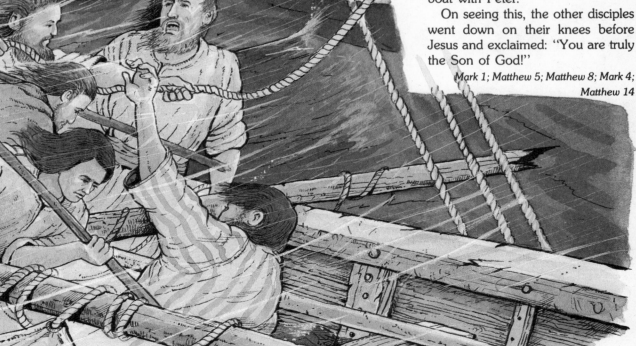

1 Jesus in the Synagogue

Mark 1

It was Saturday, the Sabbath, the feast day of the Hebrews. This was a day on which nobody worked, because it was completely dedicated to God. In the morning everybody went to the synagogue, the house of prayer. There, they read the Holy Scriptures, the Bible, and the teachings of Moses, or the prophets.

Then, anyone among the men who were present could explain or comment on what had been read.

Jesus, too, went to the synagogue, and after the readings he got up to give an explanation.

2 Jesus and the Man Possessed by the Devil

Mark 1

One day, in the synagogue of Capernaum, Jesus was explaining the Holy Scriptures, of the Bible, in a clear and precise manner. The people who were listening were amazed at his teachings.

At a certain point, however, Jesus' speech was interrupted. A poor man who had been taken over by a devil began to shout: "What are you doing here, Jesus of Nazareth? Have you come to ruin me? I know who you are: You are the saint sent by God!"

Then Jesus turned to the devil which was in this man, and shouted: "Be silent, you, and come out of that man!" At these words, the devil attempted to rebel and shook the poor man, making him scream. In the end, it left him and went away. The man was healed.

All those present grew even more amazed, and when they left the synagogue they went to tell everyone else: "We have seen amazing things! Jesus teaches with authority, not like the masters of the law. Jesus even commands the evil spirits, and they obey him!"

The news soon spread throughout the whole of Galilee, and everyone heard mention of Jesus of Nazareth.

3 Jesus Cures Peter's Mother-in-Law

Mark 1

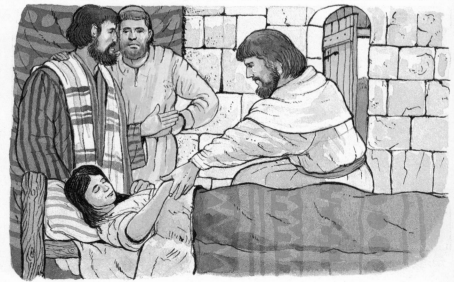

One Saturday, in the synagogue in Capernaum, Jesus had explained the law of the Lord and cured a poor man who had been taken over by the devil.

Then Jesus left the synagogue and went to the house of Simon-Peter. Simon-Peter's mother-in-law was in bed with a fever. Jesus went up to the woman, took her by the hand, and made her rise up. At once her fever disappeared; the woman was cured! So she began to prepare a meal for Jesus and the other disciples.

February

4 Jesus Cures Many Sick People

Mark 1

When the sun began to set and it was no longer too hot, people started to gather in front of Peter's house in Capernaum. Word had spread that Jesus had liberated a poor man who was possessed by the devil. A great many people came to ask Jesus to cure their illnesses, and they carried those unable to come alone. Soon there was a huge crowd. Jesus did not turn anyone away. He placed his hands on the sick, and cured them all: those who were paralyzed, blind, or possessed by the devil.

5 Where Is Jesus?

Mark 1

It was morning: a great crowd gathered outside Peter's house in Capernaum, where Jesus was living. Everybody wanted Jesus to cure his illness, or free him from evil spirits. Peter opened the door to let all the hopeful people in. Then he went to call Jesus, but his bed was empty. Where could he have gone?

Peter and the other disciples thought for a while, then they understood; they knew their master, and they knew where to go and look for him.

Peter and the disciples went out, and headed for a secluded place, up in the hills. And here they found Jesus, kneeling in prayer. Jesus was talking with his father in heaven.

Peter and his companions called to him: "Come! Everybody is looking for you!"

But Jesus replied: "We will go to the other villages so that I can take my message there too! This is why I came; I have to look after them as well!"

Thus began another day for Jesus. He traveled all throughout Galilee, followed by his disciples, and he preached in the synagogues, he cured the sick, and chased away the evil spirits.

6 Who is the Greatest?

Matthew 18

One day the disciples came to Jesus and asked him: "Who is the greatest in the Kingdom of Heaven?"

So Jesus called a child to him, stood him in front of the disciples, and said: "I tell you that if you don't become like children, you will not enter the Kingdom of Heaven.

"Anyone who becomes small like this child will be the greatest in the Kingdom of Heaven."

Jesus then added: "I dearly love little children; and whoever embraces and loves a child, embraces and loves me as well."

7 The Killing of John the Baptist

Mark 6

John the Baptist went around telling everybody what was right and what was wrong. And he even told the king.

At that time the king of Galilee was Herod Antipas, the son of the Herod who had tried to kill the baby Jesus. Herod Antipas had married Herodias, the wife of his brother, and this was evil in the eyes of the Lord. John had reprimanded him several times for this, and Herodias had sworn revenge. For this reason, John had been put in prison.

One day Herod had invited all the most important people of the kingdom to a feast. At a certain point during the feast, the daughter of Herodias, a young girl named Salome, entered the hall and began to dance. She danced so well that King Herod said to her: "Ask me what you wish and I will grant it to you!" Urged by her mother, Salome replied: "I want you to give me the head of John the Baptist."

Herod grew sad. He did not want to have John killed, but because he had made a promise before all the guests, he called a guard and ordered him to go and execute John the Baptist. In this way, the courageous prophet became a martyr.

8 The Rich Man and the Sinner Woman

Luke 7

A rich man called Simon invited Jesus to dine at his house. While they were eating, a woman entered who was well known for her many sins. She was carrying a jar of perfume. In silence she approached Jesus, she got down on her knees at his feet, and began to cry. Her tears fell on the feet of the Lord, and she dried them with her hair and sprinkled them with perfume.

When the owner of the house saw this, he thought to himself: "They say this Jesus is a prophet; but it can't be true, otherwise he would know this woman is a sinner and he would not let her touch him."

But Jesus, who had read his thoughts, said to him: "Simon, I have something to say to you." "Tell me, master," Simon replied. And Jesus continued: "A man lent five hundred coins to one person and fifty to another. As neither of them had the means to pay it back, he released them both from their debts. Which of the two do you think will love him the most?"

Simon replied: "I suppose the one who was pardoned the most." "You have answered correctly," said Jesus. Then, turning to the woman, he continued: "You see this woman? You did not welcome me into the house by washing my feet, as is done with guests. She, on the other hand, bathed my feet with her tears, and then dried them with her hair. You did not greet me with a kiss. She, on the other hand, has not stopped kissing my feet since I arrived. You did not pour perfume on my head, but she has sprinkled perfume on my feet."

Jesus concluded: "This woman has committed many sins, but they have all been pardoned, because by her behavior she has shown that she loves me very much." And turning to the woman, he said: "I forgive you your sins: go in peace."

9 The Brothers of Jesus

Mark 3

One day Jesus went into a house and a big crowd gathered outside. Then the mother of Jesus arrived with some relatives, but she was unable to enter the house because of the crowd around her son.

Someone told Jesus: "Your mother and your relatives have arrived. They are outside and they are looking for you." Then Jesus turned to the crowd and said: "I promise you that whoever listens to the Word of God and puts it into practice, is like my own family. And I will love them just as much."

10 The Son of the Widow

Luke 7

One day Jesus went to a village called Nain; he was accompanied by his disciples and a huge crowd followed him.

He had reached the first houses of the village, when he came across a funeral: on an open bier, as was the custom then, the body of a boy had been laid out, the only son of a woman who was a widow.

The poor woman, who was left all alone, followed the pallbearers and was accompanied by many of her fellow villagers. When he saw her, the Lord Jesus was moved to compassion, and said: "Do not cry!"

Then he went up to the bier, touched it, and bade the porters to stop. Then Jesus turned to the dead boy lying on the bier and said: "Boy, I am talking to you, arise!"

At these words the boy awoke, sat up, and began talking. Jesus took him by the hand and led him to his mother.

When all those present saw this incredible miracle they were amazed and began to praise God saying: "God has visited his people, sending a great prophet among us!"

They had still not realized that Jesus was not only a prophet: He was God himself.

11 Anger and Reconciliation

Matthew 5

One day Jesus gave the following lesson on how to treat people who offend us or do evil. Jesus said: "You all know the commandment that says "Thou shalt not kill." Whoever kills another man shall be brought to judgment. But I tell you now that whoever is angry with his neighbor shall also be judged.

"Therefore, if you bring an offering to the altar of the Lord and you remember that your brother has something against you, go first to make peace with him. Then return and pray and make your offering."

12 The Lost Sheep

Luke 15

One day Jesus said: "If a man has a hundred sheep and he loses one, he does not say: 'Ah, well, I still have ninety-nine.' Rather, he leaves the flock in a safe place and looks for the lost sheep. When he finds it, he lays it across his shoulders and returns home; he then calls his neighbors and friends and says: 'Rejoice, for I have found my lost sheep.''

"In the same way there is great rejoicing in the Kingdom of Heaven over every sinner who repents, changes his way of life, and comes to love God."

13 A Woman Touches the Garment of Jesus

Mark 5

There was a woman who had been suffering from a loss of blood for twelve years. She had tried everything in an attempt to get better. She had gone to see many doctors and had spent all her money, but she had only grown worse.

One day she heard people talking about Jesus and his many miracles. At this, she thought: "I must go to him. Even if I only touch his garment, I am sure I will be healed."

She set off to look for Jesus and found him, as often happened, surrounded by the crowd who pressed against him from every side. With great difficulty, the woman made her way through the crowd and eventually touched Jesus' garment. Her loss of blood stopped at once and she was cured.

At that very moment, Jesus turned around and asked: "Who touched me?" The disciples immediately answered: "The crowd is thronging around you; how can you ask who touched you?"

Jesus, however, knew that the touch had been special, and when the woman knelt fearfully in front of him, as if to beg his forgiveness, he said to her: "Daughter, your faith has saved you: Go in peace."

14 The Precious Pearl

Matthew 13, 5

One day, Jesus described the Kingdom of Heaven: "The Kingdom of Heaven is like a merchant who searches for precious pearls. On the day he finds one of great value he sells everything he owns."

On another occasion Jesus taught the following lesson: "You have been told not to swear false oaths, and to keep your word once you have sworn. But I say to you that you should never swear oaths. You should simply say yes when it is yes, and say no when it is no. Anything more comes from the devil."

15 The Law of God

Matthew 5

One day Jesus said: "I tell you truly that for as long as heaven and earth exist, the law of God shall also exist. Not one word, not even a jot of the law of God shall ever in any way be abolished!

"Therefore, whoever breaks the commandments of God's law, even the least of them, and teaches others to do likewise, shall be the least in the Kingdom of Heaven. On the other hand, he who obeys all the commandments of the law of God, and teaches them to others, will be great in the Kingdom of Heaven!"

16 A Herd of Swine in the Lake

Matthew 8

One day, Jesus arrived in the country of the Gadarenes, but before he could go into the city he encountered two men possessed by devils. The two unfortunate men were in great distress; the devils made them leap and jump like furious madmen; so much so that nobody could pass any longer by that road or the two men would attack them.

When the devils saw Jesus they spoke through the two men they had possessed and said: "What do you want of us, Son of God? Have you come to torment us?"

The devils knew that Jesus, in order to heal the two men, would throw them out of the bodies they had possessed. Nearby a large herd of swine grazed. The devils, therefore, said to Jesus: "If you cast us out of here, then at least allow us to go into the herd of swine."

"Go," Jesus said and the devils at once left the bodies of the two men and entered the bodies of the pigs. At this, the whole herd of swine threw itself into the lake and died.

The two men were healed and the men who tended the swine ran to the city, full of amazement, to tell the story of the devils and the pigs who had drowned in the lake.

17 To Do Good in Secret

Matthew 6

One day Jesus said: "Be careful that you do not do good deeds for the purpose of being seen and admired by others, or you will have no reward from God.

"Therefore, when you give something to the poor, do not let everybody know; if you do this to be praised by other people then you have already received your reward. Instead, when you help someone, do not even tell your friends what you have done. It must be a secret: and your Father, who sees even that which is hidden, will reward you."

18 A Great Banquet

Luke 14

One day, Jesus told the following parable: "A man invited many of his friends to his house for a great banquet. Everything had been prepared when the guests began to make excuses for not coming.

"'I have bought a piece of land and I must go and see it,' said one.

"'I have bought five pairs of oxen and I must go and try them out,' said another.

"'I have only just been married, so I cannot come,' said a third.

"At this, the man said to his servants: 'Go out into the streets and squares of the city and bring back the poor, the blind, and the lame.' Then, when his servants told him that there was still space, the man said: 'Go out along the roads and the ditches and find others. I want my house to be filled. And I assure you that no one I invited shall taste any part of my banquet.' "

In this parable Jesus was talking about paradise, which is a place of celebration like a great banquet. The man who prepared the banquet is God. He invites everyone and it is a grave choice to refuse his invitation. Nothing is worth more than entering into the house of God to celebrate forever.

19 Love Your Enemies

Matthew 5

One day Jesus taught the following marvelous lesson about how to treat our enemies, the people who offend us or do us harm.

Jesus said: "Do not take revenge on those who do you harm. If somebody slaps you, then turn your other cheek toward him. If somebody wants to take your coat from you, then give him your cloak as well.

"Love your enemies and pray for them. In this way you will be children of your Father who is in heaven. For it is he who makes the sun rise on the evil and the good."

20 Jesus Resurrects the Daughter of Jairus

Mark 5

One day, a man by the name of Jairus approached Jesus and threw himself at his feet, saying: "My daughter is on the verge of death. Come and touch her so that she will be healed and live!"

Jesus set off with him. On the way they met a servant of Jairus, who said: "Your daughter is already dead!"

Jairus was about to burst into tears, but Jesus said to him: "Do not be afraid. Continue to have faith!"

When they reached the house of Jairus, Jesus said to the mourners: "Why are you crying? The little girl is not dead, but merely asleep!"

When they heard him talking like this, those present were astonished. Jesus, however, sent them all outside with the father and the mother of the young girl. With his three disciples—Peter, James, and John—he went into the room where lay the body of the dead girl.

Jesus went up to her, took her hand, and said: *"Talitha cumi,"* which means "Daughter, I say to you, get up!"

As soon as Jesus had said these words, the young girl arose and started to walk. Jesus' miracle had brought her back to life.

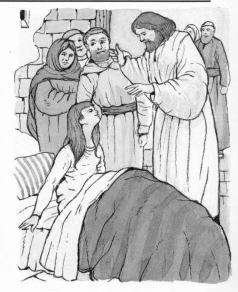

21 Like Sheep Among the Wolves

Matthew 10

Jesus moved from one village to another, announcing the good news, but he could not be everywhere. For this reason, he sent his disciples to some villages, after telling them: "Announce that the Kingdom of Heaven is at hand, but do not accept gold or silver or brass for this!"

Jesus went on to say: "I am sending you like sheep among the wolves: You must be as wise as serpents and as harmless as doves. But do not be afraid! Whoever receives you, receives me. And whoever receives me, receives our Father."

22 The Parable of the Merciless Servant

Matthew 18

One day, Peter asked Jesus: "Lord, you say that we must forgive those who offend us and do us harm. But how many times must I forgive the same person? Seven times?"

"Seventy times seven if necessary," replied Jesus. And to explain his words he told them this parable: "A king was doing his accounts with the servants who administered his kingdom. One servant arrived who owed the king the enormous sum of ten thousand gold coins. Since the servant did not have the money to pay the debt, the king gave orders, as was the custom at that time, that he and his family be sold as slaves so that the debt could be paid with the proceeds. The servant, however, threw himself at the feet of the king and said to him: 'Lord be patient with me and I will repay everything!'

"The king took pity on him. He had him released and even canceled his debt, making a gift of the money which should have been repaid.

"When that servant went out and met his fellow servants who owed him the small sum of one hundred coins, he threw himself upon him and shouted: 'Pay me what you owe me !'

"The poor servant fell at his feet and begged him: 'Be patient with me and I will repay you everything I owe!' But the first servant would not listen and had him arrested.

"Others went and told the king what had happened. The king called the servant to him and said: 'You are a wicked man. I canceled the enormous debt you owed me. You too should have had pity on your fellow and canceled his debt!" Then the king had his wicked and merciless servant thrown into prison."

After the parable Jesus added: "Your Father in heaven will deal with you in the same way if you do not forgive whoever does you harm and treat him as a brother."

23 Jesus Cures a Deaf and Dumb Man

Mark 7

Jesus found himself in a foreign land, in the region of the Phoenician city of Sidon, when a deaf and dumb man was brought to him, in the hope that Jesus would cure him.

Jesus took the poor man to one side, placed his fingers on his ears, touched his tongue, then looked toward the heavens, gave a sigh, and said: *"Ephphatha,"* or, "Open up."

At once the man was healed. Everyone present was amazed and said: "Everything he does is wonderful! He is amazing! He makes the deaf hear and the dumb speak!"

24 You Are Peter

Matthew 16

Jesus was traveling with his disciples in the region of Caesarea. As they were walking along, he asked them: "What do the people think of the Son of man? Who do they say he is?" Jesus often called himself Son of man, as the prophet Daniel had named the mysterious person who appeared to him in his vision. The disciples answered: "Some think you are the prophet Elijah, others think you are one of the ancient prophets, returned to life."

"And what about you? Who do you think I am?," Jesus asked them. Simon-Peter said: "You are the Christ, the Son of the living God!"

And Jesus said: "Blessed are you, Simon, because what you have said did not come to you by itself, but was revealed to you by my Father in heaven. And I say to you: You are Peter, which means rock, and on this rock I will build my church, and not even the devil will be able to destroy it. I shall give you the keys to the Kingdom of Heaven, and anything that you declare forbidden on earth, God shall also consider forbidden. And anything you permit, God will permit."

25 The Blind Man of Bethsaida

Mark 8

One day, Jesus, accompanied by his disciples, arrived in the city of Bethsaida. There, the people brought a blind man to be healed.

Jesus took him away from the others, and put some of his saliva on the blind man's eyes. Then Jesus placed his hands on his head and asked him: "Do you see anything?"

"I see men," he replied. "At least I think they are men, because to me they look like walking trees."

Jesus again touched his eyes with his hands and the blind man's sight was completely restored.

26 The Laborers in the Vineyard

Matthew 20

One day Jesus told the following parable: "The Kingdom of Heaven is like the owner of a vineyard who went out early in the morning to hire laborers whom he sent to work in his vineyard after agreeing on a wage of a penny a day.

"At mid-morning the owner hired other laborers, more again at midday, others in the afternoon, and, finally he hired even more laborers an hour before dark: And to all of them he promised a fair wage.

"At the end of the working day, the owner began to pay the laborers, starting with those who had arrived last. Those who had only worked the final hour came forward and received a penny each. And the same sum went to all the rest.

"Those who had worked the longest, particularly those who had been hired very early in the morning, began to complain: 'What? They have only worked for an hour and you pay them the same as us and we have worked the whole day in the heat!'

"The owner, however, replied: 'Friends, I am doing you no wrong. Did we not agree on the wage of one penny? Did I not pay you one penny? And if I choose to give the others the same wage as you, can I not do as I wish with money that belongs to me? Are you jealous because I am kind?'"

With this parable, Jesus meant to show that God is just, and gives to everyone the reward he has promised. He is also good, however, and he distributes his gifts as he sees fit.

The laborers hired earliest in the day are the Jews, who were the first to be called to enter the Kingdom of God. Then all the others came afterward; those called at the end of the day, for example, are the sinners who come to love God later in their lives, and the Lord calls them to him in paradise just the same.

27 Jesus Like Jonah

Matthew 12

One day a group of men said to Jesus: "Master, show us a miracle." They did not believe that Jesus was the Christ; they wanted a test.

Jesus was well aware of this and replied to them: "These sinners ask to see a miracle! They shall see the sign of Jonah. Just as Jonah remained three days in the belly of a fish, I shall remain for three days in the heart of the earth."

With these words, Jesus was speaking of the greatest proof he could give, that of rising from the dead on the third day.

28 The Faith that Moves Mountains

Matthew 17

One day a man approached Jesus and knelt before him, saying: "Lord, have mercy on my son! He is ill with epilepsy and suffers a great deal. When he has an attack, he often falls into the fire or into the water. I took him first to your disciples, but they could not heal him."

"Bring your son here to me," Jesus replied. When the boy came before him, Jesus spoke harshly to the devil that possessed the child and sent it away. The moment the devil left, the boy was healed.

Afterward the disciples approached Jesus, took him aside, and asked him: "Why were we not able to cast out the devil in the boy?"

And Jesus replied: "Because you have little faith. I tell you truthfully, if you had as much faith as a grain of mustard seed, you would be able to say to move this mountain. Nothing would be impossible for you!"

A short time later, Jesus again told his disciples about what was going to happen, saying: "Soon I shall be delivered into the hands of my enemies and they will kill me. But, on the third day, I shall rise up again."

This announcement made the disciples very sad.

29 The Transfiguration of Jesus

Matthew 17

One day, Jesus took his apostles Peter, James, and John with him to the top of a very high mountain. There, before their very eyes, Jesus was transfigured. His face shone like the sun and his clothing was as white as light. The prophet Elijah appeared to talk with Jesus, accompanied by Moses.

Peter then found the courage to speak and said: "Lord, it is beautiful to be here. If you wish, I will build three tabernacles: one for you, one for Moses and one for Elijah."

He was still speaking when a bright cloud overshadowed them and they heard a voice say: "This is my beloved son, whom I have sent. Listen to him well!"

When they heard the voice of God, the three disciples were filled with fear and fell facedown on the earth. But Jesus went to them, touched them, and said: "Get up and do not be afraid."

They raised their eyes and saw nothing out of the ordinary: only Jesus, looking as usual.

While they were coming down from the mountain, Jesus ordered them: "Tell no one what you have seen until I have risen from the dead."

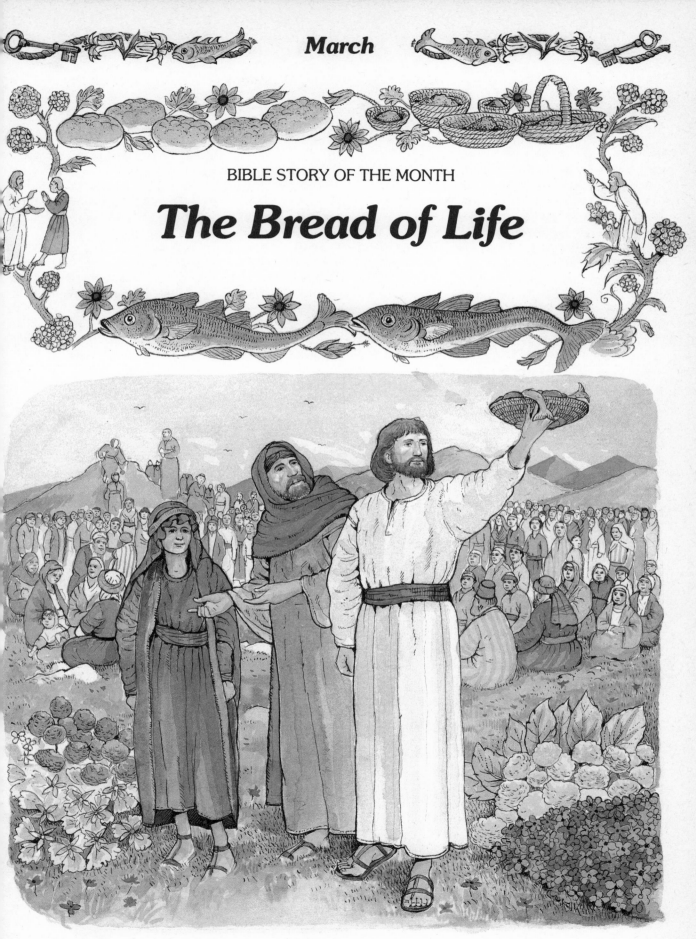

BIBLE STORY OF THE MONTH

The Bread of Life

As Jesus moved from one village to another, a crowd often followed him. Everyone loved to listen to his wonderful parables and his other teachings, and they also sought to watch him cure the sick and work other miracles.

At one time Jesus went with his disciples to an isolated place in the hills around the sea of Tiberias, and a huge crowd followed behind them. They were a long way from any village, and Jesus asked: "Where can we buy enough bread for everyone?"

He asked this question of Philip, but only to draw attention to what he was about to do. Philip replied: "Two hundred loaves would not be enough to give everybody a piece!"

Andrew, the brother of Peter, added: "There is a boy here who has brought five loaves of barley bread and two fish; but what can this do for all these people?"

Then Jesus said to the disciples: "Make them sit down." Everyone sat down on the grass, perhaps five thousand people.

When everyone was seated, Jesus took the bread from the boy, and raising his eyes to heaven he blessed it, then he broke it up and gave it to his disciples to distribute among the crowd. They all ate as much as they wanted, and did the same with the fish. Everyone present ate his fill.

When they saw the miracle that Jesus had done, multiplying five loaves and two fish into enough to feed five thousand, everyone was amazed. They said to each other: "He must really be the Messiah, the Christ of whom the prophets spoke!"

However, the time had not yet arrived for Jesus to reveal himself for what he truly was. And so he left the crowd and went up the hill alone.

When evening fell the disciples went down to the sea, got into their boats, and began making their way back to Capernaum. All of a sudden a strong wind arose, and the boat was rocked by the waves; it was dark, and the disciples began to grow frightened.

But out of the darkness they saw Jesus approaching, walking on the water. They were amazed and could not believe their eyes, until Jesus spoke. He said: "Be brave, I am here: Do not be afraid." He got into the boat and the disciples threw themselves at his feet, saying: "You are truly the Son of God!"

Then they returned to Capernaum. The next day the crowd, which had eaten the bread made by the miracle, came to look for him again, and when they found him some of them asked him: "Master, when did you come here?"

Jesus answered them: "You are all looking for me because I gave you the bread, and you are hoping that I will give you more to eat. But I tell you that you should not be looking for material food, but the food which is not consumed and gives you the strength to gain eternal life."

Then they asked him: "How can we get the food of which you speak?" "You have to believe that I was sent by God," Jesus replied.

But someone objected: "To our ancestors in the desert, God gave manna, bread which came from the sky, to eat." Jesus answered: "Manna was food to nourish the body. I am the true bread de-

scended from the sky: Whoever believes that I have come down from heaven, nourishes his soul. Your ancestors ate the manna, but they later died. Whoever has faith in me will never die!"

At these words they mumbled to each other, saying: "He is a man, he eats and sleeps like we do, we know that he comes from Nazareth . . . How can he say that he is descended from heaven?"

Jesus continued: "Do not mumble to each other. The bread that I give you to eat is myself, my body. Whoever eats my flesh and drinks my blood shall have eternal life. Whoever eats my flesh and drinks

my blood remains in me, and I in him. For this reason his life will never end, and he will live forever together with me."

The people present did not understand that Jesus was talking about faith: Whoever believes that he is the Son of God is united with him as if he were taking nourishment from him. And Jesus spoke of the Eucharist, where the communion in the faith signifies the eating of his flesh through the bread.

Jesus said all these important things while speaking in the synagogue in Capernaum. All those who heard his words were surprised. When they heard that they had to eat his flesh, many of them did not want to try and understand, and they went away.

Even some of the disciples, who until then had followed him with love, went away and no longer followed him when they heard this speech.

Then Jesus turned to his twelve most faithful disciples, the Apostles, and asked them: "Do you wish to leave as well?"

Peter answered in the name of all of them: "And to whom shall we turn, Lord? Only you speak of eternal life. We believe you, and we know that you are the Christ, the Son of the living God."

John 6

1 The Coin in the Fish's Mouth

Matthew 17

At the time of Jesus it was the law that every Israelite should pay a tax for the upkeep of the temple in Jerusalem. The temple was dedicated to God: Therefore, the Son of God, Jesus, should not have had to pay this tax. But the time had not yet come for him to reveal himself to everyone.

One day the man who had to collect the tax asked the disciples: "Does your master pay the tax for the temple?" Peter answered "Yes, he pays it."

When Jesus arrived he asked Peter: "According to you, Simon, who should pay the taxes to the kings of this world, strangers or their own sons?" "Strangers," Peter replied.

And Jesus said: "Of course the sons are not obliged to pay the taxes. But just the same I will pay this tribute to the temple of my Father. Go down to the sea, cast your hook and take the first fish that bites. Open up its mouth and you will find a coin. Take it and use it to pay the tax for us both."

Peter faithfully did what Jesus had bid: He went and cast his hook, and the first fish that he caught had a silver coin in its mouth. Peter took it to the tax collectors.

2 The Parable of the Steward

Matthew 24

One day Jesus told this parable: "A man had to go away on a journey and leave his house, so he entrusted his steward to look after it and watch over the other servants. Then one day he returned, and he thought to himself: 'I am certain that my steward has been faithful to my orders. As a reward I will entrust him with the running of all my affairs.'

"Instead, when he entered the house, the master found the steward busy eating and drinking with the drunkards and layabouts, because he had thought: 'My master will return late, and in the meantime I can do what I want.' So the lord of the house sacked the steward and forbade him ever to set foot inside his house again."

The meaning of this parable is clear. The owner of the house is the Lord. The steward is every man, to whom the Lord entrusts something to administer: his capabilities, his wealth, the authority he wields over others, and so on.

The master calls us to account when we pass from this life to the next. This often happens very unexpectedly. With this parable Jesus was telling everyone always to be ready to answer to God.

3 The Good Samaritan

Mark 12; Luke 10

One day a man asked Jesus: "Master, what must I do to enter into eternal life?"

Jesus replied: "Observe what is written in the law of Moses. The first commandment is: 'Love the Lord your God with all your heart, with all your soul, with all your mind and your strength.' The second is: 'Love thy neighbor like thyself.'"

But the man asked: "And who is my neighbor?" To make him understand Jesus told this parable.

"A man was traveling from Jerusalem to Jericho, when he was attacked by brigands who robbed him of everything and beat him, leaving him for dead. Then a priest came along; he saw the man but carried right on without stopping. Then a Levite from the temple did the same thing. Then a Samaritan came by and pitied the poor man. He treated his wounds, then lifted him onto his mule and took him to an inn to be looked after. The next day he had to continue his journey, and so he gave the innkeeper some money, saying: 'Take care of him, and if you spend more than I have given you, then I shall repay you when I return.'"

Jesus added: "According to you, which of the three behaved as a neighbor toward the man who had met with the brigands?"

"The one who took pity on him," replied the man who had asked Jesus the question.

And Jesus concluded: "Go, and conduct yourself in the same way."

With the parable of the Good Samaritan, Jesus wanted to teach us that we must always be ready to help anybody who has need of us, regardless of whether he is a stranger, or even an enemy. Because this is what Jesus did, when out of love for mankind he gave his own life.

4 Jesus and the Little Children

Matthew 19

One day a group of mothers with their children made their way through the crowd around Jesus. They wanted the Master to bless their children. But the disciples lost patience. Jesus was speaking and was not to be disturbed!

Jesus, on the other hand, turned and said: "Let the children come to me, because the Kingdom of Heaven belongs to the children and to those who are like them."

Then Jesus took the children to him, embraced them, and blessed them.

5 The Parable of the Two Sons

Matthew 21

One day Jesus said: "A man had two sons. He called the older and said: 'My son, go and work in the vineyard.' The son replied: 'I will go,' but did not. The father then called the younger and sent him. This one answered: 'I will not go,' but then went."

Then Jesus asked: "Which of the two sons carried out his father's wishes?" The people listening answered: "The second." And this was right. It is not enough to say that you love your Father, the Lord. Actions speak louder than words.

6 Jesus Meets a Rich Young Man

Matthew 19

A young man came up to Jesus and asked him: "Master, what must I do to gain eternal life?" "Obey the commandments," Jesus answered him. The young man insisted: "What commandments?" And Jesus replied: "Do not kill, do not steal, do not tell lies, honor your father and your mother . . . ."

"This I have always done," interrupted the young man. "What do I still lack?" So Jesus said to him: "If you want to be perfect, sell everything you own and give the proceeds to the poor. You will be assured a treasure in heaven. Then follow me."

But, after hearing these words, the young man went away with a sad face, because he had a great many riches and he was incapable of giving them up.

Then Jesus said to the disciples: "It is difficult for a rich man to enter into the Kingdom of Heaven! It is easier for a camel to pass through the eye of a needle than for a rich man to enter the Kingdom of God!"

The disciples were surprised at these words and they said: "So who will be saved?" And Jesus answered: "For men it is impossible, but for God everything is possible!"

7 Our Father who Art in Heaven

Matthew 6; Luke 11

One day a disciple said to Jesus: "Lord, teach us how to pray to the Father as well." And Jesus replied:
"When you pray, say:
Our father who art in heaven
Hallowed be thy name:
Thy kingdom come;
Thy will be done,
On earth as it is in heaven.
Give us this day our daily bread,
And forgive us our sins
As we forgive those who sin against us,
And lead us not into temptation,
But deliver us from evil.

8 The Parable of the Talents

Matthew 25

Jesus told the following parable: "A rich man who had to go away on a long journey, entrusted his servants with his wealth. To the first he gave five talents, to the second, two, and to the third, one.

"While the master was away, the servant who had received five talents went to invest them, and in the end he earned five more. The same thing was done by the one who had received two; in the end he made two more. The third servant, on the other hand, went and dug a hole in the ground, and in it he hid the talent he had received.

"When the master returned, he called the three servants to account. The first one gave him back ten talents, and the master said to him: 'Well done! You have been good and faithful. Feast with me.' The master said the same thing to the second servant who gave him back four talents.

"Then came the third servant with the talent he had gone to dig up, and he returned it. But to him the master said: 'You have been a bad and lazy administrator. You are not worthy to remain in my house!'"

This means that what we have was given by the Lord, but we must make it grow with good deeds.

9 The Reward for Whoever Follows Jesus

Matthew 19

"If you want to be perfect, go and sell everything that you own and give the proceeds to the poor, then come and follow me," Jesus had said to the rich young man.

Then Peter turned to Jesus and said: "Look, we disciples have abandoned everything to follow you. What reward will we have?"

It was true; to be with Jesus and follow him about from one city to another, the apostles had left their homes, their work, and their loved ones. Often, together with the Master, they had nowhere to sleep.

Jesus knew this. When a man had asked him where he lived, he had replied: "Foxes have their dens and birds have their nests. I do not even have a stone on which to rest."

But it was not always to be like this! That day Jesus revealed to Peter: "When I shall be seated on my glorious throne, you twelve will be seated on twelve thrones beside me, to reign forever along with me."

He then added: "Whoever leaves his home, his work or his family out of love for me will receive a hundredfold more and will inherit eternal life. Many who are now the first will become the last, and many who for now are last shall be the first."

10 God Listens to our Prayers

Matthew 7

One day Jesus taught prayer with faith: God is a good Father.

Jesus said: "Ask and your wish will be granted. Seek and you shall find. Knock and the door will be opened. Who out of all of you would give a rock to his son when he had been asked for a piece of bread? Who would give him a serpent if he asked for a fish? Everybody, even bad people, give good things to their own sons. All the more reason for your Father to give good things to all those who ask him for them!"

11 The First Seats at the Table

Luke 14

One day Jesus, along with a lot of other people, was invited to dinner by a doctor of the law. He noticed that some of them sought to go and sit at the best places, as close as possible to the master of the house, to show the other guests that they were more important than the others.

Then Jesus recounted the following parable, to remind all those present of the need to be humble. In fact humility is very important in gaining a place in the Kingdom of Heaven.

Jesus said: "When you are invited to dinner by someone, do not go and sit at the best places. If a more important guest than you arrives, the master of the house will come to you and say: 'Give up your seat,' and filled with shame before everyone else, you will have to take the last place.

"Instead, when you are invited to dinner, go and sit at the last seat. It is possible that the master of the house will come to say to you: 'Come, friend! Take a better seat!' And this will be a great honor for you before all the other guests."

Jesus then concluded: "In fact, remember: Whoever exalts himself will be humbled. And the humble will be exalted."

12 Invite the Poor

Luke 14

Jesus had been invited to dinner, and all around him were seated rich guests. Jesus said to the master of the house: "When you offer a lunch or a dinner, do not invite your friends, or your relatives or your rich neighbors, in the hope that they will later repay you.

"On the contrary, when you give a banquet, invite the poor, the lame, the blind, and the crippled. They do not have the means to repay your invitation. But you must take heart from this, because you will be repaid by God with eternal life."

March

13 Two Men in the Temple

Luke 18

Two men went into the temple to pray. The first man, standing up, said: "Oh God, I thank you because I am not a sinner like that other fellow. I fast, and I obey even the smallest rules of your law." But the second man had stopped a distance away. He didn't dare to raise his eyes up to heaven, but beat his breast saying: "Oh God, have pity on me, a sinner."

God pardoned the second only because whoever exalts himself will be humbled, and whoever humbles himself will be exalted.

14 The Parable of the Prodigal Son

Luke 15

Jesus told the following parable: "A man had two sons. The youngest asked, 'Give me the part of your riches that is mine.' His father gave it to him and the son set off for a distant land where he squandered all his money on evil.

"He was now reduced to poverty and was forced to become a keeper of pigs, but still he went hungry. Then he thought: Many of the servants in my father's home eat their fill! I will go back to my father and say, I have sinned against God; I am not worthy to be your son. Treat me as one of your servants.' And then he set off toward home.

"He was still a long way away when his father saw him coming and he took pity on him. He ran out to meet him, he hugged him and he kissed him. The son began the speech he had prepared, but the father didn't even let him finish. He called his servants and said to them: 'Hurry, bring him the finest clothes and dress him. Prepare a great banquet, and we will celebrate!'

"The elder son was out working in the fields. On his way home he heard the sounds of the feast from afar; he called a servant and asked him what was happening. When he found out he grew angry and he did not want to enter the house.

"Therefore his father came out to get him to come and join the joyous celebration. But the elder son said to him: 'I have worked every day for many years and no feast has ever been given in my honor. And now this brainless son of yours, who has wasted everything, comes home and you prepare a banquet for him!'

"The father replied: 'Son, you are always with me and everything that is mine is yours. But we have to feast and celebrate, because your brother was like a dead man, and now he has come back to life. He was lost and now is found!'"

15 The House Built on Rock

Matthew 7

One day Jesus said: "Whoever listens to what I say and puts it into practice is similar to a wise man who has built his house on a foundation of rock. When the rains fall, the rivers overflow and the wind blows against this house, it will still not fall, because its foundations are solid.

"Whoever, on the other hand, listens to what I say and does not put it into practice, is similar to a stupid man who has built his house on a foundation of sand: rain, rivers, and wind will hurl themselves against that house, and it will fall down."

16 Jesus Cures Ten Lepers

Luke 17

Jesus was making his way to Jerusalem when, before entering a village, he was met by ten lepers.

Leprosy was a terrible and contagious disease. Lepers could not live among other people and had to remain outside the villages, keeping well away from those not suffering from the illness.

For this reason the ten lepers kept their distance, and they addressed Jesus, shouting from afar: "Jesus, Master, have pity on us!"

Jesus replied: "Go and present yourselves to the priests." In fact the law stated that lepers who were healed had to present themselves to the priests, who would verify that they were cured. By replying in this way to the lepers, Jesus led them to believe that he would heal them. And in fact this is what happened: While they were on their way, they were all healed.

Then one of them, a foreigner from Samaria, went back to thank Jesus. Jesus then observed: "Weren't all ten cured? Well, where are the other nine? Only this foreigner has returned to give glory to God!" Then Jesus said to the Samaritan: "Get up and go! Your faith has saved you."

17 The Offering of the Widow

Luke 21

One day Jesus was in the temple of Jerusalem with his disciples, and he was teaching not far from where the coins left in offering were kept.

Raising his eyes, Jesus saw a group of rich men who were leaving abundant offerings. Then there came a poor widow who left two copper coins.

And Jesus said: "In the eyes of God, that poor widow has left more than anyone. In fact, the others only left a bit of what they don't need. She, on the other hand, gave everything she had to live with."

18 Jesus at the Feast of the Tabernacles

John 7

It was about the time of the feast of the Tabernacles, celebrated in memory of the forty years spent by the people of God in the desert. Jesus went to visit Jerusalem. In the city everyone was talking about him. Some admired his teachings. Some were amazed by his miracles. Others wondered: "How does he know the Holy Scriptures, without studying them?" Jesus answered: "I teach things that are not mine, but God's." Some people even spread the word that he was tricking everybody. In order to put a stop to all these rumors, the leaders of the people had Jesus arrested. But the guards returned empty-handed. The leaders asked them: "Why didn't you arrest him?" And the guards replied: "No man has ever spoken like he does!"

On the last day of the feast, before the crowd, Jesus stood up in the temple and said: "Whoever is thirsty, come to me and drink!"

With these words Jesus announced a promise: Whoever believed in him would receive the gift of the Holy Spirit. He satisfies every thirst for what is most important to every man: to be a friend of God.

19 The Parable of Lazarus and the Wicked Rich Man

Luke 16

Jesus said to his disciples: "There was a rich man who wore fine clothes and held splendid banquets. Outside his door sat a beggar, by the name of Lazarus, who was covered with sores and hungry.

"One day Lazarus died, and he was taken up to heaven, beside Abraham. The rich man also died, and he went to hell. When he raised his eyes and saw Lazarus beside Abraham, the rich man cried out: 'Father, have pity on me! Send Lazarus to stick his finger in the water and wet my tongue. This fire is tormenting me!'

"Abraham replied: 'My son, during your life on earth you received a lot of good things, while Lazarus suffered greatly. Between us there is an uncrossable abyss!' Then the rich man said: 'At least send him to my house, to tell my five brothers to change their way of life before they too end up in hell.' But Abraham replied: 'Let them obey!'

"The rich man insisted: 'But if someone from the dead goes to them, then they will surely change their lives.' Abraham replied: 'If they do not listen to the word of God, then they will not be convinced, even by Lazarus!'"

March

20 Jesus is a Good Shepherd

John 10

Jesus tried in various ways to explain to those who listened to him who he was and why he had come down to earth. He took examples from things the people knew well.

One day Jesus spoke of sheep and shepherds, and the difference between the shepherd who owns his sheep and the shepherd who looks after other people's sheep.

Jesus said: "I am the good shepherd. A good shepherd would give his life for his sheep. The paid guardian, on the other hand, abandons the sheep and flees when he sees the wolf coming, because the sheep are not his. Then the wolf goes among them, scatters them, and creates havoc."

"These wild beasts are like thieves," Jesus continued. "They only come to steal, kill, and destroy. But I have come to make sure that my sheep are safe and enjoy an abundant life."

"I am the good shepherd" Jesus said. The people who listened to his parable remembered the psalm: "The Lord is my Shepherd." Therefore Jesus was the Lord God! This was why his sheep, his friends, would enjoy an abundant, everlasting life.

21 The Hunchbacked Woman in the Synagogue

Luke 13

One Sabbath Jesus was teaching in the synagogue, when he saw a poor, hunchbacked woman. She had been this way for eighteen years and could not straighten up. Jesus called to the woman, touched her, and said: "Woman, you are free from your infirmity." At once she stood up straight, and she praised God.

The leader of the synagogue, however, instead of congratulating the woman, grew angry: He considered what Jesus had done as work, and all work was forbidden on the Sabbath. For this reason he turned to those present and said: "There are six days for working; come and be cured on one of those days, and not on the Sabbath!"

Then Jesus said: "You untie your oxen or your donkey and lead them down to drink even on the Sabbath, do you not? And this poor woman who has been chained to her illness for eighteen years, should she not be freed from her chains on the Sabbath?"

When they heard this, the enemies of Jesus were ashamed. The crowd, on the other hand, was delighted at the wonders that Jesus continually worked, and the teachings that accompanied them.

22 The Parable of the Lost Coin

Luke 15

Jesus told the following parable: "A woman owned ten coins. She had counted them lots of times. One day she counted them again, and found only nine. So she lit the lights and looked in every corner, took her broom and swept everywhere, and found the missing coin. She then called her friends and neighbors and said: 'Come and share my joy, for I have found my lost coin!' In the same way, there is great joy in heaven for every sinner who changes his way of life."

23 If a Donkey Should Fall on the Sabbath

Luke 14

A rich man had invited Jesus to dinner, along with a group of masters of the law who were experts in saying what was and was not permitted according to the law handed down by Moses. It was the Sabbath.

Among those present, Jesus saw a man who looked ill. So he turned to the masters of the law and asked them: "According to you, does the law allow the curing of the sick on the Sabbath?"

But the masters remained silent: They were afraid that if they said it was forbidden, they would appear heartless. Then, by example, Jesus invoked the law of Moses. He took the sick man by the hand, healed him, and sent him home.

He then explained: "Who among you, if one of your oxen or donkeys falls down a well, even on the Sabbath, wouldn't rush to pull it out?"

The masters of the law remained silent. They had understood very well: Helping a man or a woman in need is more important than any other duty.

Christians observe the day of rest ordered by God on a Sunday instead of a Saturday. But this commandment does not stop people from doing good deeds on this day.

24 The Light of the World

John 8, 10

One day Jesus said: "I am the light of the world and of life. Whoever follows me will not walk in the dark." Jesus was talking about the life without end that he grants to his believers.

Another day, the leaders of the people said to him: "If you are the Christ, then say so openly." And Jesus replied: "I have told you, and you do not believe me! But it is confirmed by the works that I do. The Father and I are a single being. He sent me to earth to give eternal life to whoever believes in me."

25 The Tree and the Fruit

Matthew 12

One day Jesus said: "Whoever is not with me is against me. And whoever does not gather in the harvest with me, throws away the crops.

"If you take a good tree, then its fruits will also be good. If you take a bad tree, then its fruits will be bad as well. Because a tree can be judged by its fruits. But people can say good things, because what comes out of the mouth does not necessarily come from the heart. Anybody who says wicked things is like a tree bearing bad fruits, and one day he will be brought to account by God."

26 Whoever is Without Sin

John 8

Jesus was in the temple when the masters of the law brought in a woman accused of having committed the sin of adultery. "Master," they said, "for this sin the law states the guilty must be stoned to death. What do you say?"

In reality these men were hoping to lay a trap for Jesus so that they could accuse him. In fact, if Jesus said that they should pardon the woman, they could accuse him of violating the law of Moses; and if he said that she should be condemned, they would say that he was cruel.

Jesus did not reply to his enemies' question. However, they persisted, and raising his head, Jesus said: "Whoever of you is without sin, let him throw the first stone against her."

When they heard these words, those present began to drift away one by one. Jesus was left alone with the woman, and he asked her: "Where are those who accused you? Did no one condemn you?"

"No one," the woman replied.

And Jesus concluded: "Neither do I condemn you. Go and sin no more." In this way Jesus wanted to show that only God can judge the hearts of men.

27 The Parable of the Rich Fool

Luke 12

One day Jesus told this parable: "A rich man had some land that yielded excellent harvests. The man thought: 'My stores are already full. Where will I put the new harvest? I must knock them down and build bigger ones, so that it will all fit. Then, without working, I will enjoy myself for many years.'

"But God said to him: 'Fool! This very night you will die. And then what will become of your riches?'

"And this is what happens to people who do not try to grow rich in the eyes of God!"

28 The Salvation of Zacchaeus

Luke 19

At the time of Jesus, the tax collectors were known as publicans. These officials worked on behalf of the emperor of Rome, who also ruled over Palestine. The Hebrews considered them traitors.

One day Jesus was walking in Jericho, surrounded by a vast crowd. The leader of the city's publicans, a man called Zacchaeus, was very curious to see this famous Jesus. When he heard that Jesus was in the city, he climbed up a tree, because, as he was small, this was the only way for him to see. When Jesus reached the tree, he raised his eyes and said: "Zacchaeus, quick, come down, because today I will stay at your house." The crowd was amazed that the Master would speak to a publican, and was even going to stay at his house.

However, Zacchaeus was beside himself with joy, and when Jesus entered his house, he said: "Look, Lord. I will give half of my belongings to the poor, and if I have stolen from someone, then I will repay him fourfold!"

Jesus then pointed out: "Today salvation has entered this house. The Son of man came to seek out and save those who were lost."

29 Jesus Heals a Man Blind from Birth

John 9

As Jesus was passing with his disciples, he met a beggar who had been blind from birth. Jesus took pity on him: He spat on the ground and made a little lump of clay which he rubbed on the blind man's eyes, saying: "Go and wash in the pool of Siloam." The man did as Jesus bid, and he could see.

All this took place on the Sabbath day and it caused heated discussion among the leaders of the people. They insisted that the man who was born blind should repeat several times how he had regained his sight.

Some of them said: "This man does not come from God, because he does not respect the Sabbath day and rest as God ordered." Others, however, replied: "But how could a sinner perform such miracles?"

Later, Jesus met the man who had been healed and asked him: "Do you believe in the Son of man?" Jesus called himself by this name, just as the prophet Daniel had foretold, to show that he was both man and God. The man who had been blind replied: "Tell me who he is, for I believe in him." And Jesus said to him: "You are looking at him." The man knelt down and said: "Lord, I believe!"

30 The Chiefs in the Kingdom of Heaven
Mark 10

One day, the brothers James and John went to Jesus and asked him: "Master, when you have established your kingdom, allow us to be second only to you in importance."

Jesus said to them: "You do not know what you are asking." And once again he explained to them that before rising up in glory, he would be captured by his enemies, made to suffer and slain. Jesus tried to make his disciples understand that, like him, they had to be ready to give their lives.

The disciples, however, did not understand this. On the contrary, when the others heard what James and John had asked, they grew angry with them, believing themselves to be no less deserving. They all wanted to be important, to be chiefs in the Kingdom of God.

Jesus then explained to them: "In my kingdom things will not be as they are in this world. Here, kings and other rulers command with force, and impose their will on their subjects. In the Kingdom of God, however, everything is different: Whoever wishes to be important shall serve the others; whoever wishes to be first, shall be the servant of all."

31 The Parable of the Wise and Foolish Virgins
Matthew 25

To explain what the Kingdom of God would be like, Jesus one day told this parable: "The Kingdom of Heaven is like ten virgins who were called to be maids of honor to a bridegroom. They took their oil lamps and went out to meet the groom. Five were foolish and forgot to take a spare container of oil. The other five were wise and took spare containers.

"The groom was late in arriving, and the virgins all eventually fell asleep. At midnight they were awakened by a shout: 'The bridegroom is coming! Go out and meet him!'

"The ten virgins awoke and found that all their lamps had gone out. The wise five relit their lamps with their spare oil, while the others were at a loss and had to go buy more oil.

"Meanwhile, however, the groom arrived and the five virgins who were waiting with their lamps lit went with him to the wedding feast. When the other five came back, they knocked on the door, shouting: 'Lord, Lord let us in!' But the groom replied: 'Truly, I do not know you!'

"Therefore," Jesus said, "Always be ready because you do not know when the Lord will come."

BIBLE STORY OF THE MONTH

Story of Lazarus

When he was in Jerusalem, Jesus often went to the nearby village of Bethany, to stay with three friends of his: Lazarus and his sisters, Martha and Mary.

They all dearly loved Jesus, and they welcomed him with great joy, each extending his best effort to please him.

Jesus said to Mary: It is good to take care of material things, but it should not be forgotten that listening to the voice of the Lord, and joining him in prayer, is of much greater importance.

It then happened that Lazarus grew sick with a very serious illness. Martha and Mary thought they should inform Jesus, who was a long way away, and they sent messengers to inform him: "Lord, your friend is ill."

When he heard this, Jesus said to his disciples: "This illness will serve to show the glory of God and the glory of the Son of God." Jesus remained for another two days in the place where he was, but he sorrowed greatly. Then he said: "Let us go to Jerusalem. Our friend Lazarus has gone to sleep, but I am going to wake him up."

"If he has gone to sleep, that means he is beginning to get better and soon he will be well," said the disciples. But they had not understood the words of Jesus; so he spoke to them more openly: "Lazarus is dead," he said, "and I am glad that none of you was there, because in this way you will believe. Let us go to him!"

When he reached Bethany, Jesus found that Lazarus had already been buried four days earlier. Since Bethany was only three kilometers from Jerusalem, lots of friends and relatives had come to console Martha and Mary over the death of their brother.

When Martha heard that Jesus was coming, she went out to meet him, while Mary stayed in the house crying. Martha said to Jesus: "Lord, if you had been here, my brother would not have died! But I also know that whatever you ask of God, God will grant you."

Jesus answered her: "Your brother will rise up."

"I know that he will rise up," exclaimed Martha, "like everyone else, at the end of the world."

Jesus then pointed out a very important thing to her. He said: "I am the resurrection and the life. Whoever believes in me, even if he dies, shall have eternal life: whoever lives and believes in me, will not die for all eternity." And he added: "Do

you believe this?''

Martha replied: ''Yes, Lord. I believe that you are the Christ, the Son of God, who has come to earth.'' Then she hurried back into the house and said to her sister: ''The Master is here, and he is calling for you.''

Then Mary arose and went out. Those who were in the house with her got up and followed her, thinking: ''Now she is going to cry at the tomb.''

When Mary reached Jesus, she fell at his feet, saying: ''Lord, if you had been here my brother would not be dead!'' When he saw Mary, and all the others who were with

her, crying, Jesus was deeply moved and he asked: ''Where have they laid him to rest?'' ''Come and see,'' they answered him. At that point Jesus burst into tears. Those present then said: ''Look how much he loved his friend.'' But others objected: ''He who gave sight to a man blind from birth, could he do nothing to stop Lazarus from dying?''

Still deeply moved, Jesus came to the tomb, which was a cave with a huge rock blocking the entrance. ''Take away the rock,'' Jesus ordered. But Mary objected: ''Lord, there is already a bad smell, for it has been four days since he was buried!'' ''As I have said to you, if

you have faith you will see the glory of God,'' replied Jesus.

Then they took away the rock. Jesus raised his eyes to the heavens and said in a loud voice: ''Father, I thank you for having listened to me.'' Then he shouted out: ''Lazarus come out!''

And Lazarus came out of the tomb alive. When they saw this, many of the people who had arrived from Jerusalem to console Martha and Mary came to believe in Jesus, and when they returned to the city they told everyone what they had seen.

Then the chiefs of the people met to decide what to do about Jesus. They said: ''He works a lot of miracles. Many people believe in him and no longer obey our commands.'' On that very day, however, they decided to have him put to death.

Six days before the Passover, Jesus went back to Bethany to see his friends. They made a meal for him. Martha served, Lazarus sat with him, and Mary demonstrated all her love for Jesus by pouring a jar of rare perfume over his head. ''What a waste,'' someone said, but Jesus defended her: ''No,'' he said. ''She did it because she loves me. I assure you that the whole world will talk about what she has done.''

Luke 10; John 11—12

1 Jesus Enters Jerusalem in Triumph

Matthew 21; Luke 19

Jesus was journeying toward Jerusalem. When he was near the village of Bethphage, between Bethany and the Mount of Olives, he called two disciples and said to them: "Go to the village before you. As soon as you enter you will find that a donkey and its colt, that no one has ever ridden, have been tied up. Untie them and bring them here. And if someone should ask you why you untie them, answer that the Lord needs them."

The two disciples went and found everything as Jesus had said. They brought the donkey to him, covered it with their cloaks, and bade the Master ride it into the city. Then someone remembered that the prophet Zechariah, speaking of the Messiah who was to come, had announced: "Behold, your king will come to you, humble and riding on a donkey."

Along the way into the city, a huge crowd gathered around him. Some of them laid their cloaks on the ground where he was passing, others waved palm and olive branches, while they all exclaimed: "Blessed is he who comes in the name of the Lord! Glory to God in the heavens."

2 A Trap for Jesus

Luke 20

The enemies of Jesus laid traps for him, to have something to accuse him of. One day they presented him with a coin and asked: "Is it right to pay taxes to the emperor?"

This was a difficult question. Whatever the reply they would have a reason for accusing Jesus. In fact, if he said it was right, they would have accused him of being a traitor to his people, a friend of the emperor in Rome and his hated soldiers who commanded in Palestine.

If, on the other hand, he had said that it was not right to pay the taxes to the emperor, they would have gone to the governor, who ruled for the emperor of Rome, and accused him of treason, to have him arrested and condemned.

Jesus knew the tricks of his accusers. Therefore he said: "Show me a coin. Whose image is shown on it? And whose name is written around it?" "The emperor's," they said. And Jesus concluded: "Then give back to the emperor that which belongs to the emperor, and to God that which belongs to God." Amazed at this reply, the enemies of Jesus remained silent, and this time, too, they were forced to go away without being able to accuse him.

3 Jesus Promises That he Will Return

Matthew 25

After his triumphant entrance into Jerusalem, Jesus was to be found in the temple every day, teaching his disciples and anyone else who wanted to listen to him, while the chiefs of the people looked for a way to have him put to death.

Jesus promised that he would return, and he announced that he, Jesus, would judge the world on the instructions of God the Father. "I will call before me all men, and I will divide them into two groups, just as the shepherd separates the sheep from the goats," said Jesus.

4 Jesus Announces the Day of Judgment

Matthew 25

On the Day of Judgment Jesus will return to judge all men. He will gather them before him and separate them into two groups.

Jesus said: "To the first group, that of the just, I will say: 'Come and enjoy the reward prepared for you, because I was hungry and you fed me, I was thirsty and you gave me drink, I was homeless and you gave me shelter, I was naked and you gave me clothes, I was ill and you came to look after me. . . .'

"And they will answer me: 'But when did we shelter you? When, O Lord, did we give you all this?'

"And I shall explain: 'Every time you helped someone in difficulty, I considered it a gift for me.'

"To the wicked people, on the other hand, I will say: 'Get away from me forever, because I was hungry and you did not feed me, I was thirsty and you did not give me drink, I was a stranger and you did not give me shelter. . . .'

"They will answer me: 'But when, Lord, did we see you in need like this and not come to your aid?'

"And I shall explain: 'Every time that you refused to help someone who was in need, it was as if you were refusing to help me.'"

5 The Parable of the Fig Tree

Matthew 24

When Jesus spoke of his return, he said that on that day this world would end and a new world would begin. But when will that day be?

"Nobody knows," said Jesus, "except for God." This is why it is always necessary to be ready to be brought to account for our actions.

"Learn this parable from the fig tree and the other plants," Jesus said. "When its branches become tender and the first leaves appear, summer is at hand. This is what you must do: be ready and prepared for the Kingdom of God."

6 The Death of Jesus Is Decided Upon

John 11

The chiefs of the people of Israel held a meeting to decide on the matter of Jesus finally. They said: "He works numerous miracles and the people follow him. If we do not do something soon they will proclaim him king. But the emperor does not allow us to have our own king; he will send his soldiers to destroy the temple and maybe even kill us all."

For this reason, they decided to have Jesus put to death, and they made an agreement with one of the apostles, Judas Iscariot. In exchange for thirty coins, he promised to lead them to where they could capture Jesus.

Jesus knew that they wanted to capture him and put him to death. He knew it; and it was for this reason that he, the Son of God, had made himself into a man! However he wanted his death to take place when he decided the time was right, after the Passover feast. With this April feast, the Jews celebrated the alliance God made with his chosen people, through Moses. Through Jesus, dead and risen again, God was going to declare a new alliance, not only with the Jews but with all men.

7 Jesus' Last Supper

Mark 14; John 6, 13

Before allowing himself to be captured, Jesus wanted to join the apostles for the Passover meal. This was a meeting full of strange events.

In those days, before sitting down at the table, the lord of the house would order the servants to wash the guests' feet. But that evening Jesus himself filled a basin with water and washed the feet of the apostles. Then he explained the meaning of what he had done. "You all call me Lord and Master. Therefore, if I, your Lord and Master, have made this gesture out of love for you, then you must all act lovingly."

Then he made an announcement to the apostles: "One of you will betray me."

They were all stunned and could hardly believe their ears. But it was true: Judas Iscariot, for thirty coins, had promised to help the chiefs of the people capture Jesus. When he realized that he had been found out, Judas crept out into the night.

The meal continued according to the rules of the Passover supper, with the roast lamb, unleavened bread, and bitter herbs. But, at a certain point, Jesus suddenly took the bread, broke it, and gave it to the apostles, saying: "Take it and eat it. This is my body which I give to you in sacrifice."

In the same way he took the chalice of wine and passed it around saying: "Take this and drink it. This wine is my blood, which flows for you and for all men. It is the blood with which God establishes a new alliance with mankind, and forgives their sins."

This command is respected every time we follow Jesus' commands. In this way Jesus brought about the promise he had made in the synagogue in Capernaum: "Whoever eats my flesh and drinks my blood shall have eternal life."

8 The Olive Grove

Mark 14

When Jesus and the eleven remaining apostles had finished the Passover meal, they left the house where they were gathered and went up to the Mount of the Olives. At its foot was an olive grove called Gethsemane that belonged to friends of Jesus, who often allowed him to spend the night there.

On this night as well, Jesus went there. When they arrived he told the apostles to sit down while he went off to pray, accompanied by Peter, James, and John.

Jesus was the Son of God, and therefore he knew how much suffering he was about to undergo. But he was also a man, and like all men he was afraid of suffering. For this reason he sought strength, asking for it in prayer to God his Father.

Jesus said: "Father, if it is possible, take this pain away from me. But your will must be done."

So great was Jesus' suffering that he sweated blood.

After he had finished praying, Jesus went back to the three apostles, and found that they had fallen asleep. He woke them up and said: "Could you not even stay awake for one hour with me? He who will betray me is close at hand."

9 Jesus is Arrested

Matthew 26

Judas Iscariot, the traitor, knew that Jesus was going to spend the night in the olive grove of Gethsemane. He was approaching at the head of a group of guards, armed with swords and clubs. He had arranged a sign with the guards, so that in the dark they would not confuse Jesus with the other apostles, and would be sure of arresting the right man.

He had said: "He is the one I shall kiss." Judas entered Gethsemane with the guards and went up to Jesus and kissed him, saying: "Greetings, Master."

Jesus answered him: "My friend, with a kiss you betray me?"

The guards rushed to arrest Jesus. Peter wanted to stop them: He took out his sword and struck a guard, cutting off one of his ears. But Jesus said to him: "Put away your sword." And he told them: "He who draws the sword, dies by the sword." Then he touched the guard's ear and healed it.

Then he said to Peter: "Do you think that if I were to appeal to my Father, he would not send an army of angels to save me? But what the prophets foretold must be fulfilled."

While the guards were leading Jesus away, the apostles fled.

10 Peter Denies Jesus

Luke 22

When Jesus was arrested and dragged off by the guards, the apostles all fled. But Peter followed behind at a distance to see where they were taking him. In fact, during the Last Supper, Peter had promised Jesus: "Even if everyone else abandoned you, I would not!"

"Really?" Jesus had answered. "Before this night is out, you will declare three times that you do not know me!"

Now Peter wanted to show that he was brave and faithful to his word. For this reason, he followed along behind Jesus, and came to the courtyard of the house of Caiaphas. But when he discovered that Jesus was being beaten and had been condemned to death, he began to grow afraid.

Peter went up to a group of people who had lit a fire in a courtyard and were gathered around it to keep warm: the night was very cold. One of Caiaphas' maidservants looked at him for a moment, and then said: "You were with that man from Nazareth, weren't you?"

Peter was afraid of meeting the same fate as Jesus, and he answered: "I do not even know who he is."

He moved away from the group, but a guard recognized him and said: "Weren't you with him in the garden of the olives?" "No" answered Peter. "It's not true."

Then other people gathered around him and they said: "Yes, you are one of his followers! Even your accent shows that you come from the same area as he." And Peter repeated: "It's not true. I tell you that I do not know him."

And at once Peter remembered what Jesus had said to him: "This very night you will declare three times that you do not know me." Then Peter went out and wept.

11 Jesus is Tried by Caiaphas

Mark 14

Jesus was taken to the house of the high priest Caiaphas to be tried. All the other chiefs of the people were there as well, and they had paid people to slander Jesus. Caiaphas asked Jesus: "If you are the Son of God, then say so!"

And Jesus replied: "Yes, I am!"

On these words Caiaphas exclaimed: "He has blasphemed. We have no further need of witnesses. He deserves to be put to death!"

And then a lot of people began to insult Jesus, and they beat him and slapped him. Some even spat.

12 Jesus is Taken before Pontius Pilate

Luke 23

The chiefs of the people could not have Jesus put to death without the permission of Pontius Pilate, who ruled over Palestine in the name of the emperor in Rome. To convince Pilate Jesus should be convicted the chiefs told him Jesus had proclaimed himself king and was therefore a rival to the Roman emperor. Pilate understood that the chiefs wanted to condemn Jesus for other reasons, so he asked him: "Are you a king?"

"Yes, I am," Jesus replied. "But my kingdom is not of this world."

13 Jesus Is Tortured

Luke 23

In order to be rid of Jesus, Pilate sent him to Herod Antipas, the king of Galilee, who was then in Jerusalem. Herod interrogated him, but Jesus did not answer and so was returned to Pilate.

The chiefs of the people had gathered a huge crowd before the house of Pilate, and they had been paid to shout that Jesus should be condemned to death. Pilate tried to calm the crowd. He ordered his soldiers to whip Jesus. And they amused themselves by torturing him and pretending that he was a king:

They draped a red cloth over his shoulders and then placed a crown of thorns on his head.

Jesus was bleeding when Pilate presented him to the crowd saying: "Here is the man." But the crowd again yelled: "Put him to death! Crucify him! Crucify him!"

Pilate made a last attempt. He said: "At Passover it is the custom that I free a prisoner. Do you want me to free Barabbas, or this Jesus?"

Barabbas was a murderer.

"But what wrong has this man done?" insisted Pilate. "I find no fault in this Jesus!"

But the crowd repeated: "Crucify him! Crucify him!"

14 Jesus Is Condemned to Death

John 19

Pontius Pilate knew that Jesus was innocent, but he was afraid that the chiefs of the Jews would tell the emperor: "Your governor is really your enemy; he freed a man who proclaimed himself king."

For this reason, he handed Jesus over to the soldiers to be crucified, and he himself wrote the tablet to be stuck onto the cross, where the reason for the punishment was written: "Jesus of Nazareth, King of the Jews." The tablet was written in the three languages spoken in Palestine: Hebrew, Latin, and Greek.

15 The Road to Calvary

Mark 15

The soldiers made Jesus bear the heavy weight of the cross and led him through the streets of Jerusalem to the place of crucifixion. It was a rocky hill called Calvary, just outside the walls of the city.

There were many people who followed Jesus on the road that led to Calvary. Some laughed at him; others were simply curious. A group of women watched what was happening and wept. Jesus suffered a great deal, and every now and then he fell to the ground under the weight of the cross.

16 Mary and John

Luke 23; John 19

Jesus was very weak from the whipping he had received and from the crown of thorns which made his head bleed. When Jesus fell to the ground under the weight of the cross, the soldiers stopped a passerby, Simon the Cyrenian, and forced him to help Jesus.

When they reached Calvary, the soldiers stripped Jesus, laid him on the cross, and nailed his hands and feet to it. Then they raised up the cross and waited for Jesus to die. While they were crucifying him, Jesus said: "Father, forgive them, for they know not what they do."

It was the custom for the soldiers to divide the clothes of a man condemned to death among themselves. Jesus had been wearing a single tunic, so, to avoid cutting it up, the soldiers decided to draw lots for the garment.

Mary, the mother of Jesus, and the apostle John stood together at the foot of the cross. Jesus turned to John to ask him to take care of his mother, and he told Mary to look upon John as her son from then on. "Woman, behold thy son," he said to Mary. And to John: "Son, behold thy mother." A large crowd had gathered as though it were a show.

17 The Good Thief

Luke 23

Two thieves had been found guilty of serious crimes and condemned to death alongside Jesus on Calvary. The soldiers had crucified them on either side of Jesus. One said to Jesus: "If you really are the Christ, then save yourself and us!" But the other thief spoke up: "Have you no fear of God? We are being justly punished, but he has done nothing wrong!" He then addressed Jesus, saying: "Lord, remember me when you come into your kingdom." And Jesus replied: "You will be with me in paradise!"

18 Jesus Dies

Luke 23; Matthew 27; John 19

Jesus had already been on the cross for some hours when an extraordinary thing happened. It was around midday when the earth was suddenly covered in a darkness which lasted for three hours. Jesus cried: "Father, into your hands I commend my spirit." And he died. At this there was an earthquake. When he saw this, the centurian in charge of the soldiers said: "This man truly was the Son of God!"

Even those who had only come to watch the crucifixion returned home beating their breasts after they had witnessed these events.

While this happened, the friends and disciples of Jesus and the women who had followed him from Galilee all stood together a little way off and watched in silence.

Since it was the day before the holy Sabbath, it was decided that the bodies be removed from the crosses. To make certain that the condemned men were dead, the soldiers broke the legs of the thieves who had been crucified with Jesus. Then they approached Jesus and saw that he was already dead. The soldiers did not break his legs, but one of them pierced his side with a spear.

19 Jesus Is Buried

Matthew 27; John 19

Out of fear of the authorities, Joseph of Arimathea had remained a secret follower of Jesus. When Jesus died, Joseph went to Pilate and asked for the body of Jesus. Pilate agreed.

The body was taken down from the cross, wrapped in a sheet and carried away at once to a nearby tomb which belonged to Joseph.

This was all done hurriedly, because the next day was the Sabbath and no work was permitted on that day. The body of Jesus, therefore, was not washed in oils and perfumed according to the custom.

Mary Magdalene and the other women who loved Jesus intended to return to the tomb the day after the Sabbath to attend to his body.

The chief priests and the elders of the people then went to Pilate and said to him: "We remember that when this impostor was alive he claimed he would rise from the dead after three days. Order a guard to be put at the tomb so that the disciples do not come and steal the body in order to tell the people that he has come back to life." And Pilate replied: "Do as you wish." Thus, they went away and sealed the stone at the entrance to the tomb and left several men to guard it.

20 The Third Day

Mark 16; John 20

Jesus had died on the cross and been buried on the day before the Sabbath. On the day after the Sabbath, several women went to buy ointments and spices for the body of Jesus and then went to the tomb.

Along the way, they asked among themselves: "Who is going to roll away for us the great stone that seals the tomb?" However, when they arrived they found that the stone had already been rolled away and the tomb was open. In amazement, they entered the tomb and saw a young man, an angel, clothed in a long white garment and they were afraid. But he said to them: "Do not fear! You are looking for Jesus of Nazareth, who was crucified: He has risen and he is here no longer. Now go and tell this to his disciples."

The women were astonished, and fled from the tomb, saying nothing to anybody of what they had seen and heard.

When Mary Magdalene returned to the tomb and found it empty, she believed that the body of the Lord had been stolen, and she began to weep. Suddenly, she heard someone call to her: "Woman, why are you weeping?" Through her tears she asked: "If you have taken the body, tell me where it is so that I can go and get it!" But the voice only called her name: "Mary!" At this, she recognized Jesus. He told her: "I will ascend to my Father. Go and give this news to my brothers!" Mary was filled with joy and ran to speak to the apostles: "I have seen the Lord!" she told them.

They did not want to believe her words. So Peter and John also returned to the tomb. When they saw that it was empty, they too began to understand that Jesus would indeed rise from the dead.

21 The Chief Priests' Deception

Matthew 28

After the resurrection of Jesus, the guards who had been watching over the tomb went to the chief priests to tell them what had happened. When they heard, the priests gave the guards a lot of money so that they would tell people that while they slept the disciples of Jesus had come by night and stolen the body. The chief priests also said to the guards: "If Pilate learns of this, we will take all responsibility and will guarantee your safety." The guards took the money and followed the chiefs' instructions.

22 The Two Disciples on the Road to Emmaus

Luke 24

On the same day that Jesus rose from the dead, two of his disciples set out on foot for the village of Emmaus. They knew nothing of what had happened that day and were still sad about the death of Jesus. As they walked, a traveler joined them and asked: "Why are you so sad?"

"You must be the only person who does not know what has happened in Jerusalem," they replied. "We had hoped that Jesus would free us from Roman rule and restore the kingdom of Israel. . . ."

The traveler was Jesus himself, but the two disciples did not recognize him. He then explained that the Messiah had not come to restore Israel, but to allow all men to enter the Kingdom of God.

When they reached Emmaus, the two disciples invited the traveler to dine with them. At the table, Jesus took the bread and broke it . . . just as he had done at the Last Supper. As he did this, the disciples recognized him, and Jesus vanished.

Filled with hope and joy, the two disciples decided to return at once to Jerusalem. There, they told the apostles what had happened on the road to Emmaus, and of how they had recognized Jesus.

23 Jesus Appears to the Apostles

Luke 24

Gathered together for supper, the two disciples who had been to Emmaus were telling the apostles that Jesus had risen from the dead and had accompanied them on their walk.

Suddenly Jesus himself appeared among them and said: "Peace be with you!"

They were all amazed and frightened. They could see that it was Jesus and yet he was not the same as before. But Jesus said: "Why are you surprised and troubled? Look at my hands and my feet. Do you not recognize me? A spirit does not have flesh and bones as you see that I have."

The apostles were overcome with joy at seeing that the Lord was alive, and they were so moved to see him that they did not know what to do. To give them further proof, Jesus asked: "Do you have anything to eat?" The apostles immediately offered him a portion of roast fish. Jesus took the fish and ate it in front of them to show that he was a real person.

"Everything has taken place as I told you it would," Jesus reminded them. "It was written that the Christ should suffer and rise from the dead on the third day."

24 Doubting Thomas

John 20

On the same day that he rose from the dead, Jesus appeared to all the apostles and said to them: "Just as the Father sent me, so I send you." He then breathed on them and added: "Receive the Holy Spirit. Whoever's sins you now forgive, shall be forgiven in heaven. Whoever's sins you do not forgive, shall not be forgiven."

The apostle Thomas was not present at this meeting. Later, the others told him: "We have seen the Lord!" But he replied: "If I do not see the marks of the nails in his hands and put my finger into them, and put my hand into the wound on his side, I will not believe you." Eight days later, the apostles were once again together with Thomas. The doors were locked, yet Jesus appeared and said, just as before, "Peace be with you!"

He then turned to Thomas and went on: "Put your finger here and look at my hands. Stretch out your hand and put it into my side. Doubt no more, but now believe!"

And Thomas answered: "My Lord and my God!" Jesus then said to him: "You have believed because you have seen. Blessed are they who have not seen and believe!"

25 Breakfast by the Side of the Lake

John 21

A short while later a group of the apostles went fishing on the Sea of Galilee. As they were returning to the shore, a stranger on the beach asked them: "Have you caught nothing?" "Nothing at all!" they replied. The stranger then said: "Throw your nets into the water on the right-hand side of the boat." They did this and the net came up full of fish. John then understood that the stranger was Jesus himself! Jesus awaited them on the shore. "Bring your fish," he said, "and we shall have breakfast."

26 Feed My Sheep . . .

John 21

By the side of the Sea of Galilee, Jesus had made a breakfast of bread and fish for himself and a group of the apostles.

After they had finished eating, Jesus said to Simon-Peter: "Simon, son of John, do you love me more than the others?" "Of course, Lord. You know that I love you," replied Peter. And Jesus said: "Feed my lambs!"

A second time Jesus asked; "Simon, son of John, do you love me?" and again Peter replied: "Of course, Lord. You know that I love you." And Jesus said: "Feed my sheep."

Then, for the third time, Jesus said: "Simon, son of John, do you truly love me?" Peter replied: "Lord, you know everything. You know that I love you."

And Jesus said to him: "Feed my sheep."

At the house of Caiaphas, Peter had denied knowing Jesus three times. Now, on the shore of the Sea of Galilee, Jesus gave him three chances to show his love.

When Jesus said: "Feed my sheep," to Peter, he was telling him to take care of and nourish the faith of those who believed in him.

27 Jesus Returns to the Father

Matthew 28; Acts 1

In the forty days which followed Jesus' resurrection from the dead, he explained many things to the apostles concerning the Kingdom of Heaven, and told them what they had to do in his name.

He gave them the power to forgive sins so that everybody could, if they so wished, come to love God and one day enter his kingdom.

Jesus also said to them: "Every power in heaven and on earth has been given to me. Go, therefore, and teach all nations what I have taught you. You must baptize whoever believes in me, and I shall always be with you!"

Jesus then said that soon he would send the Holy Spirit among them and that, therefore, they were not to go away from Jerusalem.

Exactly forty days after his resurrection from the dead, Jesus led the apostles to the Mount of Olives and there, before their very eyes, he was raised up into heaven. The apostles continued to stare at the sky until two angels clothed in light appeared to them and said: "Why are you standing here, gazing up to heaven? This same Jesus, who has left you and gone up to heaven, will one day return in the same manner."

28 The Disciple Matthias

Matthew 27; Acts 1

After the ascension of Jesus into heaven, the apostles returned to the city and prayed with Mary, the mother of Jesus, and a group of disciples. They then decided to resolve a problem. Judas Iscariot, had betrayed Jesus, had realized he had done a great evil. He had taken the thirty coins he had received as payment for the betrayal and he had given them back to the high priests. Then he had hanged himself.

There now remained, therefore, only eleven apostles. For this reason Peter ṣpoke: "We must find another man to take the place of Judas. He must be one of those disciples who has followed Jesus from the day he was baptized by John the Baptist. He must have heard all the teachings of Jesus and be able to bear witness that he rose from the dead and ascended into heaven."

Two disciples were chosen from those who fulfilled these requirements. They then all offered the following prayer: "Lord, you who know the hearts of men, show us which of these two you have chosen." They then drew lots and a disciple by the name of Matthias was chosen and thus joined the other eleven apostles.

29 Fire from the Sky

Acts 2

The feast of Pentecost fell ten days after Jesus had ascended into heaven. Jews from all around and from many distant countries had gathered in Jerusalem. Pentecost was, in fact, one of the most important Jewish feasts and was observed in celebration of the harvest.

It was nine o'clock in the morning. The apostles, Mary the mother of Jesus, and other disciples were gathered together to pray. Suddenly, a great noise like a rushing wind was heard and tongues of fire appeared over each of them.

They were all filled with the Holy Spirit, the gift promised them by Jesus. The Holy Spirit filled the apostles with courage and they all went out and began to speak of Jesus.

Drawn by the great noise, many people had gathered around the house. Every one of them, even the foreigners, realized to their great surprise that they were hearing the apostles speak in their own language. "How is it," they said, "that we hear these men speak in our own languages? Among us there are Parthians, Medes, and Elamites. Some come from Mesopotamia, some from Cappadocia, from Pon-

tus, from Asia, from Phrygia, from Egypt, from Libya, from Crete, and some of us from Arabia. There are even some of us from Rome. How can we all, at the same time, hear these men speaking to us of the marvels of God?"

Others, however, laughed and said: "Those men who are speaking are drunk!" But Peter said to them: "No. We are not drunk! It is only nine o'clock in the morning! Rather, you should know this: The Jesus who was crucified was the Christ, the long-awaited Messiah. He was the Son of God! He has risen from the dead and sent the Holy Spirit among us!"

30 Three Thousand New Christians

Acts 2

Peter explained to the crowd that Jesus was the Messiah foretold by the prophets. "Our chief priests had him crucified," Peter said. "But God has raised him from the dead!"

Struck by his words, many people asked: "What must we do?" And Peter replied: "Repent and every one of you will be baptized in the name of Jesus Christ. Your sins will be forgiven and you will receive the gift of the Holy Spirit." When they heard this, many people asked to be baptized. Three thousand believers were added that day.

May

BIBLE STORY OF THE MONTH

Peter and Cornelius

Every day the number of those who believed in the Lord Jesus grew. They listened carefully to the teachings of the apostles and prayed together often. They took part in the celebration of the various rites, especially the one then called the "breaking of bread."

All the new believers shared their personal possessions. They were of one heart and one soul, and they openly declared their faith: Jesus, who had been crucified, had now risen from the dead and was standing at the right hand of the Father in heaven.

All the believers belonged to the people of Israel and they thought that Jesus had come to bring salvation to their people only. Very soon, however, another problem arose: an ever greater number of non-Jewish people, Greeks and Romans, for example, had heard talk of Jesus and were asking to become his followers. In the church, the family of the followers of Jesus, there was much discussion as to whether or not to admit those who did not belong to the people of Israel.

And there was yet another problem to resolve. The Jews observed many special rules, some of which concerned the food they ate. They did not eat certain animals like pigs, certain birds, any shellfish, and no animal that had died by suffocation. They considered all these foods to be "impure" and even when they became Christians they continued to believe that it was a sin to eat them. Those who were not Jewish, on the other hand, did not follow these rules. If they were to be admitted into this new church, if they were to become Christians, were they to be obliged to observe the laws of the Jews? Did they have to stop eating these "impure" foods?

The Lord himself intervened to solve these problems. It happened in the following way.

An officer in the Roman army, by the name of Cornelius, lived with his family in the city of Caesarea. He was a good man who loved God and sought to do his will: He prayed regularly and gave generously to the poor. One afternoon, around three o'clock, Cornelius had a vision. He clearly saw and heard an angel who said to him: "Cornelius, God has heard your prayers and looked upon your kindness to the poor. You must send some men at once to Joppa to bring back here a certain Simon, also known as Peter. They will find him living as a guest in the house of a tanner, also called Simon. The house is by the sea."

Cornelius immediately called two servants and a soldier whom he

trusted. He explained to them everything that had taken place and sent them to Joppa.

The next day, while the three messengers from Cornelius were still making their way toward the city, Peter went up onto the terrace of the house where he was a guest, to pray. It was around midday. Not having eaten, Peter, naturally, was hungry. During his prayers he suddenly had a vision: He saw a great tablecloth descend from the sky and on it were all the animals that he had always considered impure. A voice said to him: "Rise, Peter, and eat!" "No Lord, I cannot," replied Peter, "for I have never eaten any-thing that is impure." But the Lord said to him: "Nothing of what I have created is impure."

This scene repeated itself three times, and Peter could have no doubts as to what he had seen and heard. He understood what the Lord had said: Rules about food depended on the different customs of different peoples; nobody should expect other people to follow their rules about eating. He also understood that all peoples are equal before God; we are all equally dear to his heart.

In the meantime, the three messengers from Cornelius had reached Joppa and had arrived outside the house of the tanner. The Holy Spirit spoke to Peter: "Three men are seeking you. Go with them for they are sent by God."

The next day Peter, accompanied by a group of Christians, went with them to Caesarea. He entered the house of Cornelius and said: "You know that Jews like myself do not enter the homes of men from other peoples because they consider them impure. But God has shown me that nothing and nobody is impure. In fact, I realize now that he has no preference for any type of person: Whoever lives in a way that is pleasing to God is loved by God."

Peter then went on to tell them all about Jesus, and he was still speaking when the Holy Spirit came down upon everyone who was listening.

The Christians who had accompanied Peter were astonished that the Holy Spirit had also come down on those who were not Jewish. But, having seen what had happened, Peter said: "We cannot refuse to baptize these people who have received the Holy Spirit in the same way as ourselves."

Cornelius and the other members of his household were all baptized at once. They were the first non-Jewish people to become followers of Christ and enter the Christian family: the first of a long line that continues to this day.

Acts 2, 10

1 The Lame Man at the Beautiful Gate

Acts 3

One afternoon, about three o'clock, the apostles Peter and John went up to the temple in Jerusalem to pray.

When they reached the temple, they entered by a gate known as the "Beautiful Gate." There they saw a cripple who had been carried every day to the gate in order to beg.

The lame man asked Peter and John for alms, but Peter looked at him and said: "Look at us." The cripple obeyed, hoping to receive a few coins. Instead, Peter said to him: "I have neither gold nor silver, but what I have I will give you. In the name of Jesus Christ, get up and walk!"

As he said these words, Peter took the man by the right hand and lifted him up. And immediately the feet and ankles of the lame man grew strong. He leapt to his feet and began to walk around and then to jump for joy, before following the apostles into the temple to give thanks to God.

There were many people coming and going by the "Beautiful Gate" and they all knew the lame man who sat there to beg for alms: Every one of them was amazed when they saw him walking and jumping for joy.

2 Barnabas, a Generous Apostle

Acts 4

The first Christians shared all their possessions, so that everybody had what he needed. If one of them owned fields or houses, he sold them and brought the proceeds to the apostles, who then distributed the money to the neediest.

One of the men who did this was Joses, a Jew from Cyprus, whom the apostles called Barnabas. This name means "Son of Encouragement" and Barnabas, in fact, began to work closely with the apostles and was very active, speaking to everyone about Jesus.

3 Peter and John are Brought before the Council

Acts 4

Peter had healed the lame man at the Beautiful Gate of the temple. He explained to the crowd that he had acted in the name of Jesus.

Suddenly, however, the guards arrived and arrested Peter and John and put them in prison. The next day, the chiefs of the people questioned the two apostles: "Who has given you the power to do such a thing?" they asked.

Peter was filled with the Holy Spirit and he replied with great courage: "Jesus of Nazareth! The same Jesus that you put to death and God has resurrected, for Jesus alone can free us from evil!"

The chiefs of the people feared that the news of Peter's miracle might lead more people to become Christians, so they ordered the apostles not to speak about Jesus anymore. Peter and John, however, answered them: "You can judge for yourselves whether it is right to obey God or to obey you. We cannot help speaking about great things!"

Once again the chiefs of the people threatened Peter and John and then they released them, in fear of all the people who praised them for the miracle they had just performed.

4 Touched by his Shadow

Acts 5

Every day the apostles went to the temple and sat under Solomon's porch. There they taught the doctrines of Jesus, and performed many miracles among the people. They were respected by everyone and every day the number of those who believed in the Lord grew.

From all over Jerusalem and the nearby villages, people carried the sick on stretchers and laid them in the streets, so that when Peter passed by, at least his shadow might touch them. And every one of them was healed.

5 The Story of Two Liars

Acts 5

A certain man named Ananias and his wife Sapphira sold a field in order to distribute the proceeds among the poor. But, secretly, they kept some of the money apart.

Peter found out about this and said to Ananias: "As you well know, nobody forced you to sell your field. And even after you had sold it you could have done as you wished with the money. But you should not have said that you had given it all away! You did not lie to us, you lied to God!"

Ananias was so dismayed at what he had done that he fell to the ground, dead. A group of young men wrapped his body in a sheet and carried it off for burial. Sapphira, who did not know what had happened, arrived three hours later.

Peter asked her at once: "Sapphira, did you really sell the field for this amount of money?" Her reply was "yes," and Peter then went on: "You and your husband agreed to cheat the Lord! Look, the men who buried your husband are just returning. Now they shall also bury you!"

And, in fact, at that moment Sapphira too fell down dead and everyone understood that it was a great sin to lie to the Lord.

6 Seven Helpers for the Apostles

Acts 6

The numbers of the disciples of Jesus continued to grow and the twelve apostles could no longer carry out their work with all of them. Thus, they called a meeting and said: "It is not right that we should set aside the Word of God and concern ourselves with feeding people. Brothers, you must choose seven men of faith and wisdom from among you to be our helpers." This proposal pleased everyone, and seven men, including Stephen and Philip, were chosen to help the apostles distribute food.

May

7 Stephen, the First Martyr

Acts 6–7

Stephen was one of the seven helpers of the apostles and he was full of faith and love for the Lord Jesus. He argued very ably with the Jews in order to show them that Jesus was the Messiah sent by God.

Because they could not defeat him in argument, several of the Jews began to accuse him falsely. They said that Stephen had blasphemed against Moses, against the law of God, and against the temple. They repeated these false charges until Stephen was brought to trial before the high priest.

The high priest asked Stephen if the accusations made against him were true. Stephen then made a long speech: He reminded them that the people of Israel had often behaved badly toward God; they had not listened to the prophets and even ignored Moses; they had received the law from God, but had often failed to obey it.

Stephen then added that God had decided to make himself known to man and had therefore sent Jesus, his Son. Just as the Jews had killed the prophets sent by God in the past, so had they killed Jesus.

The chief priest and all those with him were enraged at Stephen's words. Stephen, however, said: "Behold, I look unto the heavens and see Jesus, standing at the right hand of the Father."

In this way, Stephen was proclaiming that Jesus, too, was God. The chief priest and the judges were shocked and angry and they condemned Stephen to be stoned to death. They dragged him outside of the city at once and began to throw rocks at him. Stephen began to pray and, like Jesus on the cross, he said: "Lord, accept my life." Then, knowing that he was close to death, Stephen fell to his knees and added: "Lord, forgive them for what they are doing."

8 Saul Against the Christians

Acts 6–7

Stephen was the first Christian martyr, the first of many men and women to give their lives for love of Jesus. The people who stoned him to death had given their cloaks to a young man named Saul to hold.

In those days, there was a great deal of persecution against the Christians in Jerusalem. Saul would go into houses and arrest men and women and have them thrown into prison. Many fled to other cities where they could speak of Jesus and spread his teachings throughout the land.

9 Philip and the Magician Simon

Acts 8

Philip, one of the seven helpers of the apostles, went to a city in Samaria. There, he began to speak of the Lord and he accompanied the Word with many miracles.

In this way, many of the inhabitants of the city came to believe and were baptized. Among them, Simon the magician, who had enchanted many people with his spells for a great many years. Even Simon spent all his time at Philip's side and came to marvel at the many miracles and wonders that he saw Philip perform.

10 Peter and the Magician Simon

Acts 8

The apostles Peter and John went to Samaria to visit those who had received the Word of God. They prayed for the Samaritans and laid their hands on them and, in this way, the Samaritans received the Holy Spirit.

When Simon saw that the Holy Spirit was bestowed through the laying of hands, he went to the apostles and offered them a great deal of money, saying: "Give me this power, so that those on whom I lay my hands will receive the Holy Spirit!"

At once, however, Peter grew angry and replied: "Leave, and take your money with you! You believe that a gift from God can be bought for money: You must cease to believe such things. Pray to the Lord to forgive your wickedness! I see now that you are full of bitterness and a slave to evil!" Peter, of course, had remembered what Jesus told the apostles when he spoke to them of God's gift to us: "What you have freely received, that you must freely give!"

When he heard the words of Peter, Simon at once repented and said: "Pray to the Lord for me, that I might be forgiven."

11 The Minister of the Queen of Ethiopia

Acts 8

An angel of the Lord said to Philip: "Get up and go toward the south, on the road from Jerusalem to Gaza."

Philip set off, and while he was traveling he came across a chariot, inside of which a man was reading. He was an Ethiopian, the superintendent of the treasury of Candace, the queen of Ethiopia. He was a believer in God, and he was returning from Jerusalem where he had gone to pray in the temple.

Along the way, the superintendent had been reading the book of the prophet Isaiah, and when he met up with Philip he was reading the passage which says: "Like a sheep that is led to the slaughterhouse, and like a lamb that is dumb, he does not complain. . . ."

The Ethiopian asked Philip: "Tell me, please, who is the prophet speaking about?"

Philip explained that Isaiah announced the death of the Messiah, Jesus. He spoke so well, that when they reached a spring, the man said to Philip: "Look, what is to stop me from being baptized?" The superintendent stopped the chariot and they both got into the water, and Philip baptized him.

12 Saul on the Road to Damascus

Acts 9

Saul had decided to destroy the disciples of Jesus. For this reason, he asked the chiefs' permission to go to Damascus and arrest the Christians. He obtained their permission and an armed escort.

He was traveling toward Damascus when, suddenly, a light came down from the sky and wrapped itself around him. He fell to the ground and heard a voice that said: "Saul, Saul, why do you persecute me?" Who are you?" replied Saul. And the voice continued: "I am Jesus, whom you persecute."

13 Saul and Ananias

Acts 9

There, on the road to Damascus, Jesus revealed himself to Saul, the persecutor of the Christians. Jesus also said to him: "Get up and enter the city: Someone there will tell you what you have to do."

Saul got up from the ground and realized that he was blind. His guards led him into the city.

In Damascus there lived a Christian named Ananias. In a vision the Lord spoke to him in the following way: "Go to Straight Street, and look for a man from Tarsus called Saul. At this moment he is praying, and in a vision he has seen you arrive and place your hands on his eyes to give him back his sight."

Ananias replied: "Lord, I know of all the evils that he has done to the faithful in Jerusalem." But the Lord said: "Go and put your hands on his eyes. For me, he is a tool that I have chosen in order to make myself known among all peoples."

Ananias went, he placed his hands over Saul's eyes and said: "Saul, my brother, the Lord has sent me to you." And Saul regained his sight and was baptized. And to show everyone that he was a different man, Saul changed his name to Paul.

14 Paul Lowered in a Basket

Acts 9–13

Saul had received baptism and had become Paul, a new man who believed in the Lord Jesus. He immediately began going around announcing his faith in the synagogues of Damascus. The Hebrews were astonished and said: "But isn't he the one who threw the Jews into prison in Jerusalem? How is it that now he has become a Christian?"

Some of the Hebrews decided to put him to death. But Paul found out about their plans, and at night he had himself lowered from the walls of Damascus in a basket.

15 Peter at Lydda

Acts 9

The Church was enjoying a period of peace, and it was growing continually.

Peter, the leader of the Church, decided to go and visit the different Christian communities. When he reached the city of Lydda, he found a man named Aeneas, who had been lying paralyzed on his bed for eight years. Peter said to him: "Aeneas, Jesus Christ heals you. Get up and make your bed." At once the paralyzed man arose. The inhabitants of Lydda saw him and were converted to the Lord.

16 Peter Raises up Tabitha

Acts 9

Peter was visiting the community of Lydda, when, in the nearby city of Jaffa, a Christian woman grew ill and died. Her name was Tabitha, which means "gazelle," and she was much loved by everyone because she never tired of doing good and giving charity to the poor.

The Christians were very sad over the death of Tabitha, and when they heard that the apostle Peter was in Lydda they sent two men to call him, and they said to him: "Come with us at once."

Peter went, and as soon as he arrived they took him into the room where the woman's body had been laid out. There were a group of widows present and, in tears, they showed Peter the clothes that Tabitha had made for them.

Then Peter told everyone to leave, and he knelt down to pray. Then, turning to the body, he said: "Tabitha, get up!" She opened her eyes, saw the apostle and sat up; he took her by the hand and raised her up, then he presented her to the widows and the other Christians.

All of Jaffa heard of the resurrection of Tabitha, and because of this, many people came to believe in the Lord Jesus, becoming Christians.

17 Herod Has Peter Imprisoned

Acts 12

In Jerusalem King Herod began to persecute the Christians, and had the apostle James put to death. Seeing that this pleased the Hebrew leaders, he had Peter arrested as well and placed him under heavy guard: four squads of four soldiers each.

It was a few days before the Passover feast, and the king planned to try the leader of the Church in public after the feast.

While Peter was in prison, an incessant prayer went up from the Church to God for his safety.

18 Peter Is Freed from Prison

Acts 12

The day was approaching on which Herod planned to try Peter before the people. The night before the trial Peter slept in prison, bound in chains and watched over by the soldiers. And then a bright light filled the cell, and an angel of the Lord came down. The angel woke Peter and said: "Get up, hurry!"

At these words the chains dropped from his hands. The angel continued: "Put on your belt and your cloak and tie your sandals." Peter did so. Then the angel said: "Follow me."

Peter could not believe that what was happening was real. He was convinced that he was having a vision. He followed the angel, and with him he passed the first guard and then the second, until they were before the iron gate which gave access to the road from the prison. The door opened by itself before them.

They went out and walked a little way along the road; then Peter realized that the angel had disappeared. Only then did he truly realize what had happened, and he thought to himself: "The Lord has sent an angel to free me. He has delivered me from the hands of Herod, who sought my ruin."

19 A Girl Named Rhoda

Acts 12

The prayers of the Church had been answered: The Lord had sent his angel to free Peter from prison. Now in the streets of Jerusalem, Peter thought that as soon as the guards noticed he was gone from his cell they would come to look for him.

He had to find somewhere to hide himself. After thinking about it, he decided that the best place was the house of some friends of his: the house of Mary, the mother of John, also called Mark, who was later to write one of the Gospels.

In that house there were a fair number of Christians, gathered together in prayer. As soon as they heard a knock on the door, they sent a girl named Rhoda to find out who it was.

She went up to the door. But when she recognized the voice, she was so overcome with joy that she forgot to open the door and instead rushed to announce to the others that Peter was outside.

"You don't know what you're saying!" was the reply. And meanwhile Peter continued to knock. When they finally got around to opening the door and saw him, they were speechless. And he told them what had happened.

20 The Community of Antioch

Acts 11

Those who had fled from Jerusalem, when the persecutions began at the time of Stephen, had been scattered far and wide. Some had gone to the great city of Antioch, in Syria.

There, they began to announce the Lord Jesus again, to both the Hebrews and the non-Hebrews, the pagans. The hand of the Lord was with them, and so a great many believed and were converted to the Lord.

In Antioch, for the first time, the disciples of Jesus were called Christians.

21 Paul and Barnabas are Sent by the Holy Spirit

Acts 4–13

One day the community of Antioch was gathered in prayer and there were many Christians present who were known for their faith and for their good works. As they were worshiping the Lord, the Holy Spirit came to them and said: "Tell Barnabas and Paul that I have chosen them especially to do difficult work for me." This work meant spreading the word of Jesus in places where it had never been heard before.

After they had fasted and prayed together, the Christians of Antioch laid their hands on Paul and Barnabas and said good-bye to them. Thus Paul and Barnabas departed on their long journey to the island of Cyprus.

Paul and Barnabas at once began to preach the word of the Lord in the various cities on the island. They decided that it was right to give the good news first to the Jews, and so every Sabbath day they went into the synagogues and spoke of the Lord Jesus.

On many occasions their words were heard with interest by the Jews; and some of them were converted to Christianity. But often they chose not to listen to the words of the apostles.

22 Paul and Elymas the Sorcerer

Acts 13

In the city of Paphos on the island of Cyprus, the Roman governor Sergius Paulus had called for Paul and Barnabas because he wished to hear the word of God. Among the servants of the governor was a sorcerer called Elymas the Jew, who did everything in his power to prevent his master from believing the apostles.

At this, Paul turned to Elymas and said: "When will you cease to work against the will of the Lord? Behold, for one whole season you shall be blind as a warning from the Lord!" And that was what happened.

23 Paul Is Persecuted

Acts 13–14

After they left the island of Cyprus, Paul and Barnabas continued on their voyage and they disembarked in Asia Minor, which today is Turkey. Here, they proclaimed the Word of God, first to the Jews, and then to the Gentiles.

Often the Jews opposed them in every way imaginable. At Lystra it was a group of Jews who persuaded the crowd to stone Paul so badly that they thought they had killed him. They dragged his body out of the city and dumped it. Fortunately, a number of disciples found Paul.

24 Paul and Barnabas Are Mistaken for Gods

Acts 14

On their long journey as missionaries, Paul and Barnabas had arrived in the city of Lystra.

There, Paul began to preach, and while he was speaking he noticed a man listening to him whose legs had been paralyzed from birth. Paul looked straight at him and said in a loud voice: "Get up and stand on your feet!" And, with a leap, the cripple got up and began to walk.

When they saw this miracle, the pagans immediately said to each other: "The Gods have come down among us in human form!" For they believed that Barnabas was the god Jupiter, and Paul was the god Mercury.

It was the custom of the pagans to offer animals to their gods in sacrifice. Thus, the priest of Jupiter then arrived, followed by a large crowd, with a bull that he intended to offer in sacrifice to Barnabas. However, when Paul and Barnabas saw this, they raced into the crowd shouting: "Citizens, do not do this! We are men like you! We came here especially to tell you not to worship these false gods and to turn instead to the Father, the one true God!" Finally, Paul and Barnabas convinced the crowd not to offer them a sacrifice.

25 Paul Is Sent to Europe

Acts 16

After he had returned to Antioch, Paul once again departed, this time with a disciple named Silas, to spread the Word of God. At Lystra, Paul met a young Christian by the name of Timotheus whom he took with him on his journey. When they reached Troas, a doctor, Luke, joined the group. One night Paul had a vision. He saw a man from Macedonia who begged him: "Come and save us!" The vision was given to him by the Lord, and Paul set sail at once for Europe.

26 Lydia, the Seller of Purple Dye
Acts 16

On his second journey as a missionary, the apostle Paul was accompanied by Timotheus and other disciples. One of these disciples was Luke, a young physician.

After the vision had told Paul to move from Asia into Europe, the little group boarded a ship which took them to Neapolis in Macedonia. From there they proceeded on foot to the important city of Philippi.

That Sabbath day they decided, as usual, to spread the good news first among the Jews. They went where the Jews met, outside the city, on the banks of a river.

When the apostles arrived, they came across a group of women. They immediately sat down and began to speak with them. Among those was Lydia, a seller of purple dye. The Lord opened her heart and she became a convert at once and was baptized along with all her family. She then invited Paul and the other disciples to her home: "If you are convinced that I have really heard the word of the Lord, then you can come to my house." And Paul and the others accepted.

27 Paul Is Imprisoned in Philippi
Acts 16

In the city of Philippi Paul succeeded in forming a small group of Christians. Many citizens, however, were opposed to him. One day, some of them grabbed Paul and his disciple Silas and dragged them both before the judges.

Here, they accused them in the following way: "These two men are spreading disorder by preaching practices different from ours." The crowd that was gathered grew angry at Paul and Silas when they heard these words and the judges ordered them to be thrown into prison.

28 An Earthquake at Philippi
Acts 16

Paul and Silas had been thrown into prison at Philippi. During the night, while they prayed and sang hymns of praise to the Lord, a great earthquake shook the foundations of the prison, opened all the doors and broke the chains of the prisoners.

When the warden saw all the doors lying open, he thought that the prisoners had escaped. He knew that he would be held responsible and drew out his sword in order to kill himself. When Paul saw this, he shouted loudly: "Do yourself no harm, we are all here!"

The warden could not believe it. He took a lamp and rushed into the cell of Paul and Silas. When he saw that they really were still there, he was very glad. He led them outside and said to them: "I see that you are better men than others. I have faith, therefore, in the words you speak. What must I do?"

"Believe in the Lord Jesus and you will be saved," replied Paul and he then explained who Jesus was.

The prison warden at Philippi heard Paul's words and believed in them and was baptized at once. He then took care of Paul and Silas, washing their wounds and inviting them to his own house to eat.

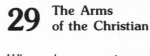

29 The Arms of the Christian

Ephesians 6

When he was in prison, Paul watched the soldiers who were guarding him closely. The arms that they carried led him to think of every Christian as a type of soldier, armed by God to conquer evil. This is what Paul said:

"Brothers, the truth is your belt. Good works are your armor. The sandals on your feet should be the readiness to spread the good news. Your faith is your shield and the salvation brought by Jesus is your helmet. Your sword is the Word of God!"

30 Paul, the Citizen of Rome

Acts 16

At Philippi the judges had ordered Paul and Silas to be beaten and thrown into prison. The next day they gave orders that they should be freed. Paul, however, said to the guards: "First they beat us with sticks and imprison us without a trial though we are citizens of Rome! And now they wish to release us in secret? No, the judges must come and release us themselves, thereby recognizing before all the people that we have done nothing wrong."

The guards repeated these words to the judges, who became very frightened when they heard that Paul and Silas were citizens of Rome. The laws of Rome were very severe; it was forbidden for anybody to beat one of its citizens.

The judges, therefore, went straight to the prison to apologize to Paul and Silas for what had happened the previous day and to set them free.

The apostle and Silas left the prison and went to the house of Lydia, the seller of purple dye, and remained as her guests. Here they had many meetings with the Christians of Philippi and they filled them with faith and courage before departing.

31 Like Runners in a Race . . .

1 Corinthians, 9

When he spoke, Paul often used examples that his listeners could understand, like the following sporting example.

"Brothers, you know that many runners take part in a race, but only one will win the prize. In a way, all of you are running in a race to win a prize that is offered by the Lord.

"You also know that runners train and suffer for long periods in order to win a crown of glory that soon disappears. We, on the other hand, are running for a prize that lasts forever, the glory of the Lord!"

BIBLE STORY OF THE MONTH

Paul Preaches In Greece

Paul, who had persecuted the Christians, had had a dramatic encounter with the risen Christ on the road to Damascus. From that moment on, he dedicated himself tirelessly to spreading the Word of God. Either alone or in the company of other disciples, he went on long and difficult journeys through Europe and Asia, and he succeeded in converting many people. Paul journeyed by ship or on foot, usually in the company of other Christians. Of these Mark and Luke each wrote one of the Gospels.

When Paul arrived in a city, he would await the Sabbath and then go into a synagogue to talk about Jesus with the Jews. A few of these would follow, but the majority would always oppose him and Paul would then preach to the pagans.

When he reached Athens, the most important Greek city, Paul had a strange adventure. The city was full of magnificent temples dedicated to gods. Paul trembled within himself when he saw all of these false gods and idols. He went at once to the main square and began to talk to the people that he met. Paul even argued with the philosophers, many of whom were highly respected in Athens. Some of them said: "What has this charlatan come to teach us?" Others, however, said: "He has come to talk of strange gods."

And since the most popular pastime in Athens was listening to and talking about the latest news and gossip, Paul was invited to speak before the council of the city, which was called the Areopagus.

In front of the most important people of the city, Paul began to speak: "Citizens of Athens, I see that you are very religious people. I have walked through your city and I have noticed that you build temples to many gods. As I walked through one part I even came across an altar dedicated to "The Unknown God." Good! For I have come to show you the God whom you worship and do not yet know."

The citizens of Athens were astounded at these words, but Paul went on: "This God created the world and everything in it. He is the Lord of heaven and earth and, truly, he does not live in the temples built by men. He does not need men to serve him, for he lacks nothing. On the contrary, it is he who gives life and everything else to all things. He created the first man and gave him as his descendants other men and all the peoples who live on the earth. And since he has made us in his image, we must not believe that he is made of gold or silver or marble. We must not believe that statues built by men for their own gods

are images of the true god."

Paul now had to explain the most delicate aspect of his message to the Athenians and he did it using these words: "God has decided to forgive us for the past, when men lived in ignorance. He has sent his only son, Jesus, among men. He will judge all men righteously at a time decided by God, when all men rise from the dead, just as Jesus himself died and rose again. . . ."

When they heard this explanation from Paul, some of the Athenians began to laugh and others mocked him. Those who did not believe Paul joked: "We will have to go over this point again, later!" and

many of them walked away. A few of the Athenians, however, believed the words of Paul and became Christians.

The life Paul led really was extraordinary. After he had completed his third journey he was arrested and held prisoner for a long time in Palestine, before being transferred to Rome. He then was freed and went on other journeys, always taking care to spread the Word of the Lord wherever he went. In a letter to the Christians of the city of Corinth, he told the following story: "I have received five times the Jewish penalty of thirty-nine lashes. Three times I have suffered the Roman

penalty of being beaten with rods. And once I was stoned."

"I have been shipwrecked three times," Paul went on, "And I have spent a day and a night on the open sea. I have traveled a great deal and I have faced every kind of danger: danger on rivers, danger in cities, danger in the desert and at sea. I have been attacked by brigands and by those who were not Christians, and I have been attacked by those who only pretend to follow Christ. I have borne great burdens and have spent entire nights without sleep. I have endured famine and thirst. Often, when I have not eaten, I have remained out in the cold because I had nothing with which to cover myself.

"Over and above all this, I have concerned myself every day with the well-being of the whole Christian community. If someone is in difficulty, I too am worried. If someone is weak in his faith, I suffer."

But where did Paul find the strength to confront all these problems? He himself told us: "Fourteen years ago I was taken up into heaven. There I heard words which were so marvelous that it is impossible for a man to repeat them." God, therefore, had granted to Paul a taste of the great joy that he would certainly be given when he had completed his work.

Acts 17; 2 Corinthians 11–12

1 Paul at Corinth

Acts 18

After Paul had been to Athens, he went on to Corinth. In this city, he met a Jew, Aquila, who had fled to Corinth from Rome with his wife Priscilla, after the emperor had ordered all Jews to depart.

Paul was welcomed under their roof, and since he was an expert in the work they did, the sewing of tents, he began to help in their business. Paul, in fact, always tried not to impose on other people, but to pay his way by working. And then, every Sabbath day, he would go to the synagogue.

2 Paul's Dream

Acts 18

In Corinth, Paul went to the synagogue on every Sabbath day to preach to everyone, Jews and Greeks, in order to convert them. To all of them he explained that Jesus was the Messiah sent by God. The Jews, however, did not want to believe him and they refused to listen and insulted him.

When this happened, Paul showed his anger. "I am doing everything I can to save you. If you will not be saved, it is your own fault! I will now go out and seek to save those who are not Jews!" Thus Paul left and went to the home of a Greek. One night the Lord appeared to Paul in a dream and said to him: "Do not be afraid! Continue to spread the Word and do not fall silent, for I am with you!"

Paul stayed for a year and a half in Corinth and preached the Word of God. As the Lord had promised, many Jews were converted. Among these was the chief of the synagogue, Crispus.

A group of pagans also became converts and together all these people formed a large Christian community. Paul taught them in the faith with the help of his disciples Silas and Timotheus.

3 Gallio's Reply

Acts 18

One day several of the Jews of Corinth carried Paul before the Roman Governor Gallio. "This man," they said to him, "tries to persuade people to worship God in a way which is against the law."

Paul did not even have time to defend himself, before Gallio said: "If you are talking about a crime, an attack, or an evil deed, I will listen to you, O Jews! But since you are arguing over the subtleties of your own laws, you must decide for yourselves. I do not wish to judge such matters!"

4 Apollos Preaches in Ephesus

Acts 18

In the city of Ephesus a Christian by the name of Apollos spoke with great love of Jesus to both the Jews and the pagans. Aquila and Priscilla, the married friends of Paul, heard him speaking and realized that Apollos said many things that were not true, because he had never been instructed in his faith in Jesus. Therefore, they took him aside and carefully taught him everything he did not yet know. In this way, Aquila and Priscilla helped Apollos to spread the work of the Lord.

5 Paul in Ephesus

Acts 19

Paul left Corinth and the country of Greece in order to return to Asia Minor. He crossed the mountainous regions and arrived in the large and important city of Ephesus. There were already a number of believers in the city and Paul asked them: "Did you receive the Holy Spirit when you became Christians?" And these believers replied: "We do not even know what the Holy Spirit is. We were baptized in the way of John the Baptist."

Paul then explained to them that the baptism of John was for those who agreed to change their way of life and to believe in the one who was to come, namely Jesus; only by receiving the Holy Spirit could they now become Christ's followers.

When they heard this the disciples of Ephesus all asked to receive the Holy Spirit. Paul laid his hands on each and they were filled with the Holy Spirit. At once they began to speak in strange tongues and to prophesy and to bear witness for the Lord Jesus. Through Paul, God performed great miracles. People would take handkerchiefs and clothes that had been in contact with Paul and lay them on the sick, who would suddenly be healed.

6 The Magicians of Ephesus

Acts 19

When people saw the miracles performed through Paul, many tried to profit from them. One day, seven Jewish brothers went to a man possessed by a demon and said: "In the name of the Jesus whom Paul worships, be gone from this man."

The evil spirit, however, replied: "I know Jesus, and I know who Paul is, but who are you?" And immediately the possessed man threw himself upon them, overcame them, and beat them until they fled. After this, many magicians and sorcerers confessed and became Christians

7 A Young Man Named Eutychus

Acts 20

During one of his journeys Paul performed another great miracle. It was the anniversary of the resurrection of Jesus, and Paul was celebrating a meal in the name of the Lord. A young man named Eutychus was sitting on the window ledge until overcome with fatigue, he fell asleep, and fell from the third floor. They found him dead.

Paul went down to the young man and, taking the body in his arms, said: "Do not be sad. The boy is alive!" Eutychus was carried back into the house safe and sound!

8 The Silversmiths of Ephesus

Acts 19

At the time when the apostle Paul was working in Ephesus, a revolt broke out because of him.

A silversmith by the name of Demetrius earned his living making silver shrines for the goddess Diana, whereby he reaped profits.

One day, Demetrius called together all those who did the same work as he and said to them: "Have you not heard what the foreigner called Paul is saying? He says that the things we make with our hands, and which bring us such wealth, are not true gods. He has persuaded many people to stop worshiping the goddess Diana, and there is the risk that our trade will be ruined."

All the silversmiths then began to shout together: "How great is Diana, the goddess of the Ephesians!" They then went around the city, rousing the people. The crowd ran to the great open-air theater and began to shout and protest against Paul and his helpers.

After a while, two of Paul's companions, Aristarchus and Gaius were dragged into the theater. Paul feared for their safety and wanted to go into the theater in order to speak to the crowd, but the other Christians of the city stopped him, fearing it was too dangerous.

Meanwhile, there was great confusion in the theater. Some people said one thing and some another. For two hours many kept up a chorus of "Diana is great, the goddess of the Ephesians!"

The city chancellor then arrived, and with great difficulty succeeded in getting the crowd to listen to him. He told them: "You have dragged these men here, but they have not offended our goddess Diana. If Demetrius and the others believe they have been harmed, let them appeal to the court. The rest of you go home." The crowd obeyed and Gaius and Aristarchus were freed.

9 Farewell at the Port of Miletus

Acts 20

While traveling by ship, Paul arrived at the port of Miletus. There, he gathered the Christian community around him and said to them: "Now I intend to return to Jerusalem and I foresee that we shall not meet again. The Holy Spirit has warned me that I will have to face many difficulties. But the most important thing of all is that I continue to carry out my task: to tell everyone of God's love!"

Everyone burst into tears at the thought of not seeing Paul again, and when he left, they accompanied him to his ship.

10 By Sea toward Jerusalem

Acts 21

Paul was returning from one of his long, tiring, and dangerous missionary journeys. He was heading for Jerusalem, where he planned to celebrate the feast of Pentecost with his fellow believers.

He knew, and had told several of his companions, that many difficult times awaited him. The chiefs of the Jews were still opposed to his work as an apostle of Jesus, and in Jerusalem they would seek some new means of preventing him from carrying out his mission.

When the ship that Paul was traveling on reached Tyre, he took advantage of the long delay to meet the Christians who lived in that city. They, too, understood that it was very dangerous for Paul to return to Jerusalem and they urged him not to go.

Paul, however, was resolute: He considered it his duty to go, even if this meant he had to give up his life as Jesus had done. Thus, when the hour of his departure arrived, the Christians of Tyre, along with their wives and children, accompanied Paul to his ship. They knelt on the beach and prayed together before saying an affectionate farewell. Then Paul boarded his ship and set sail.

11 Some of Jesus' Words

Acts 20

The Gospels, which recount the life and works of Jesus, do not tell us everything about him, but only the parts that each evangelist considered most important.

One day, in one of his speeches, the apostle Paul told of a phrase spoken by Jesus which is not written in the Gospels. Jesus was telling his listeners to be full of love for their neighbors, and to particularly help those most in need. Paul then told them to remember what Jesus had said: "There is more joy in giving, than in receiving."

12 The Prophecy of Agabus

Acts 21

The ship in which Paul was traveling to Jerusalem stopped at the port of Caesarea. There Paul and his companions went to visit Philip, who was one of the seven who first helped the apostles.

They had been at Philip's house for several days when a prophet by the name of Agabus arrived from the region around Jerusalem. When Agabus came into Philip's house, he picked up Paul's belt and tied it around his own hands and feet. He then said: "This is what the Holy Spirit foretells: The man who owns this belt will be bound with it by the Jews of Jerusalem and handed over to the Gentiles."

When they saw and heard these things, Paul's traveling companions, Philip, and his other friends, all wept and begged him to change his plans and not travel to Jerusalem.

Paul, however, replied to them: "Why are you doing this? If you continue to cry in this way, you will break my heart. I am ready not only to be tied and bound, but to die in Jerusalem for my love of Jesus."

Just as he said he would, after he had completed his preparations several days later, Paul set out to finish his journey to Jerusalem.

13 Paul is Arrested in Jerusalem

Acts 21

After all his travels, Paul returned to Jerusalem where the other Christians greeted him joyfully. Paul first greeted James, who, after Peter had departed, had become the head of the Christian community.

Then, like every good Jew, Paul went to pray in the temple. Once there, however, he was seen by a group of non-Christian Jews from Asia Minor, who leaped on him and began to shout out: "Help us, men of Israel! This is the man who teaches all men everywhere to go against our faith!"

The people dragged Paul out of the temple, and were about to kill him when the Roman soldiers arrived.

When they saw the soldiers, the Jews stopped beating Paul. The captain of the soldiers arrested Paul and then asked the people around what crime he had committed. Everyone began to shout at the same time and they all said different things. At this, the captain decided to transfer the prisoner to the fortress to question him calmly. In order to save Paul from the violence of the crowd, the soldiers had to carry him on their shoulders. Many Jews shouted: "Put him to death!"

14 Paul's Defense

Acts 22

As Paul was being carried into the fortress, he asked the Roman captain if he could be allowed to address the crowd. "How is it that you can speak Greek?" the captain asked him, and then gave him permission to speak to the crowd.

Paul spoke to them in Hebrew, saying: "Brothers, listen to my defense. I am a Jew and I used to persecute the followers of Jesus, but then he himself spoke to me on the road to Damascus." Paul told them what Jesus had said, but the crowd shouted: "Put him to death!"

15 Paul Is Comforted by Jesus

Acts 22–23

Paul's defense before his own people in Jerusalem had proved useless. The crowd shouted that he was a traitor and should be put to death. The Roman soldiers led Paul into the fortress and tied him up in order to whip him. Just as he had once before pointed out to Philip, Paul now said: "Roman law forbids you to whip a Roman citizen, and I am a citizen of Rome!" When the captain of the guards heard these words, he was afraid, so he decided to send Paul to be tried before the highest court of the Jews.

When Paul appeared before the Jewish court, a great argument started at once over how to judge him. There were some who saw nothing wrong with what he had done, and there were some who wanted him put to death. The argument grew so heated that the captain feared for Paul's life and decided to take him to safety to a cell in the fortress where the Jews could not enter. That night, in his cell, Paul had a vision in which Jesus appeared to him and said: "Have courage! You have publicly declared yourself to be my disciple, here in Jerusalem. Now you must do exactly the same thing in Rome!"

16 Paul Escapes From a Plot

Acts 23

The apostle Paul had been imprisoned in the Roman fortress in Jerusalem. Several Jews who were his sworn enemies vowed they would kill him.

They decided on the following plan: They would convince the leaders of the people to try Paul before the court again. then attack and murder him. This plot, however, came to the attention of a young relative of Paul, who passed the information on at once to the Roman commander. Paul was immediately sent in secrecy to Caesarea.

17 A Letter to the Roman Governor

Acts 23

The Roman commander in Jerusalem wrote the following letter in which he entrusted the responsibility for Paul's life to the governor of Palestine. "I am sending you this man who has been arrested by the Jews. They were about to kill him when I intervened. Since he is a Roman citizen, I freed him and sent him before the Jewish court, to find out what the accusations against him were. The Jews have prepared a conspiracy against him and I am therefore sending him to you!"

18 Paul Appeals to the Roman Emperor

Acts 25

In order to save his prisoner from death at the hands of the Jews of Jerusalem, the commander of the Roman guards had taken Paul to Caesarea, where he could be tried in person by the Roman governor who ruled over Palestine.

The leaders of the Jewish people traveled from Jerusalem to Caesarea in order to accuse Paul of preaching a new faith. This was not a crime under Roman law. However, in order not to displease the Jewish chiefs, he ordered Paul kept in prison.

Two years later a new governor arrived in Caesarea. He retried Paul but could not condemn him. He therefore announced his intention of sending Paul, once again, back to Jerusalem.

Paul, however, knew that once he was in Jerusalem his enemies would find it very easy to put him to death. At this point there was only one course of action open to him. As was permitted by law to citizens of Rome, Paul announced his intention to appeal to the emperor, to be judged by the courts of Rome. "You have turned to the emperor, and so to the emperor you shall go!" the governor replied.

19 Paul Is Brought Before King Agrippa

Acts 25–26

A few days later, King Agrippa and his sister Bernice arrived in Caesarea as guests of the Roman governor. The governor told them the story of Paul, and King Agrippa said: "I want to hear what this man has to say."

The next day, Paul was brought before King Agrippa, who was a learned Jew. Paul explained to the king all the reasons that proved that Jesus was the Messiah. Paul also told his own story. Paul spoke so well that Agrippa said: "You have almost persuaded me to become a Christian!"

20 Storm and Shipwreck

Acts 27

Under the guard of several Roman soldiers commanded by the centurion Julius, Paul was sent from Caesarea to Rome to be judged by the emperor's court. Two of his companions were sent with him.

Their ship sailed very slowly, arriving at the island of Crete in winter, so they could sail no farther. However, the captain of the ship wanted to set off again at once in order at least to reach a more hospitable port. Unfortunately, a hurricane came up and the ship was caught in a whirlwind.

The ship drifted for fourteen days, driven and buffeted by the winds and the waves. The passengers had lost all hope of ever reaching safety, but Paul encouraged them saying: "Do not be afraid! Last night an angel of my God appeared to me and comforted me by telling me that I shall reach my destination, Rome, and that none of the people on the ship will perish. You should eat something now to give yourselves strength, and have faith in me."

Paul was the first to start eating and then all the others, with new hope, did the same. Meanwhile, the sailors had the impression that there was land nearby, so they cast out the anchors and waited for dawn to find out where they were. When day came, they noticed a creek and tried to steer toward it. The ship, however, ran aground a long way from the shore and began to break up in the violent waves. The soldiers feared that the prisoners would escape by throwing themselves into the sea and so they decided to kill them. But the centurion Julius stopped them. He ordered those who could swim to throw themselves into the water, then everybody else, clutching onto planks of wood. Just as Paul had predicted, every one of the people on board safely reached the shore.

21 Bitten by a Viper

Acts 28

Paul and all who had escaped from the shipwreck had reached the shore of the island of Malta. The natives of the island greeted them with a huge fire.

Paul, too, gathered a bundle of twigs and branches to throw on the fire: but a viper that was awakened by the heat leaped out and fastened onto his hand. When they saw this, the people present thought: "This man must certainly be a murderer. He must pay for his crime!" But Paul simply shook his hand and the viper dropped into the fire.

22 Paul in Malta

Acts 28

Paul had been shipwrecked and had arrived on a beach on the island of Malta. He had gone to gather wood for the fire which the natives had lit. A viper had leaped from the wood and fastened itself to Paul's hand. The people who saw this expected to see Paul's hand swell up or even watch him fall down dead from the venom. But after seeing that nothing was wrong, they concluded he was a god. "This man must be a god!" they whispered.

A few days later they witnessed another miracle. The governor of the island was a man named Publius and he invited Paul and his companions to stay with him as his guests and he treated them with great courtesy. While they were staying there, the father of Publius fell ill with a high fever. Paul went to see him, prayed, laid his hands on the sick old man, and cured him.

When this became known, all the other people of the island who were sick came to Paul, and they too were cured by him. As a result of this, Paul was treated with great respect by everyone. Three months later he set out again, and the Maltese supplied all the provisions needed for the voyage.

23 On the Via Appia

Acts 28

It was impossible to sail during the winter and, so, in spring, Paul and his two companions, Luke and Aristarchus, set out once again on their journey to Rome. There, Paul was to be tried at the court of the emperor. Several Roman soldiers escorted him. The ship on which they set sail left Malta to the east, and sailed for Sicily. They crossed the Straits of Messina and arrived at Rhegium. The following day the south wind blew strongly and they quickly reached Puteoli.

At Puteoli, Paul was met by other Christians who invited him to stay with them for a week. He then set off once more, this time on foot, for the capital of the empire. The Christians of Rome were informed of his imminent arrival and went to meet Paul on the Via Appia.

When Paul saw them, he thanked the Lord and felt greatly heartened. And when they reached Rome, while he was awaiting trial, permission was immediately granted for Paul to live alone, with a single soldier as a guard.

Paul spent two years in his house in Rome. To every one of the many people who came to visit him he told the good news about Jesus.

24 Paul Teaches of Love

1 Corinthians 13

Paul was tireless in teaching everyone about Jesus Christ and what is pleasing to him. And what Jesus loves most of all is Love.
Though I might speak all the
    languages of men and of angels,
If I do not have love
I am like a clanging bell
Or a tinkling cymbal.
Even if I were a prophet
And I understood all of the
    mysteries
And I had a faith that could move
    mountains,
Without love it has no meaning.

Love is patient.
Love is thoughtful.
Love is not envious
And never boasts.
Love never swells with pride
And is always respectful.
Love forgives and has faith in
    everything.
Love hopes for everything and
    bears it all.
Love will have no end.
Now we do not see God clearly
But as if through an ancient mirror,
But, one day, we shall see him face
    to face.
Three things only have true value:
Faith, Hope, and Love.
And the greatest of these is Love.

25 Paul Helps a Runaway Slave

Letter to Philemon

The apostle Paul was a prisoner in Rome when he met a man named Onesimus. This man was a slave who had robbed his owner and fled. Paul spoke with Onesimus and persuaded him to become a Christian. He even convinced him to go back to his owner, taking a letter from Paul.

Paul already knew the owner of Onesimus. He was a man called Philemon, and he was a Christian who welcomed other Christians of the city to pray with him.

Thus, Paul wrote to Philemon: "I have sent Onesimus back to you: He has become like a son to me. If he has offended you, forgive him. If he still owes you something, I will pay his debt. Since I am still kept prisoner because of the love I have for the Lord Jesus, I would have been glad to keep Onesimus with me. You must not treat him like a slave, but rather as a brother. If you consider me your friend, then you will greet Onesimus."

Everything went just as Paul wished. Philemon received his fugitive servant and instead of punishing him, he treated him like a brother. This was just as Paul had asked and as Jesus had taught.

26 The Rich Man and the Pauper

_*James 1*

Among the followers of Jesus there was a man named James who almost certainly later became the head of the Christian community in Jerusalem.

James wrote: "Brothers, if one of you is poor, let him rejoice because God has honored him. If one of you is rich, however, he should be glad for God to humble him. The rich man passes away like a flower in a field. The sun comes up and its warmth dries the land and the flower falls and its beauty vanishes forever."

27 A Life Offered in Sacrifice

_*2 Timothy 6*

Paul's imprisonment in Rome lasted for two years. At the end of this period his innocence was acknowledged and he was set free. Paul at once began to travel again, to carry the Word of God to as many people as possible. He visited Christian communities that were already established and he founded many others. When Nero became emperor, however, Paul was once again arrested and brought to Rome.

In his twenty years of traveling and teaching, Paul had taken and spread the Gospel over the entire Roman empire. His life, however, was now drawing to a close, and he himself knew that his martyrdom was at hand. Knowing this, Paul wrote to his friend Timothy and said: "I am about to offer my life in sacrifice to God. The time has come for me to set out on my very last journey. I have fought the good fight. I have reached the end of my road and I have kept the faith. A winner's crown has been set aside for me as my reward. The most righteous judge of all, the Lord himself, shall give it to me. On the last day he will reward not only me but all men who await his return with love."

28 Actions Speak Louder than Words

_*James 2*

The Word of God is full of the most marvelous lessons for us. One of the most important of these lessons is that words alone do not suffice; actions, too, are essential. James wrote: "Brothers, what does it mean if a man says he has faith and then does not show it in his actions? Suppose you meet a man with no clothes or with nothing to eat. If you say to him: 'Cover yourself' or 'Eat as much as you want!' they are words without sense if you do not give him clothing and food with which to satisfy his hunger!"

29 The True Christian Loves Peace

James 3

According to James, what is it that makes a true Christian? The true Christian is both good and mild, and his heart is full of the desire for peace. He is a man to whom God has given wisdom, and the wisdom that comes from God is pure, peaceable and gentle, expressed through good works. People who work for peace will enjoy the fruits of justice.

To be peaceful we must also know how to moderate what we say. James wrote: "The tongue is only a tiny part of our body and yet it is responsible for a great deal. The tongue is like the helm of a ship; if the helm steers properly then even a large and heavy vessel which is buffeted by great winds will go where the pilot directs it."

The true Christian is patient and awaits with faith the return of the Lord. He is like the farmer who waits for his crops to grow out of the earth, and awaits patiently the spring and autumn rains.

The true Christian is sincere and does not swear in the name of heaven or of earth. He simply says yes when he means yes and no when he means no! It was Jesus himself, remember, who told us this.

30 I Am the First and the Last

Revelation 1

John was a follower of Jesus who, because of his faith, was sent to live in exile on the island of Patmos in the Aegean Sea. Not only did he write the Fourth Gospel, the Gospel according to John, but he also wrote another book of the New Testament which is called The Revelation, which describes the many visions which John saw.

"One day," he wrote, "while I was in exile on the island of Patmos for having spread the Word of God, I heard a voice like a trumpet blast which said: 'Write all that you see in a book and send it to the seven churches.' "I turned and saw seven golden candlesticks and, a figure like the Son of Man, holding seven stars in his right hand.

"When I saw him I fell at his feet. But he placed his hand on me and said: 'Do not be afraid. I am the First and the Last. I am he who lives. I was dead and now I live forever. Write down what you have seen and what you will see and send it to the seven churches, which are symbolized by the seven candelabra and the seven stars.' "

It was Jesus himself, the Son of God, who commanded John to spread the Word of God.

Index

October

BIBLE STORY OF THE MONTH

Absalom, Son of David

1. The Lord Is My Shepherd
2. A Prophecy for David
3. The Gratitude of David
4. For Love of Jonathan
5. Solomon Is Crowned King
6. Solomon's Dream
7. The Judgment of Solomon
8. A House for the Lord
9. The Temple on Mount Zion
10. The Sanctuary of the Temple
11. The Holy of Holies
12. Offerings to the Lord
13. Priests and People in the Temple
14. The Lord Enters into his Temple
15. Pilgrims on the March
16. The Gratitude of the Pilgrims
17. The Pilgrims' Departure
18. The Feasts of Pentecost and the Day of Atonement
19. The Feast of the Tabernacles
20. The Ships of Solomon
21. The Greatness of Solomon
22. A Throne of Gold and Ivory
23. The Queen of Sheba's Caravan
24. Solomon and the Queen of Sheba
25. The Kingdom Divided
26. The Prophets of the Lord
27. The Lord Appears to the Prophet Isaiah
28. Amos the Prophet
29. Amos Speaks of Salvation
30. The Trials of Jeremiah
31. Jeremiah Goes to the Potter

November

BIBLE STORY OF THE MONTH

Jonah

1. King Ahab and the Prophet Elijah
2. Elijah Is Fed by the Ravens
3. The Widow's Flour
4. Elijah and the Widow's Son
5. The Faith of Obadiah
6. Elijah Challenges the Priests of Baal
7. The Return of the Rain
8. Elijah in Flight
9. Elijah Meets the Lord
10. The Vocation of Elisha
11. Naboth's Vineyard
12. The Prophet Elijah Confronts King Ahab
13. Into Heaven in a Chariot of Fire
14. The Spirit of Elijah Remains with Elisha
15. The Healing of the Waters
16. The Widow's Oil
17. The Breath of Life
18. Naaman's Leprosy
19. The Ax Head in the Water
20. Joash, the Little King
21. The Lesson of the Arrows
22. Josiah and the Rediscovered Book
23. The Temple Is Destroyed
24. Four Boys in the Court of Babylon
25. The Statue and the Little Stone
26. Nebuchadnezzar and the Statue of Gold
27. The Fiery Furnace
28. The Writing on the Wall
29. Daniel Prays
30. Daniel in the Lions' Den

December

BIBLE STORY OF THE MONTH

Esther the Queen

1. By the Waters of Babylon
2. The Visions of the Prophet Ezekiel
3. The Return from Exile
4. The Joy of the Returning Exiles
5. Nehemiah and King Cyrus
6. Nehemiah Rebuilds the Walls
7. The Renewal of the Covenant
8. Job Is Put to the Test
9. Job Is Struck Again
10. Job and his Three Friends
11. Job Questions God
12. Job Is Rewarded
13. Waiting for the Messiah
14. The Vision of the Son of Man
15. The Long-Awaited One Is Here
16. Zacharias and Elisabeth
17. Zacharias and the Angel
18. Zacharias Returns Home
19. A Young Woman Named Mary
20. Mary, the Mother of God
21. Mary Goes to See Elisabeth
22. His Name Is John
23. Joseph the Carpenter
24. The Journey from Nazareth to Bethlehem
25. Jesus Is Born
26. The Song of the Angels
27. The Good News Given to the Shepherds
28. Mary Praises the Lord
29. The Homage of the Shepherds
30. Zacharias Gives Thanks to the Lord
31. Unto us a Child Is Born

January

BIBLE STORY OF THE MONTH

Baby Jesus in the Temple

1. The Wise Men From the East
2. They Will Bring Gold and Incense
3. The Journey of the Magi
4. Herod, King of the Jews
5. King Herod and the Magi
6. The Adoration of the Magi
7. King Herod and the Children of Bethlehem
8. The Flight into Egypt
9. Jesus in Nazareth
10. John Preaches Repentance
11. John and Jesus: "Behold the Lamb of God"
12. The Baptism of Jesus
13. Jesus Defeats the Devil
14. Jesus Announces the Good News
15. The First Disciples
16. Jesus Calls Philip and Nathanael
17. The First Miracle at Cana
18. Jesus Drives the Merchants from the Temple
19. A Nocturnal Visit
20. The Parable of the Sower
21. The Kingdom of God and the Grain of Mustard Seed
22. The Son of the Nobleman
23. The Yeast and the Treasure
24. Jesus Heals a Leper
25. Jesus Calls Levi Matthew to Him
26. The Fishing Net
27. The Man Lowered from the Roof
28. The Man with the Withered Hand
29. Jesus Chooses the Twelve Apostles
30. A Group of Women Help Jesus
31. The Parable of the Weeds

February

BIBLE STORY OF THE MONTH

Jesus and His Disciples

1. Jesus in the Synagogue
2. Jesus and the Man Possessed by the Devil
3. Jesus Cures Peter's Mother-in-Law
4. Jesus Cures Many Sick People
5. Where Is Jesus?
6. Who Is the Greatest?
7. The Killing of John the Baptist
8. The Rich Man and the Sinner Woman
9. The Brothers of Jesus
10. The Son of the Widow
11. Anger and Reconciliation
12. The Lost Sheep
13. A Woman Touches the Garment of Jesus
14. The Precious Pearl
15. The Law of God
16. A Herd of Swine in the Lake
17. To Do Good in Secret
18. A Great Banquet
19. Love Your Enemies
20. Jesus Resurrects the Daughter of Jairus
21. Like Sheep Among the Wolves
22. The Parable of the Merciless Servant
23. Jesus Cures a Deaf and Dumb Man
24. You Are Peter
25. The Blind Man of Bethsaida
26. The Laborers in the Vineyard
27. Jesus Like Jonah
28. The Faith that Moves Mountains
29. The Transformation of Jesus

March

BIBLE STORY OF THE MONTH

The Bread of Life

1. The Coin in the Fish's Mouth
2. The Parable of the Steward
3. The Good Samaritan
4. Jesus and the Little Children
5. The Parable of the Two Sons
6. Jesus Meets a Rich Young Man
7. Our Father who Art in Heaven
8. The Parable of the Talents
9. The Reward for Whoever Follows Jesus
10. God Listens to our Prayers
11. The First Seats at the Table
12. Invite the Poor
13. The Men in the Temple
14. The Parable of the Prodigal Son
15. The House Built on Rock
16. Jesus Cures Ten Lepers
17. The Offering of the Widow
18. Jesus at the Feast of the Tabernacles
19. The Parable of Lazarus and the Wicked Rich Man
20. Jesus is a Good Shepherd
21. The Hunchbacked Woman of the Synagogue
22. The Parable of the Lost Coin
23. If a Donkey Should Fall Down a Well on the Sabbath. . . .
24. The Light of the World
25. The Tree and the Fruit
26. Whoever Is Without Sin
27. The Parable of the Rich Fool
28. The Salvation of Zacchaeus
29. Jesus Heals a Man Blind from Birth
30. The Chiefs in the Kingdom of Heaven
31. The Parable of the Wise and Foolish Virgins

April

BIBLE STORY OF THE MONTH

Story of Lazarus

1. Jesus Enters Jerusalem in Triumph
2. A Trap for Jesus
3. Jesus Promises that he Will Return
4. Jesus Announces the Day of Judgment
5. The Parable of the Fig Tree
6. The Death of Jesus Is Decided Upon
7. Jesus' Last Supper
8. The Olive Grove
9. Jesus Is Arrested
10. Peter Denies Jesus
11. Jesus Is Tried by Caiaphas
12. Jesus is Taken before Pontius Pilate
13. Jesus Is Tortured
14. Jesus Is Condemned to Death
15. The Road to Calvary
16. Mary and John
17. The Good Thief
18. Jesus Dies
19. Jesus Is Buried
20. The Third Day
21. The Chief Priests' Deception
22. The Two Disciples on the Road to Emmaus
23. Jesus Appears to the Apostles
24. Doubting Thomas
25. Breakfast by the Side of the Lake
26. Feed my Sheep
27. Jesus Returns to the Father
28. The Disciple Matthias
29. Fire from the Sky
30. Three Thousand New Christians

May

BIBLE STORY OF THE MONTH

Peter and Cornelius

1. The Lame Man at the Beautiful Gate
2. Barnabas, a Generous Apostle
3. Peter and John Are Brought before the Council
4. Touched by his Shadow
5. The Story of Two Liars
6. Seven Helpers for the Apostles
7. Stephen, the First Martyr
8. Saul Against the Christians
9. Philip and the Magician Simon
10. Peter and the Magician Simon
11. The Minister of the Queen of Ethiopia
12. Saul on the Road to Damascus
13. Saul and Ananias
14. Paul Lowered in a Basket
15. Peter at Lydda
16. Peter Raises up Tabitha
17. Herod Has Peter Imprisoned
18. Peter Is Freed from Prison
19. A Girl Named Rhoda
20. The Community of Antioch
21. Paul and Barnabas Are Sent by the Holy Spirit
22. Paul and Elymas the Sorcerer
23. Paul Is Persecuted
24. Paul and Barnabas Are Mistaken for Gods
25. Paul Is Sent to Europe
26. Lydia, the Seller of Purple Dye
27. Paul Is Imprisoned in Philippi
28. An Earthquake at Philippi
29. The Arms of the Christian
30. Paul, the Citizen of Rome
31. Like Runners in a Race

June

BIBLE STORY OF THE MONTH

Paul Preaches in Greece

1. Paul at Corinth
2. Paul's Dream
3. Gallio's Reply
4. Apollos Preaches in Ephesus
5. Paul in Ephesus
6. The Magicians of Ephesus
7. A Young Man Named Euthycus
8. The Silversmiths of Ephesus
9. Farewell at the Port of Miletus
10. By Sea toward Jerusalem
11. Some of Jesus' Words
12. The Prophecy of Agabus
13. Paul Is Arrested in Jerusalem
14. Paul's Defense
15. Paul Is Comforted by Jesus
16. Paul Escapes from a Plot
17. A Letter to the Roman Governor
18. Paul Appeals to the Roman Emperor
19. Paul Is Brought before King Agrippa
20. Storm and Shipwreck
21. Bitten by a Viper
22. Paul in Malta
23. On the Via Appia
24. Paul Teaches of Love
25. Paul Helps a Runaway Slave
26. The Rich Man and the Pauper
27. A Life Offered in Sacrifice
28. Actions Speak Louder than Words
29. The True Christian Loves Peace
30. I am the First and the Last